TRANSFORMATIVE FAMILY THERAPY

Just Families in a Just Society

TRANSFORMATIVE FAMILY THERAPY

Just Families in a Just Society

RHEA V. ALMEIDA

Institute for Family Services

KEN DOLAN-DEL VECCHIO

Private Practice Morristown, New Jersey

LYNN PARKER

Denver University School of Social Work

PEARSON

Boston ■ New York ■ San Francisco
Mexico City ■ Montreal ■ Toronto ■ London ■ Madrid ■ Munich ■ Paris
Hong Kong ■ Singapore ■ Tokyo ■ Cape Town ■ Sydney

Senior Aquisitions Editor: *Patricia Quinlin*
Editorial Assistant: *Nakeesha Warner*
Marketing Manager: *Laura Lee Manley*
Production Supervisor: *Roberta Sherman*
Editorial-Production Services: *Progressive Publishing Alternatives*
Composition Buyer: *Linda Cox*
Manufacturing Buyer: *Debbie Rossi*
Electronic Composition: *Progressive Information Technologies*
Cover Administrator: *Elena Sidorova*

For related titles and support materials, visit our online catalog at www.ablongman.com

Between the time website information is gathered and then published, it is not unusual for some sites to have closed. Also, the transcription of URLs can result in typographical errors. The publisher would appreciate notification where these errors occur so that they may be corrected in subsequent editions.

Library of Congress Cataloging-in-Publication Data

Almeida, Rhea V.
  Transformative family therapy: just families in a just society / Rhea V. Almeida,
  Ken Dolan-Del Vecchio, Lynn Parker.
      p. ; cm.
  Includes bibliographical references and index.
  ISBN-13: 978-0-205-47008-2
  ISBN-10: 0-205-47008-4
  1. Family psychotherapy.   2. Social justice. I. Dolan-Del Vecchio, Ken. II. Parker,
  Lynn. III. Title.
  [DNLM: 1. Family Therapy—methods. 2. Social Justice. WM 430.5.F2 A447t 2008]

  RC488.5.A4668 2008
  616.89'156—dc22   2007010166

Printed in the United States of America

10   9   8   7   6   5   4   3   2   1   11   10   09   08   07

TO THOSE WHO SUPPORT LIBERATION THROUGH SEEKING JUSTICE AND EQUITY AND REMEMBERING

All who have hated oppression to the point of death,
all who have loved freedom to the point of imprisonment
and have rejected falsehood to the point of revolution

—**Nawal El Saadawi, 1982**

CONTENTS

CHAPTER 3

Expanding Gender Identities 55

CHAPTER 4

Families as Subsystems 76

CHAPTER 5

Healing as a Community Effort: Culture Circles   96

CHAPTER 8
Special Issues: Domestic Violence and Substance Abuse   165

FOREWORD

As the world flattens, our cultural context enlarges. In the process of globalization, we become accountable to each other. Thus, what happens to our sister in India eventually "happens" to us.

To survive in this new reality, we need to reformulate our identity. Such transformation, similar to speciation or the process whereby animals modify their biology to accommodate to novel surroundings, helps us to resonate with our context. Our transformation signals liberation. In our new identity—liberation practitioners—we help to transform ourselves, others, and society in general. We examine the legacies of inequalities, raise consciousness, master the art of democracy, value partnership, and commit to civic engagement. Our transformation is not about survival; it is about revolution and evolution. We assert the adage that the test of courage comes when we are in the minority. Therefore, to be fully emancipated in the global context, we are required to liberate others. We revolt against oppression and create a just society by becoming agents of change. We evolve by making ethical choices grounded in truth, reason, and compassion.

Liberation practitioners promote empowerment, reconciliation, and healing. But first, we must liberate our professional selves. Mainstream mental health tends to be decontextualized, apolitical, and ahistorical. Therefore, if psychotherapy remains silent on the central role of history and sociopolitical factors in life, it will become obsolete. As James Baldwin (1955) stated, people are trapped in history and history is trapped in them. The work of Frantz Fanon, Albert Memmi, Paulo Freire, and others encourages our transformation. These scholars taught us to see individuals not only in relation to their culture, race, and gender, but also in relation to their sociopolitical and historical context. Their work brings to life E. T. Hall's exhortation that we cannot be free until we allow others to be themselves.

The authors of this book continue with this tradition. They demonstrate how to reformulate our identity in order to become liberation practitioners. They speak the truth when they promote a viable paradigm for healing relations. Moreover, the authors help us heal, transform, and liberate. Since the philosopher's stone in mental health and in life is the ability to recognize yourself in the other, the authors help us to do this. This book provides a roadmap to become members of the global family.

Lillian Comas-Diaz, Ph.D.
Executive Director, Transcultural Mental Health Institute
Clinical Professor, George Washington University
Department of Psychiatry and Behavioral Sciences

PREFACE

Transformative Family Therapy: Just Families in a Just Society presents clinical strategies that connect relational healing and liberation from the oppressive patterns that structure all institutions in our society, including communities, educational institutions, religious organizations, workplaces, and families. The book represents the culmination of the three authors' more than 25 years of respective experience as social workers and family therapists. Working in mental health, the public schools, hospitals, corporations, private practice, institute-based practice, academia, and other training programs, the authors each came to see that social justice values, while often spoken, rarely translate into actual practice. The authors individually developed a commitment to bringing justice, fairness, and equality to the center of clinical work. In keeping with their social justice value base, the coauthors shared the writing of this book.

With roots in Paulo Freire's educational pedagogies, liberation theology, critical psychology, postcolonial race/gender theories, feminism, and contemporary masculinities and queer theories, the book offers both theoretical and practical applications for therapists in a variety of settings. We invite practitioners to engage in dialogue and inquiry regarding these theories and applications. We offer strategies that challenge patterns of power, privilege, and oppression at the foundation of all relationships, across multiple systems levels. The concepts in this book arise largely from Rhea Almeida's cultural context model. Rhea's unique personal journey informs the model. She was born in Uganda to Asian Indian parents from the West Coast of India, the firstborn child and grandchild to both of her parents' families. Her 13 aunts and uncles gathered around the hospital bed to welcome her, and the family celebrated her birth for months thereafter. Although they decided that Almeida's skin could have been lighter, they agreed that it was light enough, and her remarkable eyes more than made up for her darker skin color. When she was 3, her brother arrived. Her parents felt blessed to have two beautiful, able-bodied children. Six months later, Rhea contracted polio. For years thereafter, Rhea and her parents traveled from country to country seeking a cure. Finally, they accepted that there would be no cure, only rehabilitation.

Instead of relegating their daughter to an adoptive institution or maltreating her for being female and disabled, Almeida's parents viewed her as a *Harijan*—one of god's children who brought added value. Her parents' childrearing challenged community norms. When she turned 5 years old, Rhea's father decided that, since she would never marry and receive the buffering experiences that marriage might bring, he would be her teacher. Instead of taking his son to the men's activities, he took his daughter. The men in the family and community criticized him harshly. They believed that Rhea's father, by bringing a girl child into the world of men, was breaking too many traditions. There were others, however, who celebrated his choices.

Shortly after he seized power in 1970, Idi Amin decreed the exile of Uganda's citizens of Asian heritage. Rhea's extended family dispersed—some fleeing to Canada and others to the United States Each family was allowed to take only one suitcase and no money. Along her journey, Rhea encountered angels, people who believed in her spirit. Years later, having experienced military violence and racism, and being protected from the worst of sexism by her extraordinary parents and community, Rhea was determined to bring the connection between justice and healing into her chosen profession.

Ken Dolan-Del Vecchio, who currently works as the employee assistance director at a major international corporation and as a family therapist in private practice, met Rhea when he was a postgraduate family therapy trainee. Rhea invited him to join her institute's faculty, and they have collaborated on training and writing projects for the past 10 years.

Lynn Parker came to know Almeida and Dolan-Del Vecchio when she began doing research on feminist and social justice approaches to therapy. Lynn is a family therapist, social worker, researcher, and professor who has devoted her professional life to addressing power, privilege, and oppression in therapeutic work and more broadly in society.

ACKNOWLEDGMENTS

All of my thinking, writing, and doing has been informed by my community of family, friends, clients, students, mentors, and colleagues.

Thanks go to Michele Bograd for getting into print my first work on sponsorship.

I am thankful to Robert Jay Green for hours he spent interviewing clients to elucidate the concept of sponsorship. Robert contributed to the development of a flow chart for the cultural context model.

My special thanks go to Lynn Parker, who has contributed years collecting client, staff, and community narratives to create a research representation of a social justice model.

A very special thank you goes to Pilar Hernandez, who has taken these ideas across borders of practice into research and supervision. I thank Miguel Hernandez and Darielle Watts Jones for always promoting these ideas.

I am ever grateful to all my friends, family, and colleagues for bearing with my single-mindedness through the past year. I am thankful to my coauthors, Ken and Lynn, who worked hard to bring the complexity of theory and practice into a text grounded in social justice principles.

I thank Judith Lockard for effortlessly reading numerous versions of the text, offering her seasoned insights, keeping the fires down at the Institute—and for bringing Joy Stocke, our editor, to us. To Lisa Dressner, Andrae Brown, and Eun-jung Ryu for reading numerous versions of the text and pushing us toward greater clarity, thank you. To Etiony Aldorando for daring us to be a little less humble and write about the work he witnessed, to Jane Ariel, who has always embraced these ideas and most importantly been a great friend through some difficult times, and to Louise Silverstein, whose stimulating conversations challenged and inspired me throughout the writing of this book, a special thank you.

I cannot say enough about Robin Keegan, who tirelessly worked and reworked the graphics, always with a smile. To Christina Ginter, who handled the toxic job of finding and correcting references from books to movies throughout this project, thank you!

I must remember our beloved editor, Joy E. Stocke, whose calm and assured assistance in shaping this long and unwieldy text was invaluable. She has become a trusted friend.

Most importantly, to my daughters, Arielle and Lara, whose deep commitment to justice and equity offer me great hope for our future generation.

— *Rhea V. Almeida*

I thank my coauthors, Rhea and Lynn, for making the writing of this book a transformative journey. Rhea has been a mentor for years, and Lynn has become a dear friend during our work on this project. I thank the men, women, and families who over the years have trusted me enough to seek my counsel. They teach me volumes about love, courage, and justice. I thank Monica McGoldrick, Nydia Garcia Preto, Roberto Font, Theresa Messineo, and Rosemary Woods for empowering me to understand white male supremacy and challenge it in myself and in the world. I thank Judith Lockard for her countless contributions to this text and for her friendship. I thank Joy E. Stocke, my writing coach, editor, and friend. My connection to Joy proves Alice Walker's assertion that a mysterious providence sometimes brings the right people into our lives at precisely the right moment. I thank Tim Garrett, my life partner, for his love, endless understanding, and sage comments on everything that I write. I become a better writer and a better person because of you. I thank Lynn Dolan, the mother of my son. Loving, wise, and good humored—she is the best co-parent one could hope for. Finally, I thank my son, Erik Dolan-Del Vecchio, for his gentle teenaged cynicism and fierce kindness toward all living things. You inspire me to believe that your generation can remake the world.

— *Ken Dolan-Del Vecchio*

I acknowledge first my parents, Martha and Chalmerse Parker. Their unconditional love and quest for making the world a better place has guided my every step. And, there is no one more fun or able to provide candid feedback at just the right moment than my brother Walter. I have cherished him from his first breath. I thank my life partner, James Moran, for his ever-present encouragement and patience and for being willing to grapple with all the nuances of creating an equitable partnership, especially when it's difficult. Thank you to my students and clients who challenge and inspire me to live my principles in my practice, teaching, and life. Muchas gracias Gerardo Debbink, Gerardo Thijssen, Gloria Cruz, Ofelia Laureano, and the families of Cuernavaca, Mexico, for opening my eyes and heart to our common struggle for liberation. You inspire me to live more simply and with a pointed commitment to justice for all.

Finally, thanks to Rhea and Ken for walking this journey with me. I can't think of better partners or more able teachers. I am forever transformed by your willingness to allow me into the intricacies of your amazing work.

— *Lynn Parker*

TRANSFORMATIVE FAMILY THERAPY

Just Families in a Just Society

CHAPTER ONE

REMEMBERING CONTEXT: TRANSFORMING FAMILY THERAPY

Well, the first thing is that truth and power for me form an antithesis, an antagonism, which will hardly ever be resolved. I can define, in fact, can simplify, the history of human society, the evolution of human society, as a contest between power and freedom. And whether this contest is being performed along ideological lines or along religious lines, ultimately, really what we have is truth versus power. Truth for me is freedom, is self-destination. Power is domination, control, and therefore a very selective form of truth which is a lie. And the polarity between these two, in fact, forms for me the axis of human striving in the creation of an ethical society, an ethical community.

—Wole Soyinka (1998)

Healthy families, whose members demonstrate love, mutual respect, caring, support for differences, reciprocity, and equal distribution of power among adults, thrive with the support of communities that embody these values. But where do we find such communities?

Too often, we live and work in communities that glorify competition, consumption, revenge, war, and conquest—communities that prize "might makes right," greed, and the ranking of people according to their differences. We see compartmentalized and fragmented communities, a coast-to-coast suburbia where interpersonal relationships can grow shallow, fleeting, and unreliable. Many people spend less time and energy relating to other people than they do relating to their favorite television reality and news shows. Given these conditions, is it any wonder that so many family relationships are deeply troubled?

1

The boundary that separates families from the larger world exists more in our imaginations than in reality. In the real world, human beings live, learn, and change communally. We learn to understand ourselves and relate to others from experiences within our homes, schools, neighborhoods, workplaces, communities of faith, organizations, and other places of belonging. We gather our perspectives from what we see on television, hear on the radio, read, and absorb from authority figures: child care providers, teachers, employers, and community leaders. Families, communities, and ultimately the societies in which we live create one another in an endless cycle.

Transformative Family Therapy is written for social workers, family therapists, counseling psychologists, students, and practitioners who wish to translate social justice values into everyday clinical practice. We offer a model for social justice practice, the cultural context model, which places the connection between family and society at the center of therapeutic thinking and intervention strategies. We remind helping professionals that too often the world surrounding families encourages values and actions that undermine health and sanity.

This chapter introduces

- A sociopolitical perspective on family life.
- A critical overview of the family therapy movement's relationship to social justice.
- The cultural context model, a family therapy model based on social justice.
- The challenge of transformative change.
- Concepts useful for understanding and delivering social justice–based intervention.

Despite the progress won by liberation movements, inequity persists. Traditional gender patterns still cause most married heterosexual women of all colors to shoulder more than half of their family's service work, including laundry, cleaning, food preparation, and managing child and elder care arrangements.

If the world modeled fairness across differences, it would be much easier for intimate partners to create fairness within their relationships. Individual couples do not invent this unjust division of labor or the underlying power imbalances. Similarly, single mothers and fathers do not invent school systems and workplaces that expect one parent to always be available. Nor do single parents invent the drastic choice they often have to make between focusing on work as a priority or on their children's education. Instead, we learn these patterns from the larger world.

The dynamic interplay between families and their broader contexts requires professional helpers to expand their focus beyond the individual and beyond relationships forged by blood and household connections. The professional helper faces the challenge of helping clients construct not only couple partnerships and families governed by just values but also communities that sustain these values.

THE FAMILY THERAPY MOVEMENT
AND SOCIAL JUSTICE

During the last two decades, with the advent of **multiculturalism**,* family therapy approaches emerged that recognize the importance of race, ethnicity, culture, and social class. While this scholarship greatly advanced the field by opening pathways to honor cultural differences and inequities such as racism and social class, the conceptual analysis's practice methods rarely addressed how power, **privilege**, and oppression interconnected. Furthermore, the intersectionality of gender, race, class, culture, and sexual orientation were absent from the multicultural scholarship. A social justice approach was missing, one that would weave all these threads into therapeutic practice.

Why this omission? Power, privilege, and oppression remain dirty little secrets that most therapy approaches continue to deny. Many family therapy approaches acknowledge cultural differences but rarely address injustice. Feminist family therapy charged the landscape around gender and family life. This scholarship challenged sexism but rarely other abuses of power. Some progressive therapists acknowledge cultural differences and injustice beyond sexism, but they address injustice only from the perspective of those victimized. They rarely challenge those who use their power to victimize others. The notion of accountability escaped this analysis (Tamasese & Waldegrave, 1993). Seldom were clients helped to organize against power inequities. An exception to this are the just therapy team in New Zealand who offered a paradigm that would bring all of these intersections to the therapeutic context. Most therapy approaches collude with the status quo of power, privilege, and oppression.

For example, a female client described how she became furious after telling her previous female therapist about sexist promotional practices at her workplace: "Twice within two years, I trained men who recently had been hired into my area, and both of them were subsequently chosen for supervisor positions. When I asked my director why I didn't get the job, he said, 'You do a great job, but we needed someone who could keep this team in line—someone who is aggressive.' He might as well have told me that he would only hire a man."

"Yes, I agree with you," the therapist replied. "It's tough to be a woman, but that's the way the world operates. It's much too big to take on alone. You have to find ways to adapt."

While the therapist's statement rightfully acknowledged the woman's dilemma, it also supported acquiescence—unmindfully adhering to what is considered normative. How different it would be for the therapist to send an empowering message: "You and all women find yourselves on the downside of a power equation to an extent that varies according to other factors such as race, sexual orientation, and class. Let's figure out how you and the people closest to you can organize with others to help change this injustice." Unfortunately, the therapist in our example did not see this possibility for herself or her client.

***Bold face** words are defined at the end of this chapter.

Though some theorists and practitioners do address the connections between family therapy and social justice, much of family therapy and social work practice has not moved beyond a shallow awareness of differences. Why?

We live in conservative times. Social work, family therapy, and the broader mental health field reflect the current social and political climate in which national policies lack compassion for the conservation of diverse families. Lack of accountability for increasingly large military spending exists in stark contrast to the lack of funding and support for hard-working families. This inequity has increased homelessness and the number of working families without health care. Emergency food requests increased 14.4% from 2003 to 2004, and in 2004, 81% of major cities turned people away from shelters because they were filled to capacity. Health coverage has declined fairly steadily from 1995–2004. According to US Census studies in 2004, 45.8 million individuals or 15.7% of the population did not have health insurance, as compared to 14.1% in 1995. (Wollman, Yoder, Brumbaugh-Smith, Largent, 2005). In contrast, Canada's health care, education, and social programs, together with a military budget that has decreased over the past two decades, reflects a different picture of equity than the dilemma for the middle and working class families in the United States. With increased pressure from the United States and its War on Terror, however, the military budget in Canada is rising against the wish of the people (Pizzigati, 2004). Moreover, the fields of family therapy and social work, like most academic and professional disciplines, adhere to a worldview that suffers from "patriarchal fragmentation."

Patriarchy depends on "this" being different and separate from "that," because difference and separation provide the rudiments of hierarchy. In other words, the differences between men and women, blacks and whites, and straights and **queers** must be punctuated and rigidly upheld in order for the pyramid of privilege to stand. Despite their often avowed systemic perspective, the patriarchal ordering of the world keeps most family therapists, and therapists in general, at a distance from the work of sociopolitical theorists (Cesaire, 1972; Collins, 1989; Crenshaw, 1994; Memmi, 1967). The path forward requires synthesis: simultaneous attention to multiple oppressions and privileges, the skills to link public and private matters, and the ability to connect the work of relational healing and social justice.

The term *postcolonial analysis* describes a simultaneous accounting for current and historical repercussions of oppressive social forces, including colonization, sexism, racism, homophobia, and classism (Said, 1993; Soyinka, 1999; Spivak, 1987; Spivak, 1989), Duran and Duran (1995) and Yellow Bird (1995, 2001) write about their therapeutic work with Native Americans in which it is essential to emphasize and acknowledge the Native American genocide and its intergenerational impact. They may situate a client family's experience of domestic violence or substance abuse within the family's multigenerational history of violent colonization. Liberation becomes available by situating current experience in its historical context.

We are not implying that colonization should be used as an excuse for domestic violence or alcoholism. We believe it is essential to help a family review the social context in which problems emerge, including a community's historical relationship to power, in order for clients to make informed decisions as they move forward. For Native Americans, this history includes their exile onto reservations and the mass kidnapping of their children into Christian boarding schools, where children were abused and forced to accept an alien religion. Highlighting history of colonization authenticates the therapeutic endeavor by bringing it in line with the family's longstanding efforts toward cultural resistance and survival alongside the issues for which they have sought therapy.

Similarly, an examination of domestic violence and/or incest in the African American community warrants a consideration of the history of slavery and racism in America, as well as white America's ongoing exploitation toward communities of color in the US and globally. Contextualizing the family's presenting crisis within larger crucibles of historical and contemporary public abuse toward marginalized groups brings integrity to the therapeutic process and identifies, evaluates, and addresses the multiple challenges each family member faces.

Acknowledging pressures from outside the family does not discount the existence of patriarchy within groups, such as the African American community. Nor does it mean that perpetrators of abuse are not held accountable. Much of the controversy surrounding incest and domestic violence in the African American community and other populations including immigrants of color is driven by an either-or approach to gender and race. Inequities related to gender and sexism are often obscured in the effort to highlight the injustices of racism. Brian Stevenson (2006) describes the connection between racism, domestic violence, and the plethora of black men on death row. He documents that many death row occupants experienced domestic violence for which neither they nor their parents received constructive intervention. We do not mean to suggest that alcoholism is unique to Native Americans, or domestic violence or incest is unique to African Americans. Of course people of all communities experience these problems. We suggest, instead, that these and other human problems be assessed with consideration for their larger contexts. Such problems within a white family therefore need to be considered within the "white" historical context of superiority, greed, instant gratification, pressure to succeed, and ownership. Other post-colonial scholars (Said, 2003; Spivak, 1990; Stoler, 1995) point to the significance of not elevating an ethnic, national, or racial identity over the politics of intersectionality. Romanticizing ethnicity or culture enforces a predefined and limited identity. Dismantling the ways in which colonized and enslaved cultures resisted domination provides the backdrop to liberation. For white families, the backdrop of imperialism and ongoing domination is the backdrop for problem inquiry.

Challenging the trajectory of privilege is as crucial as voicing the subjugation of oppression. Imagine consulting with a white husband and wife, both top executives at Fortune 500 firms, whose 13-year-old son has been caught stealing from classmates. Many therapists would help the family seek the origin of the boy's stealing by exploring intergenerational legacies of loss and displacement. Most therapists would not, however, initiate a conversation about the wave of corporate crime grabbing headlines these past several years, nor would they ask the parents to describe their own business practices. While the individual sense of responsibility must be balanced within the collective, these legacies are at least as likely as multigenerational patterns to contribute to the presenting problem, and they need to be examined (Thandeka, 1999; Wise, 2001).

Exploitation and domination, cornerstones of colonialism, are part of all national, ethnic, and cultural legacies. Illuminating this reality broadens understanding of the ways that we replicate domination. An Irish male employer's mistreatment of his Puerto Rican employee can be placed alongside 500 years of British colonization in Ireland and numerous other countries. The invitation of Irish immigrants into "whiteness" in the United States in order to prevent their alliance with blacks and Native Americans is another important reference point. Raising these historical realities in conversation and bringing them into consciousness provides employers (and employees) with a more informed and compelling challenge: Will they choose to perpetuate or transform such legacies?

In the therapeutic setting, raising these historical realities in a matter-of-fact manner provides a framework for making sense of clients' present-day issues. Seeing the connection between individual problems and the broader context helps clients recognize that they are part of a network of domination. They can then envision being part of a framework for liberation. With more options, they are freed from the burden of individual pathology and empowered toward change through social action.

THE CULTURAL CONTEXT MODEL

The cultural context model, an approach to therapy originated by Rhea Almeida, links social justice to many aspects of intervention (see Chart 1.1 for a flowchart of the cultural context model).

The model revises the endeavor of family therapy to include the pursuit of justice at every level, using tools and techniques that:

- Invite clients' critical awareness of diversity and power.
- Emphasize how "normal" hierarchies of power, privilege, and oppression perpetuate suffering.
- Experientially demonstrate the link between fairness and relational healing.
- Expand the therapeutic encounter to include a community with **critical consciousness** rather than one family at a time.
- Define **empowerment** in collective rather than individual terms.
- Link social activism to therapy as a means for empowering communities, families, and self.
- Invite and embrace systems of **accountability** for all participants, including therapists.
- Create a basis for developing authentic relationships across diverse communities.
- Help people think about ways to connect past, present, and future legacies within the matrix of critical consciousness, empowerment, and accountability.

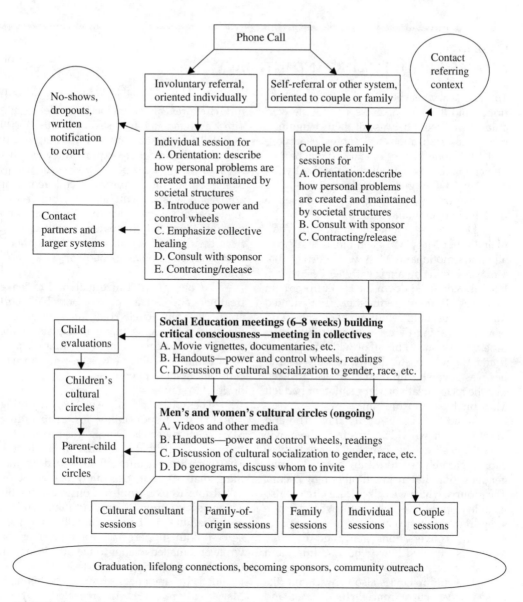

CHART 1.1   Cultural Context Model Flowchart

As you read the case that follows, notice the similarities and differences between therapy as it is usually practiced and therapy described in Case 1.1. In the following chapters, we clarify questions you may have regarding our approach, and we encourage you to consider ways to incorporate aspects of this model into your practice.

■ ■ ■ ■ ■

CASE 1.1

AFFAIRS: TRUTH TELLING AND INTIMACY

Tim and Mary, married 25 years, are a white, upper middle-class, heterosexual couple who entered treatment because of their daughter's recent hospitalization for anorexia nervosa and Tim's long history of extramarital affairs. The couple has two adult children, Kathy, 20, and Dan, 24. (See genogram figure 1.3A–1.3B.) The genogram is a family therapy tool used to track intergenerational patterns.

During the intake session, Tim complained that Mary had abandoned him sexually and emotionally. Mary was worried that Tim was having an affair with her best friend, Lauren, who lived down the street from them and was Kathy's godmother. Tim denied Mary's accusation, rebutting her "vivid fantasy life," saying that it was "working overtime." As a result of his affair with Mary's best friend, the relationship between the two families was severely ruptured. Tim also insisted that the recent death of Mary's mother had left Mary unable to nurture him.

To address issues of loss, both Tim and Mary were shown video clips from the movie *Steel Magnolias*. The partners viewed these clips separately, each within a small same-gender group that included other new clients. The groups, which we call **culture circles**, also included sponsors—volunteers who provide **support** in a variety of ways.

The conversations generated by *Steel Magnolias* explored how gender, culture, and class shape responses to loss.

The culture circles also viewed and discussed video clips from *Pretty Woman* and *Jungle Fever*. These movies were used to initiate conversations about the different forms of entitlement open to men from different race and class backgrounds and how men's actions create the oppression experienced by women. Figures 1.1 and 1.2 provide language to describe tactics of oppression.

Further discussions within Mary's culture circle revealed convincing evidence that Tim was in fact involved sexually with Mary's friend. The sponsors within Tim's culture circle helped him begin to explore the ways that he, like many men, placed his own desires over those of his partner and children. This admission was difficult for Tim, but it was made easier by the voices of other men who reminded him that this pattern resulted more from their shared socialization into manhood than from Tim's being a "bad" or "sick" individual.

At one point, Tim threatened to leave treatment and seek a "more responsible" therapist. His men's circle confronted him about his history of seeing many therapists in the past. They challenged him to consider the possibility that the real issue was his reluctance to confront issues openly and honestly. He decided to stay.

Therapists and sponsors began urging Tim to take responsibility for disregarding Mary on many levels. During this process, the truth emerged about his affair with her friend. The therapists encouraged Tim to do something that may surprise many readers: they asked him to claim full responsibility for his actions by informing Mary and their children of his affair. He balked initially, but then agreed. With support from the other men, he wrote and mailed a letter to the other woman, officially terminating their affair. Then, surrounded by members from both his and Mary's culture circles, Tim revealed the truth to his wife and children. Although understandably upset, Mary was also relieved to hear the truth, which confirmed that she wasn't crazy or overly suspicious.

Mary spent many hours in her culture circle discussing her confusion over her responsibilities within her marriage and at

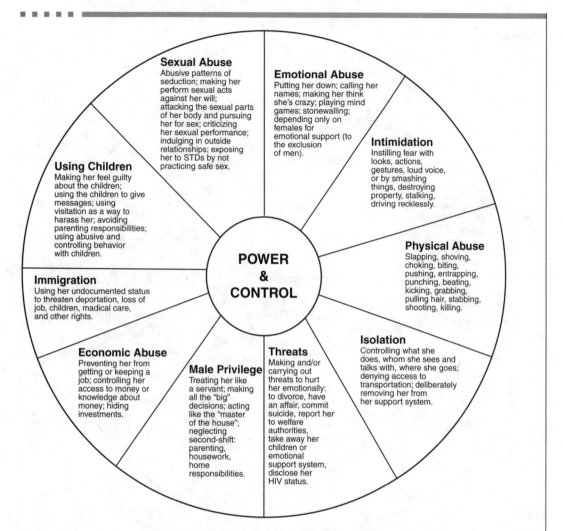

FIGURE 1.1 **Private Context: The Misuse and Abuse of Power within Heterosexual Relationships**

Adapted from Ellen Pence, founder of the Domestic Abuse Intervention Project (DAIP) in Duluth, Minnesota: www.tamu.edu/wcenter/ruralfamilyviolence/pence.htm

work. She and Tim owned and operated a printing and office supply store, where Tim assumed responsibility over Mary and the staff. Slowly, Mary acknowledged the many ways in which Tim subordinated her at work and at home. At work, he cut her off in staff meetings, overrode her decisions, and always second-guessed her investment choices. In the home, he helped with household duties only when invited. If he happened to be watching a

(continued)

■ ■ ■ ■ ■

CASE 1.1   CONTINUED

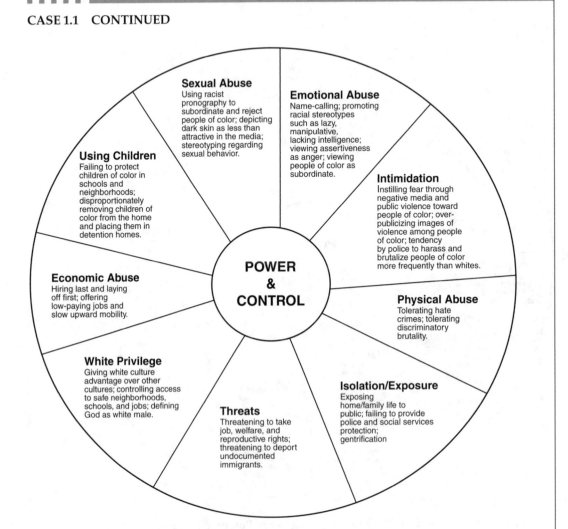

FIGURE 1.2   White Privilege/Public Context: The Misuse and Abuse of Power toward People of Color

Institute for Family Services (IFS) 3 Clyde Road, Suite 101, Somerset, NJ 08873

ball game and they were getting ready for invited guests, Tim felt no obligation to assist Mary in the dinner preparation. Within his culture circle, Tim was also becoming aware of the ways in which he abused his privileges,

assuming Mary would nurture him without the need for reciprocity.

Tim and Mary's children each participated in a series of sessions with their same-sex parent. In the initial session with Mary and her daughter Kathy, which included female sponsors and Mary's culture circle, Kathy vented her anger toward Mary for choosing to stay with Tim despite the horrible way he treated Mary.

In later sessions, Kathy voiced understanding of her mother's choices and described the different choices she would make if she found herself in a similar predicament. Kathy's participation helped her develop a different perspective of her mother as woman. She became more compassionate toward her mother as she came to understand the complexities of her mother's choice. She was also able to confront her father about her sadness and disappointment with his choices. Her symptoms of anorexia nervosa dissipated as the secret of his affair was made public. Dan, Tim and Mary's son, was noncommittal. In Dan's circle, he was exposed to **social education** and conversation among the men regarding traditional

gender roles that often embrace a rigid sense of masculinity and homophobia.

Tim described feeling a new sense of freedom and calm, having relinquished the stress that comes with secrecy and a posture of domination. He began to love the camaraderie of the men's culture circles. Like many men, he had relinquished most of his friendships many years ago and was now rediscovering the joy such connections bring. Tim and Mary transitioned into more egalitarian marital and business partners. They organized the household responsibilities, sorting them into daily, weekly, monthly, and seasonal jobs that are fairly negotiated. They met with a financial planner and redefined their roles as business partners, placing Mary as codirector with equal control over the finances. Tim and Mary continue their involvement with the therapeutic community but primarily as participants in social and community projects.

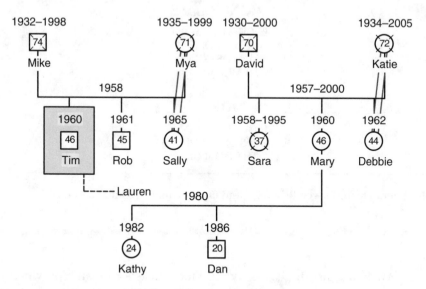

FIGURE 1.3A   Tim and Mary Genogram

(continued)

■ ■ ■ ■ ■

CASE 1.1   CONTINUED

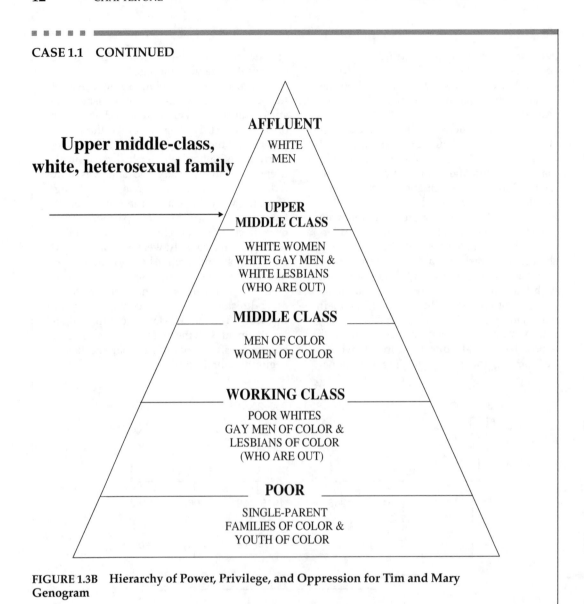

Upper middle-class, white, heterosexual family

AFFLUENT
WHITE
MEN

**UPPER
MIDDLE CLASS**

WHITE WOMEN
WHITE GAY MEN &
WHITE LESBIANS
(WHO ARE OUT)

MIDDLE CLASS

MEN OF COLOR
WOMEN OF COLOR

WORKING CLASS

POOR WHITES
GAY MEN OF COLOR &
LESBIANS OF COLOR
(WHO ARE OUT)

POOR

SINGLE-PARENT
FAMILIES OF COLOR &
YOUTH OF COLOR

FIGURE 1.3B   Hierarchy of Power, Privilege, and Oppression for Tim and Mary Genogram

We know that this case may raise more questions than it provides answers. For example, why involve the kids in a parent's affair? Isn't that an issue for adults? Are appropriate boundaries being set and respected? Is it healthy and constructive to be so honest? Why was a group approach used? Isn't privacy better?

Please note your questions and any initial discomfort you may feel with the approach. We hope that your questions will be answered as you read this book.

THE CHALLENGE OF CHANGE

Until the 1970s, it was considered highly unorthodox for a therapist to meet with more than one family member. The family therapy movement arose as a radically different mental health approach—a necessary expansion of the prevailing emphasis on the individual and intrapsychic dynamics. Borrowing heavily from early social work models, a variety of systemic approaches emerged, each offering unique conceptual and technical contributions. Multiculturalism began to influence writers and clinicians, though many did not know how to introduce the ideas into the therapeutic process.

Although activist approaches, such as feminist consciousness-raising groups, became part of some therapists' work in the 1970s and 1980s, activist practice has mostly disappeared from therapeutic models. Most therapeutic approaches today involve conversations between one therapist and a client or client family in which socially mandated hierarchies of power are rarely mentioned and even more rarely challenged.

For example, a heterosexual couple seeking assistance for a "communication problem" is typically engaged in an exploration that, in keeping with their expectations, locates their problem within the bounds of their dyad. The therapist proceeds as though only the emotional and behavioral dimensions of the couple's partnership are relevant. Consequently, the following questions are *not* routinely asked: Who manages the family money? Who handles second-shift responsibilities such as housework, child care, and maintenance of the couple's connections to family and friends? What are the couple's decision-making and conflict resolution patterns? How does the couple negotiate the fulfillment of each other's sexual needs?

When these questions are pursued, the answers are rarely challenged because of the therapist's pursuit of remaining neutral. Underlying gendered prescriptions are rarely explored. If one or both members of the couple are people of color, it is unlikely that the impact of racism both outside and within the couple's relationship will be investigated. Questions about this include: What does your support circle at work look like? If or when your children experience bias or discrimination in school, who handles it? Similarly, a therapist working with a same-gender couple will likely not inquire into the impact of homophobia on the couple's relationship either within extended families or with the outer world. The focus in each case often remains on verbal, behavioral, and emotional transactions that the couple describes and exhibits during therapy sessions.

The therapist is also likely to enforce mainstream societal prescriptions in many ways. For example, therapists often search for psychopathology in one or both members of the couple. Since most diagnoses were developed by men and about women, a female client is more likely than a male to be pathologized. Similarly, a woman's emotional response, and not the man's lack of one, is likely to be labeled problematic.

Solution-focused or strengths-based approaches avoid some of these pitfalls, yet they often fail to consider the broader contextual issues. Though often unintentionally, therapists regularly replicate and reinforce socially prescribed norms during therapy sessions, often to the serious detriment of their clients. The most dangerous examples, of course, include those in which therapists hold women clients responsible for their own physical battering by abusive partners or strangers.

Transformative, social justice approaches not only acknowledge gender, race, culture, sexual orientation, and class as matters of significance, but also address the varying histories around issues of power, privilege, and oppression that accompany these factors. We do not address culture by focusing on ethnic enclaves. Instead, we bring culture into the therapy room through popular films, printed literary material, and other media. Clients learn and participate in sharing their knowledge about various cultures. We encourage therapists to merge this learning about culture in context with their readings from multiculturalism. More specifically, we ask them to consider a transformative versus an ameliorative approach when it comes to the unfairness often linked to cultural differences.

Transformative family therapy moves the focus away from simply searching for problems (or solutions) or navigating adaptation to existing systems. It includes a search for reciprocity and resilience and a demand for change in the current economic, social, and political structures. Transformative family therapy requires bold evaluation and revision of much that we professionals find comforting. We hope this book illuminates ways to accomplish this transformation, and we invite you to join us in this project.

The chapters that follow describe elements of the cultural context model in detail and discuss how you can adapt these elements to all practice settings. While theory is essential, the following chapters emphasize practical application. Over the years, we have witnessed the important link between social justice and relational healing as they become a reality in the lives of our clients and also in our lives as practitioners. We are eager for you and your clients to enjoy the same rewards.

ESSENTIAL CONCEPTS

We provide below a list of terms that will prove useful as you read the book.

Accountability: Accountability begins with acceptance of responsibility for one's actions and the impact of those actions upon others. However, accountability moves beyond blame and guilt. It results in reparative action that demonstrates empathic concern for others by making changes that enhance the quality of life for all involved parties.

Critical consciousness: Critical consciousness is awareness of the political foundation of relationship patterns. Transformative family therapy works to develop critical consciousness as both a catalyst and map for positive change. In subsequent chapters, we extensively explore critical consciousness.

Paulo Freire (1978; 2000) originated the term *critical consciousness* to describe the awakening of his literacy students to the impact of social class dynamics on their life circumstances. As critical consciousness develops, we no longer see current realities as "the unquestioned and unchangeable nature of things." Instead, we see options for change. For example, those who view men as genetically programmed for aggression also accept war and domestic violence as the natural order of things, whereas those who view men's aggression as a learned tactic of domination see the possibilities for peace on all systems levels.

Culture circle: Another term borrowed from Freire, culture circles are heterogeneous helping communities involving members of families who seek treatment, volunteer helpers from the community who work with the families, and a team of therapists. Within the cultural context model, culture circles provide the primary context for treatment. Culture circles, discussed in detail in subsequent chapters, promote healing through development of critical consciousness and resistance to norms that maintain hierarchies of power, privilege, and oppression.

Empowerment: Social justice–based empowerment promotes "power with" rather than "power over." For example, a woman gains empowerment by pursuing an education and employment that allows her to fulfill a lifelong dream while also financially supporting herself and her children. A man who has neglected his wife and child gains empowerment through his letter of accountability to them and through his subsequent reparative actions. He is empowered through just action—and so are those on the receiving end. This definition initially confuses some practitioners, whose patriarchal vision presumes that when a man takes responsibility for his actions, he experiences humility rather than empowerment.

Genogram: The genogram is a tool used to gather information on family process and generational patterns. Tables 1.1, 1.2, and 1.3 explain the legends used in genograms.

Intersectionality: Intersectionality is the dynamic interplay of gender, race, sexual orientation, social class, age, disability status, and other diversity markers in

TABLE 1.1   GenoPro Emotional Relationships Legend

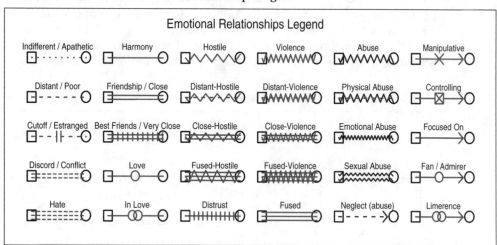

GenoPro Beta. Genogram Soft Wave www.genopro.com

TABLE 1.2   GenoPro Family Relationships Legend

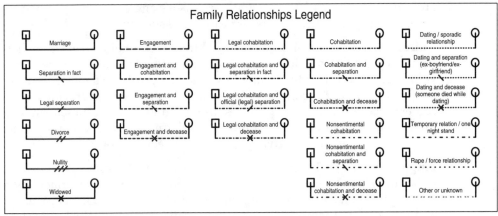

GenoPro Beta. Genogram Soft Wave www.genopro.com

an individual's life circumstances. Intersectionality also includes the resources and lack of resources these identity aspects convey upon the individual. Mindfulness of intersectionality interrupts the usual pattern of discussing differences in a fragmented manner. More specifically, the impact of a person's race cannot be evaluated apart from his or her gender, class, sexual orientation, age, and disability status. For a visual representation of a person's social location, see Figure 1.4, which illustrates the way power, privilege, oppression situate us relative to one another.

We want you to become familiar with the concept of social location (intersectionality) when you consider family genograms. The family genogram depicted in red is an illustration of the family's social location on this hierarchy. Each family member reflects a different nodal point experience: together they represent multiple intersections. Reggie, African American son of sharecroppers, moved to middle class via education, a stable job and income, and a small inheritance from the sale of his parents' farm. He was able to purchase a home when he married (asset accumulation). He married Lily, a dark-skinned Latina whose single mother, a

TABLE 1.3   GenoPro Genogram Symbols Legend

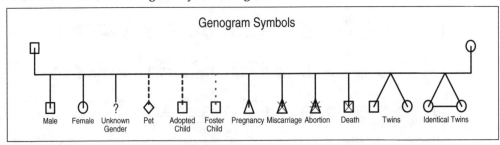

GenoPro Beta. Genogram Soft Wave www.genopro.com

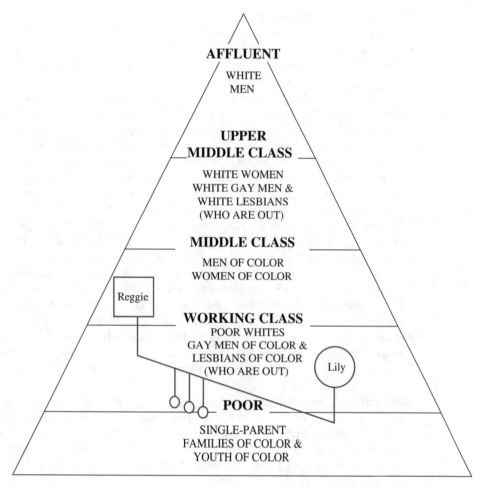

FIGURE 1.4 Hierarchy of Power, Privilege, and Oppression

Black Cuban working-class woman, experienced multiple oppressions of racism, sexism, and classism. Lily's mother struggled to support Lily and her brother on a stable but modest income working as a janitor in a hospital (stable working class but no asset accumulation to pass on to her children).

With Tim and Mary, whose case we examined earlier, asset accumulation was abundant in addition to race privilege. These points of intersection are not static but fluid. Consider the case of a poor white family who might occupy the same position as a poor family of color but simultaneously experiences race privilege as they interface with police, judicial system, teachers, bank representatives, realtors, and other "officials." Racial, cultural, and economic standards define inequality in this country. With a white, working class or poor family, many of the intersects would be different, Historically, wealth to all white families was passed on through GI bills, subsidized housing through the VA loans, no discrimination with education, and work that included benefits and social security. Today, many adults of color whose parents were domestic workers or engaged in forms of employment that lacked a contribution into social security have to take care of elderly parents with no governmental support for basic needs (Lui, et. al., 2006).

While individuals within all races and genders can achieve wealth, the hierarchy is a depiction of collectives and their varying access to wealth. Why do hard-working Americans of all nationalities not participate equally in the accumulation of wealth? For centuries, laws, discriminatory practices, and violence restricted people of color from participating in wealth-building programs. Since this nation was founded, U.S. government policies that enabled white Americans to accumulate wealth were not accessible to people of color. For example, during the 1800s when Chinese American citizens attempted to purchase property, they were faced with the politics of identity: Were they white or immigrant? Congress hurriedly passed a law defining them as nonwhite citizens, rendering them unable to purchase property. Misogyny laws were enacted to ensure that Chinese men who married white women would not be allowed the legitimate purchase of property. Lui et al. (2006) telegraph the roots of economic divisions: "White Americans typically have assets more than ten times greater than Americans of color. This difference was created not only by government policies that impeded wealth building for people of color but also by policies that actually boosted white wealth—policies like land grant and homestead programs, low-cost mortgages, farm loans, and Social Security checks, all at times available mostly to white people" (p. 225).

Multiculturalism: Multiculturalism is a catchall term that usually refers to race but also commonly extends to other categories of diversity: socioeconomic class, gender, language, culture, sexual orientation, and disability. Writers in the field describe not one but several multiculturalisms. We make the distinction here between definitions of multiculturalism that focus on superficial valuing of differences and critical multiculturalism.

What we consider to be a superficial view of multiculturalism more often describes family patterns and historical legacies and promotes celebration of foods, traditional styles of dress, holiday rituals, and belief systems across the spectrum of diversity. By compartmentalizing various ethnic groups, this definition avoids acknowledging systems of power, privilege, and oppression. Moreover, whiteness is not deconstructed, nor are Eurocentric norms. These omissions bolster those with power to acknowledge and romanticize differences while denying their own relative power, privilege, and accountability for the oppression of others.

We instead embrace a critical multiculturalism based in postcolonial theory. Critical multiculturalism "is dedicated to the notion of egalitarianism and the elimination of human suffering" (Espin, 1999; Kincheloe & Steinberg, 1997, p. 24). It is concerned with issues of justice and social change: how domination occurs and how it shapes human relations in families, the workplace, the schools, and everyday life.

Patriarchy: Patriarchy is a worldwide, cross-cultural system of male domination—men over women and men over men. Patriarchy is a system that values power over life, control over pleasure, and dominance over happiness. As a foundation, patriarchal hierarchy relies on rigid categories of difference. Transgender people, for example, threaten patriarchy by obscuring the definitional boundary between those who rule (men) and those who serve (women). In ordaining power over rather than power with, patriarchy provides the structure for all other systems of privilege and oppression (racism, classism, and homophobia). Refer to Figure 1.4 to see the resulting matrix.

Postcolonial: The term *diaspora*, within postcolonial studies, suggests both a breakthrough in cultural politics and social justice. It interrogates the final stage in the ascendancy of migrant, "cosmopolitan," and first-world metropolitan biases in representations of the "postcolonial experience." The prefix *post* does not imply that colonialism is a past, historical phenomenon but rather an ongoing meta-perspective, A postcolonial analysis recommends that therapists consistently attend to both precolonial and postcolonial history because they inform identity through the intersectionalities of social location. A fundamental tenet of postcolonial analysis is that attention be paid to the standpoint and social location of the author scholarship (therapist) and the audience.

Privilege: An individual gains an advantage, or privilege, when he or she possesses certain identity characteristics such as white skin, maleness, heterosexuality, middle- or upper middle-class status, and able-bodied status. An individual loses an advantage, or privilege, when he or she possesses characteristics such as femaleness, queerness, skin of color, and low-income or poverty status (McIntosh 1990).

Queer: An umbrella term for lesbians, gay men, bisexuals, transgender people, and others who do not identify themselves as heterosexual, *queer* is a "reclaimed" affirmation favored by activists for its inclusiveness. A growing number of "queer studies" programs at universities mark this usage as the term favored within academia. However, its historically pejorative meaning of "strange" continues to offend some within the GLTB (gay, lesbian, transgender, bisexual) communities.

Reparations: Corrective actions that serve to restore equity after injustices have been committed, reparations include the gift of services, currency, property, or other assets. Social justice–based therapy includes these corrective exchanges as a means for rebalancing damaged relationships in a way that facilitates healing.

Social education: An integral part of social justice–based therapy, social education promotes critical consciousness. Popular movies, songs, magazine and newspaper articles, along with handouts that list norms of masculinity and femininity, patterns of power and control within relationships, and other social patterns (Figure 1.2 is an example of such a tool) can be used to initiate discussions with clients about contemporary sociopolitical realities.

Support: Support within the framework of social justice never serves to elevate one individual at the expense of another. Men, therefore, are encouraged to support one another in a manner that values the needs of each man's partner and children equally with his own needs. Women are supported in valuing their own needs no less than their partner's needs. Whites are supported in their collective and personal ability to take responsibility for racism. People of color are encouraged to interrogate their own systems of internalized racism, power, and privilege.

REFERENCES

Cesaire, A. (1972). *Discourses on colonialism*. New York: Monthly Review Press.

Collins, P. H. (1989). A comparison of two works on Black family life. *Signs: Journal of Women in Culture and Society, 14*(4), 875–884.

Crenshaw, K. (1994). Mapping the margins: Intersectionality, identity politics, and violence against women of color. In M. Fineman & R. Mykitiuk (Eds.), *The public nature of private violence* (pp. 93–118). New York: Routledge.

Duran, E., & Duran, B. (1995). *Native American postcolonial psychology*. Albany, NY: State University of New York Press.

Espin, O. (1999). *Women crossing boundaries: The psychology of immigration and the transformations of sexuality*. New York: Routledge.

Freire, A. A., & Macedo, D. (2000). *The Paulo Freire reader*. New York: Continuum.

Freire, P. (1978) *Education for a critical consciousness*. New York: Seabury Press.

Kincheloe, J. L., & Steinberg, S. R. (1997). *Changing multiculturalism*. Philadelphia: Open University Press.

Lui, M., Robles, B., Leondar-Wright, B., Brewer, R., & Adamson, R., with United for a Fair Economy. (2006). *The color of wealth: The story behind the U.S. racial wealth divide*. New York: The New Press.

McIntosh, P. (1990). White privilege: Unpacking the invisible knapsack. *Independent School, 49*, 31–39.

Memmi, A. (1967). *The colonizer and the colonized*. Boston: Beacon Press.

Pizzigati, S. (2004). *Good and greed: Understanding and overcoming the inequality that limits our lives*. New York: Apex Press.

Said, E. (1993). *Culture and imperialism*, London: Chatto and Windus.

Soyinka, W. (1999). *The burden of memory, the muse of forgiveness*. New York: Oxford University Press.

Spivak, G. (1987). *In other worlds: Essays in cultural politics*. New York and London: Methuen.

Spivak, G. (1989). A response to "The difference within: Feminism and critical theory." In E. Meese & A. Parker (Eds.), *The Difference Within: Feminism and Critical Theory* (pp. 207–220). Amsterdam/Philadelphia: John Benjamins.

Spivak, G. (1990). *The post colonial critic: Interviews, strategies, dialogues*. S. Harasym (Ed.). London: Routledge.

Stevenson, B. (2006). Commencement speech at Bard College, Annondale-on-Hudson, NY. May 20.

Stoler, L.A. (1995). *Race and the education of desire: Foucault's history of sexuality and the colonial order of things*. Durham, NC: Duke University Press.

Tamasese, K., & Waldegrave, C. (1993). Culture and gender accountability in the just therapy approach. *Journal of Feminist Family Therapy, 5*(2), 29–45.

Thandeka, (1999). *Learning to be white—Money, race and God in America*. New York: Continuum.

University of California, Berkeley, Institute of International Studies. (1998, April). *Wole Soyinka*. Retrieved March 19, 2007, from: http://globefrotter.berkeley.edu/Elberg/Soyinka.

Wise, T. (2004). *White like me: Reflections on race from a privileged son*. New York: Soft Skull Press.

Wollman, N., Yoder, B., Brumbaugh-Smith, J. & Largent, J. (2005). *Trends in homelessness, health, hunger and dropout data suggest a 'society at risk'*, North Manchester, Indiana: Manchester College's Peace Studies Institute.

Yellow Bird, M. (1995). Spirituality in First Nations storytelling: A Sahnish-Hidatsa approach to narrative. *Reflections: Narratives of Professional Helping. A Journal for the Helping Professions, 1*(4), 65–72.

Yellow Bird, M. (2001). Critical values and First Nations peoples. In R. Fong & S. Furuto (Eds.), *Cultural competent social work: Interventions* (pp. 61–74). Boston: Allyn and Bacon.

RECOMMENDED READINGS

Ashcroft, B., Griffiths, G., & Tiffin, H. (1998). *Key concepts in post-colonial studies*. London and New York: Routledge.

Anthony, A. K., & Gates, H. L., Jr. (1996). *The dictionary of global culture*. New York: Alfred A. Knopf.

Bhabha, H. K. (1991). The postcolonial critic: Homi Bhabha interviewed by David Bennett and Terry Collits. *Arena*, 96, 47–63.

Brophy, A. L. (2004) Reparations talk: Reparations for slavery and the tort law analogy. *Boston College Third World Law Journal*, 24, 81–138.

Brophy, A. L. (2004). The cultural war over reparations for slavery. *DePaul Law Review*, 53, 1181–1213.

Connors, J. (1996). The women's convention in the Muslim world. In Mai Yamani (Ed.), *Feminism and Islam: Legal and literary perspectives*. Berkshire: Garnet.

Prashad, V. (2000). *The karma of brown folk*. Minneapolis: University of Minnesota Press.

Said, E. (1989). Representing the colonized: Anthropology's interlocutors. *Critical Inquiry*, 15, 2 (Winter), 205–225.

Said, E. (1990). In the shadow of the West: An interview with Edward Said. With P. Mariani and J. Crary. In R. Ferguson, W. Olander, M. Tucker, & K. Fiss (Eds.), *Discourses: Conversations in postmodern art and culture* (pp. 93–103). Cambridge, MA: New Museum of Contemporary Art, MIT Press.

Sharabi, H. (1992, Fall). Modernity and Islamic revival: The critical task of Arab intellectuals. *Contention*, 2(1).

Sharoni, S. (1997, October–December). Women and gender in Middle East studies: Trends, prospects, and challenges. *Middle East Report*, 27(205).

Spivak, G. (1983). Displacement and the discourse of woman. In M. Krupnick (Ed.), *Displacement: Derrida and after* (pp. 169–196). Bloomington: Indiana University Press.

Spivak, G. (1985). The Rani of Simur. In F. Barker, P. Hulme, M. Iversen, & Diana Loxley (Eds.), *Europe and its others* (Vol. 1, pp. 129–151). Colchester, UK: University of Essex.

Spivak, G. (1986). Imperialism and sexual difference. *Oxford Literary Review*, 8(1–2), 225–240.

Spivak, G. (1989). The political economy of women as seen by a literary critic. In E. Weed (Ed.), *Coming to terms: Feminism, theory, politics* (pp. 218–229). New York: Routledge.

Spivak, G. (1992). *Outside in the teaching machine*. New York: Routledge.

Stannard, D. *The American holocaust: The conquest of the New World*. New York: Oxford University Press.

Vaid, U. (1997). *Virtual equality: The mainstreaming of gay and lesbian liberation*. New York: Random House.

CHAPTER TWO

CRITICAL CONSCIOUSNESS: RECOGNIZING THE SOCIAL AND POLITICAL CONTEXT OF DAILY LIFE

There is no discussion taking place in the world today that is more crucial than the debate about strategies of resistance.
—(Arundhati Roy, 2004, p.55).

Critical consciousness brings with it an awareness of the sociopolitical context of daily life. It often illuminates realities that we take for granted about how the world operates—for example, the manner in which family therapy and mental health service delivery systems are structured according to hierarchies of class, profession, gender, race, sexual orientation, disability status, and most importantly, funding sources. Critical consciousness empowers therapists to avoid replicating domination within intervention practices, and it empowers clients to gain a comprehensive perspective (meta-perspective) on the distress they are experiencing.

For example, a client who develops critical consciousness may learn that her depression is not exclusively a medical illness driven by organic factors she cannot change. Instead, she discovers that expectations rooted in patriarchy—her husband's desire that she take care of him, her unsatisfying employment, her financial worries—also contribute to her depression.

A strictly medical model gives her two choices: to consume or not consume a prescribed antidepressant medication. But a broader understanding of her situation, awakened by critical consciousness, opens up a range of options, including strategies for gaining equal power within her intimate partnership, opportunities for more satisfying employment, and steps toward a more secure financial status.

She moves from being simply a patient to becoming an agent in her own process of evolution.

At the same time, the therapist who gains critical consciousness becomes a collaborator and fellow explorer in the client's healing process instead of taking a dominant role.

In this chapter, we examine

- The elements of critical consciousness.
- The role critical consciousness plays in therapy.
- How to help therapists develop critical consciousness.

Consciousness raising should be fundamental to any social justice–oriented therapy. We agree with liberation theorists and feminists who assert that the personal is political—that a person's gender, race, sexual orientation, sexual identity, culture, and ethnicity have a profound impact on personal and social relations. Moreover, the failure to break down the broader social dimensions in the therapeutic process makes us complicit with practices of domination.

WHAT IS CRITICAL CONSCIOUSNESS?

What tools do we need to build critical consciousness? First, we must ask important questions: "What? Why? How? To what end? For whom? Against whom? By whom? In favor of whom? In favor of what?" (Freire & Macedo, 2000, p. 7).

These questions force us to consider issues broadly, including our reason for being, our purpose in life, and how we handle life's unique challenges. When this process is integrated into therapy, clients are empowered toward liberation. They also become aware of the cost to themselves and their families when others are marginalized.

A prominent Latin American liberation psychologist, Ignacio Martin-Baro, wrote:

> There is no person without family, no learning without culture, no madness without social order, and therefore neither can there be an I without a We, a knowing without a symbolic knowing, a disorder that does not have reference to moral and social norms. (1994, p. 41)

CRITICAL CONSCIOUSNESS: INTEGRATING COLLECTIVISM, SOCIAL EDUCATION, AND SOCIAL ACTION

Through educator Paulo Freire's direct experiences teaching literacy to Brazilian peasants, he developed the process of "awakening consciousness" (1971), which emphasizes the link between intrapersonal dynamics and sociopolitical context. Freire originated the use of culture circles as his teaching forum. Collective discussions prompted critical reflection and dialogue about the life circumstances of the participants. Freire believed that individuals could develop an increased aware-ness of their own place in the world via reflective dialogue combined with social action.

Freire's work was originally used to organize working-class communities in Brazil to challenge their social and economic disenfranchisement. This process is similar to the liberatory base Christian communities in Mexico and South America that help marginalized people improve their social conditions.

Freire's concept of critical consciousness focused primarily on social class and political power. We expand his concept to include all dimensions of a person's social location: gender, race, sexual orientation, ethnicity, religion, and physical ability. An inclusive critical consciousness provides a platform for family therapy that incorporates social justice.

We suggest that, like Freire, therapists work to bring together clients from diverse backgrounds and ask them to consider their respective places in life, soci-ety, and the political process. When clients are grouped together, they move from a pointed focus on individual personal problems to empowerment as they develop an understanding of the social conditions that cause and contribute to problems.

Therapists, clients, and communities working together to develop critical con-sciousness provide a first step toward building more just relationships for all involved parties. Critical consciousness propels therapists and clients through expe-riences of empowerment and accountability, which are cornerstones for liberation.

This approach, which works within a framework of social justice, promotes balance between self-interest and the interests of one's community and family. For example, in an Asian family in which the revered, newlywed older son was accustomed to placing his own desires above those of the women in his life, social justice–oriented therapy offered him the opportunity to engage in discussions with other men. Through such discussions, the son learned to counter his self-focus and pay equal attention to the dreams of his new bride.

In another example, a lesbian client in her late 30s, because of her self-centerdness, experienced difficulties with colleagues and partnerships. Her rigid self-focus evolved from her childhood: She was one of many children and little attention was paid to her daily well-being. Neglected by her mother, she fell prey to the focus by her alcoholic father only in the service of his own needs. She coped by becoming overly self-reliant, competitive, and by elevating achievement at work. These rigid traditional norms, as well as her tendency to denigrate feminine sensi-bilities and nurturing skills, constrained many of her relationships. These internal-ized male norms kept her from being vulnerable and nurturing in relationships.

We asked her to learn to cook, buy kitchenware, nurture herself with baths, and cook one dish a week for others in her friendship circle. Simple tasks like these help clients challenge hierarchies of power, privilege, and oppression. They help to resocialize people toward a more collective understanding of their lives and cir-cumstances. This experience normalizes the issues for which clients have sought therapy and empowers them, offering a new and expanded vision of self and rela-tionship to others.

These tasks also help clients distinguish rights from privileges. We have a right to necessities, such as the air we breathe, shelter, and safety. Privileges convey unearned advantages based upon gender, race, sexual orientation, age, family background, ableness, and other human characteristics. The critical consciousness curriculum addresses the entire matrix of human diversity and social context, including broader social issues.

Because of their social status, race, sexual orientation, and religion, those who have the privilege of defining "reality" are often people with powerful and privileged social positions. Consequently, they have little incentive to explore the experiences of those who are "less fortunate." While people are often acutely aware of those who hold more power and privilege than they do, they are usually less aware or concerned about those who have less power.

The process of building critical consciousness requires that we simultaneously transform ourselves while we transform our relationships with others and our communities. Through dialogue, reflection, social education, and action, families remodel their lives along with their communities.

Family interaction normally takes place within a societal context that teaches people to judge and value others according to their identity characteristics: skin color, gender, sexual orientation, immigrant status, class, and the like. These variables infuse interactions within the family and within society with patterns of inequality that too often go unacknowledged and unchallenged. It is crucial to examine and expose these patterns in order to heal.

WHAT ROLE DOES CONSCIOUSNESS-RAISING PLAY IN THERAPY?

Critical consciousness develops as clients examine their own expressed concerns against the backdrop of the sociopolitical realities of the larger world. Developing critical consciousness can be supported in a number of ways. Clients may be encouraged to get involved in social action projects relevant to their own issues, to read, or to watch popular films and documentary clips pertinent to the issues. These activities must have a context for dialogue and inquiry.

Therapy has historically been a Western, cognitive, intellectual enterprise. As a result, its structure has been less useful for people who are not introspective or who lack the ability, willingness, or inclination to articulate their thoughts and feelings. The use of films, narratives, music, and supporting handouts—in English and other languages—can engage clients and make therapy more accessible. In addition, these tools can help clients build their critical consciousness as they link their personal concerns to patterns in society.

Developing critical consciousness is especially important because many institutions that make up our society, and especially workplaces, indoctrinate us with values that promote hierarchy, domination, and discrimination. This point is demonstrated in Case 2.1.

■ ■ ■ ■ ■

CASE 2.1

FACING POWER, PRIVILEGE, AND OPPRESSION IN THE WORKPLACE

Clyde, a middle-aged white male corporate director, manages outside vendors for his corporation. To get better service, Clyde's boss, a vice president, encouraged Clyde to verbally chastise those vendors. Clyde saw his harshness toward the vendors as loyalty to the corporation. After all, he was "just trying to make the vendors deliver on their contracts." Obscured within his "naive" consciousness were the ties between the corporate culture and his increasing dehumanization of self and others.

He believed that his commitment to the corporation was mutual. In fact, that was not the case. The corporation showed no interest in reciprocating Clyde's loyalty. Corporations have a legal mandate to create short-term profits for their shareholders. Few modern corporations offer loyalty to employees, their families, or communities.

Yet Clyde, like many other organizational employees, committed his life to his employer, devoting 50 to 60 hours per week to his job. When his loyalty was not rewarded, he became enraged. In therapy, Clyde was asked to broaden the examination of his rage. Rather than focusing solely on his rage at incompetent vendors, the therapeutic team encouraged him to consider the politics of the vendor–corporation contract. He was asked to consider how his corporation operates within the larger political and social context. This exploration mobilized Clyde's rage and underlying depression in a new way, transforming them into a healthy anger. Like others who have been oppressed, Clyde began to feel that he deserved equity.

In spite of the many reasons for his investment in the status quo, as Clyde examined his own family history of upward mobility and how it was connected to other people within the corporation of different status, he was willing to entertain the links between his personal story and larger patterns of power, privilege, and oppression in society.

For Clyde and for others dealing with corporate abuses of power, critical consciousness requires critical inquiry into the prevailing capitalist narrative: Who benefits? Who loses? Are there alternative options? How has the current age of corporate globalization been reshaping cultural sensibilities?

The 2002 International Forum on Globalization identified the following corporate values:

- Profit motive is sacred.
- Everything, including time and health, is regarded as a commodity.
- What you can get people to believe is more important than truth.
- The costs of social responsibility can and should be avoided.
- Immediate profit gain is prioritized (look no further ahead than quarterly return on investment).
- Knowledge and experience are compartmentalized.
- Accountability goes in one direction only: up the chain of command.
- Rigid hierarchy is the dominant social structure.
- Job security for employees is sacrificed to maximize economic gain for senior executives (and other stockholders).

For clients who are struggling with corporate or workplace issues, lists like this one can lift problems out of the personal realm and into the social realm; help them normalize their feelings, often of depression or rage; and can propel them into action.

We also recommend using excerpts from popular films as starting points for consciousness raising around corporate life. Relevant films include *Roger and Me*, *The Corporation*, *Wal-Mart: The High Cost of Low Price*, *In Good Company*, and *Working Girl*.

- *Roger and Me*, a 1989 documentary directed by Michael Moore about the abandonment of Flint, Michigan, by General Motors, is both a dark comedy and a compelling indictment of an American Dream gone awry. Using the premise that he is trying to get an interview with the president of General Motors, Roger Smith, Moore explores the tragic fallout of closing down the GM plant in Flint: 25 percent unemployment; record rates of suicide, spousal abuse, and alcoholism; and skyrocketing rates of violent crime. Through live footage of the citizens, Moore shows the differential cost levied by the imbrications of race, class, and gender.
- *Wal-Mart: The High Cost of Low Price*, a 2005 film directed by Richard Greenwald, explores the retail giant's assault on families and American values. Mixing statistics and employee testimony, Greenwald details the giant's business practices: coerced unpaid overtime, foreign sweatshop labor, and health-insurance packages that have forced thousands of employees to rely on Medicare.
- *The Corporation*, a 2004 film directed by Mark Achbar and Jennifer Abbott and written by Joel Bakan, explores the origins and nature of the dominant institution of our time. It illuminates the corporation's grip on our lives with footage from pop culture, advertising, television news, and corporate propaganda. Taking corporate legal status as a "person" to its logical conclusion, the film assesses the institutions, which have the rights of an individual but neither the social nor legal constraints of a human. The film includes 40 interviews with corporate insiders and critics—including Milton Friedman, Noam Chomsky, Naomi Klein, and Michael Moore—along with case studies and strategies for change.
- *In Good Company*, a 2004 film written and directed by Paul Weitz, depicts the corporate culture in which plundering victims and looting assets are shown on the books as growth. Dennis Quaid plays a middle-aged advertising executive who, the victim of a merger, gets new boss who is half his age. While telling a romantic and amusing story, the movie raises the issues of mergers, downsizing, demotions, and ageism and explores their impact on male norms and family life.
- *Working Girl*—directed by Mike Nichols, written by Kevin Wade, and starring Melanie Griffith, Harrison Ford, and Sigourney Weaver—is a movie about life in the corporate jungle. While telling an entertaining Cinderella story, it explores class relations among women, corporate ladders and their dangerously serrated edges, and the way women can internalize male norms and mistreat each other as brutally as any patriarchal club wielder.

After the clients view these films on their own or view excerpts within a circle that the therapist arranges, follow-up discussions help the client define the cost of corporate life to individuals, families, and communities. Therapists must bring what is unseen, and perhaps unpleasant, to the surface. The challenge is to raise the issues—to make what has been invisible, visible; what has been comfortable, less comfortable; what has been absent, present—and to not lose the clients.

Raising difficult issues for scrutiny is not unique to therapy. What is unique is the objective: confronting issues of power, privilege, and oppression. Underlying the process is the sense that people's problems have roots in patriarchy, colonization, racism, and capitalism. The shared goal is to unravel the problems, the social and cultural system affecting the lives of the individual, couple, family, and community.

STRUCTURING SESSIONS FOR CONSCIOUSNESS RAISING

How sessions are initially organized sets the social justice course by defining what issues are relevant. The therapeutic team and the client must assess which issues are being addressed and which are not. We advocate that therapists initiate social education respectfully yet matter-of-factly. When clients enter therapy, they can be invited into a process of dialogue and inquiry. Social justice therapists intentionally ask questions and sequence events so that clients make a connection between their concerns and the distribution of power and privilege in their relationships.

A first session may be structured by asking questions that raise arenas of power and privilege for discussion and analysis. For example:

- How much money do you earn?
- How are resources allocated?
- Who makes decisions?
- Who accommodates?
- How are household and family-care responsibilities distributed?
- Are you employed?
- Do you work out of the home?
- If so, what is your line of employment?
- How is your workplace organized?
- What is the diversity of your workplace?
- How are management decisions made?

The specifics of these arrangements help clients begin to move beyond what is likely a denial of disparities of power and privilege in their relationships and lives. In-session exercises, education, and homework assignments are other structural means for eliciting power issues and raising partners' consciousness of such issues in their relationships.

The organization of the session should provide power-issues literacy training for clients by raising specific, concrete questions that probe power inequities. It can also be done by working with genograms, whereby therapists help partners examine the transmission of power issues down through generations and in a social and political context. Hardy and Laszloffy's (1995) cultural genogram and Halevy's (1998) "genogram with an attitude" provide good examples of this process. This information allows therapists to connect issues for which the clients came to therapy with power and privilege at the outset and establishes the tone for the therapy.

Homework tasks provide other tools to help couples reconsider their current arrangements and to get role inequities on the table. Partners can be asked to consider, and then list, what each one actually does regarding household and caregiving chores in a given day.

We often ask people to bring in a list of what their partners do in a day. When clients argue about whether or not the male partner in a heterosexual relationship is really helping out, we might say, "Pick one day, say Tuesday, and before you go to bed, write down what you did that day that relates to the children or household. Do not compare notes; just write it down." Partners then bring the lists to the next therapy session for examination and the inequities immediately become apparent in the lists each brings.

Sex, Money, and Laundry, a survey (see Table 2.1A on page 36) developed by Marianne Ault-Riche (1994), provides a structured way to achieve the same understanding. The survey divides responsibilities into daily, weekly, biweekly, monthly, bimonthly, seasonal, and annual tasks. Homework or in-session assignments focus on rebalancing inequities discovered through clients' responses to the survey.

Clients might also be asked to read Arlie Hochschild's (1990) *The Second Shift* and reflect on the three gender ideologies—traditional, transitional, and egalitarian— outlined in the book. Reading about other couples who suffer inequity in their relationships can make it easier for the couple seeking therapy to see themselves in the book's examples.

In conjunction with reading *The Second Shift*, a therapist might ask partners to think about whether they are a traditional, a transitional, or an egalitarian couple and in what ways. Then, they can start working on where they would like to be and how they might begin to get there. The exercise is quite effective because when the couple comes back, the wife usually has a very long list of the things she takes care of in the home, while the husband has just a few items on his list. At that point, the couple can begin to ask themselves, "Is this what we want?"

Finally, therapists can help family members examine the positive and negative consequences of current arrangements as a way of keeping them engaged in conversations about power and privilege. Each might be asked to examine the pluses and minuses of topics for conversation: What is acceptable, and what is not? How long is too long for such discussions?

The consequences of each of the following arrangements warrant examination:

- One partner consistently acquiescing to the other's desires
- Taking the other partner's name
- The effect of one partner bearing the primary financial, household, or family care responsibilities

It is more powerful if partners themselves, rather than the therapist, reveal the consequences of current arrangements.

Each of these examples makes it easier for clients to examine issues of power and privilege. Once these issues are on the table for discussion and inquiry, the client and therapist can examine their impact on the client's primary relationships and relationships with others.

In the cultural context model, social education toward critical consciousness is built into the structure of the therapy. After an initial intake session, all clients enter a same-gender social education orientation group. This component of therapy critically locates clients within their social, cultural, and political lives. Clients learn a new language for communicating about the complex ways in which people experience their communities of family, work, religion, and recreation. All clients complete a basic genogram. They use the language from the power and control wheels (see Figures 2.1, 2.2, 2.3) to launch conversations regarding various film vignettes as well as stories of other participants. In Chapter 1, we introduced the critical consciousness wheel, the heterosexual wheel, and the hierarchy of power,

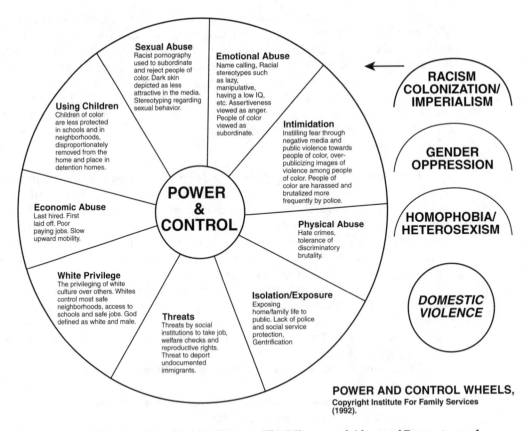

POWER AND CONTROL WHEELS,
Copyright Institute For Family Services (1992).

FIGURE 2.1   White Privilege/Public Context: The Misuse and Abuse of Power toward People of Color

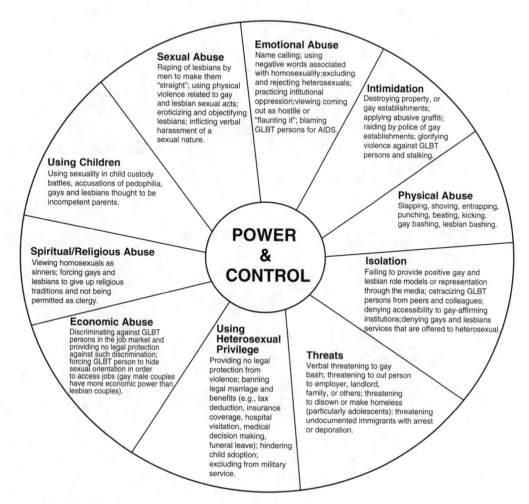

FIGURE 2.2 Public Context: The Misuse and Abuse of Power in Gay, Lesbian, Bisexual, and Transgendered Relationships

privilege, and oppression. Here we have the gay, lesbian, bisexual, transgendered (GLBT) wheels within multiple contexts.

Films and other multimedia aids, music videos, music CDs, poetry, and readings all help clients distinguish the impact of such issues as race, culture, and sexual orientation on themselves, their family, and community. The tools are intended to detoxify personal issues while simultaneously inviting conversation about the broader Issues of gender-role socialization and the implications for GLBT people. From the outset, film and multimedia restructures therapeutic intervention, taking it from the personal to the political, from the intrapsychic to the social, and from the interior to the exterior. This process is crucial because it provides a foundation from which future therapeutic interventions will be made.

FIGURE 2.3   Family Context: The Misuse and Abuse of Power in Gay, Lesbian, Bisexual, and Transgendered Relationships

For example, with GLTB clients, we may use the movie *Torch Song Trilogy,* a story about a Jewish gay man whose lover is killed by a gay-bashing gang. The movie shows the relationship between the man and his mother as well as the relationship between the gay couple and society. We would use the language in the various wheels to launch conversations about intimate, family, and community experiences for GLBT persons. The various permutations of homophobia, loss, religion, culture, and heterosexism provide the landscape for dialogue and inquiry leading to critical consciousness.

The social education aspect of therapy begins in the first session with new clients and continues for a period of 6 to 8 weeks of weekly sessions, which last from 60 to 90 minutes. At the end of the eighth week, clients are absorbed into a larger circle community with films used intermittently. Clients' personal problems are thereby maintained in a holding pattern while participants examine historical

■ ■ ■ ■ ■ ▬▬▬▬▬▬▬▬▬▬▬▬▬▬▬▬▬▬▬▬▬▬▬▬▬▬▬▬▬

CASE 2.2

EXAMINING CLASS, RACE, AND DOMESTIC ABUSE IN FILM

Four women in a meeting were in the process of raising critical consciousness. Elaine, one of the therapists, showed two film clips, one from *Sleeping With the Enemy* and the other from *Straight Out of Brooklyn*. Before showing the films, Elaine explained to the women what they were about to see. She also asked them to view the tapes not from a personal stance, but from an objective viewpoint and to look for the dynamics happening between the characters.

After viewing the tape, the women wanted to talk about how the movies resembled their lives. Most therapists, at this point, might allow the women to tell their personal narratives. However, by using the power and control wheels, Elaine was able to guide them from focusing on their personal narratives. She asked them to think about the movie clips and then discuss where on the wheel they saw the characters in the movie.

The women engaged in this discussion and dissected the power and control issues portrayed in the film. Then Elaine asked, "What options did each woman have?"

Reflecting on this question enabled the women to begin to understand the differences in options for poor women of color and for white women of privilege. Further dialogue and inquiry braids the women's personal stories into transformative narratives.

and cultural prescriptions for choices they are making in their lives. In addition, participants examine how choices others make impact them as well.

Case 2.2 an example of a family therapy trainee's response after witnessing clients' social education process. In this case, the women's social education circle viewed film clips from two movies that highlight issues of domestic abuse, but from radically different social class and racial backgrounds.

As Case 2.2 shows, social education alters the perspective with which clients enter therapy. Clients rarely mention the dynamics of white privilege, diversity, and power because such issues are not considered polite conversation within our society.

Examining these matters is, however, essential to developing critical consciousness and changing family dynamics. For example, a conversation with a middle-aged, socially conservative Cuban woman struggling with her Americanized teenage daughter might be augmented by viewing film clips from *Real Women Have Curves*. The film can stimulate conversations on a range of topics, including the depiction of Latinas in film, the relationship between mothers and daughters, and the meaning of desire and being desired for women who are moderate to heavy in stature, dark-haired, and dark-skinned, as opposed to thin, fair-haired, and fair-skinned women.

A film clip from *Real Women Have Curves* could be juxtaposed with one from *Pretty Woman* or *Legally Blonde* as a way of probing the forces that create cultural standards of beauty, value, and correct behavior. Or, it could be shown with a clip from *Boyz n the Hood* in which the young man, Tré, is dealing with competing life experiences: his expectations of going to college and his intimate relationships with gang members. How does he reconcile these "middle-class" dreams with the daily urban nightmare that his friends must confront?

Films can be used to explore issues such as domestic violence, colonization, and family structure *(Sleeping with the Enemy, Straight Out of Brooklyn, The Great Santini, Once Were Warriors)*; gendered expressions of loss, grief, and family life *(Steel Magnolias)*; familial and societal oppression of GLBTs *(Torch Song Trilogy)*; and the impact of colonization *(Dirty Pretty Things)*, immigration *(A Day without a Mexican)*, and intersecting social positions *(Quinceañera)*.

Film vignettes can then be paired with other social educational tools such as critical consciousness and power and control wheels. All offer clients and therapists a way to locate the social and political aspects of personal experience, and are helpful to clients with limited literacy.

After viewing the relevant power and control wheel, clients can be instructed to identify how they have used or experienced power and control in their relationships. When therapists incorporate social education into the therapeutic process, they and their clients see that clinical practice is context bound, inseparable from societal dynamics of dominance and subordination.

THE ROLE OF COURAGE

And there comes a time when one must take a position that is neither safe, nor politic, nor popular, but one must take it because one's conscience tells one that it is right.

Cowardice asks the question, "Is it safe?"
Expediency asks the question, "Is it politic?"
Vanity asks the question, "Is it popular?"
But, conscience asks the question, "Is it right?"

—Martin Luther King, Jr.

In order to promote the development of critical consciousness among our clients, we must work continuously to develop our own. Therapists must be ever mindful of the world around us and must gain knowledge of that world from many different sources, especially sources whose perspectives run counter to that of the mainstream. And therapists must be courageous. We must help our clients critically explore cultural practices and prejudices operating within all the institutions that govern our lives, including institutions of faith.

Therapists must initiate and encourage discussion and information sharing that challenge oppressive belief systems. For example, current rhetoric by fundamentalist Christians seeks to deny gay and lesbian partners the rights guaranteed heterosexual partners, such as the right to marry. Oppressive dogma is often couched in religious ideologies that proclaim heterosexuality to be "natural" and all other sexual orientations "unnatural."

Homophobia within communities of faith demonizes gay and lesbian relationships as a threat to family life, despite all the evidence to the contrary. Many nations have granted legal recognition to gay and lesbian partners, and hetero-sexuality in those countries has not declined in membership; family life continues to flourish. Indeed, many argue that family-centered community norms gain strength through the legal inclusion of family-minded gay and lesbians.

A growing body of research affirms that children fare as well in gay and les-bian parent families as they do in heterosexual parent families. Studies also indi-cate that lesbian and gay couples tend to be more egalitarian than heterosexual couples (Green, Bettinger, & Zacks, 1996). It is important for clients of all sexual orientations to be made aware of these findings.

We invite therapists to challenge ideologies that privilege some people—heterosexuals, men, whites, able-bodied, or other so-called "majorities"—over others, and we feel that not doing so is unethical. Therapeutic efforts to build criti-cal consciousness run counter to today's mainstream quest for individualism.

Clients can begin to identify patterns of power, privilege, and oppression through discussion with others who are critically conscious. It also helps them locate where, how, and when these patterns are formed, and what purposes they serve.

We believe these goals can best be accomplished in a collective process in which a community of others remains committed to personal, familial, and com-munity change. The ability to critically question perceived reality develops through a learning process with others and through the transformation of one's beliefs and experiences with others. In dialogue and inquiry, people—clients and therapists alike—deconstruct current dynamics of their world, learn to see how domination and oppression operate, and develop the tools for positive change. We would like to conclude this chapter with a guide to the use of popular films.

Film Guides to Social Education: Using Popular Films

Following are several examples of films that therapists can use to augment social education with clients. Film clips are selected in order to facilitate dialogue and inquiry of the social location and intersectionality of each person's identity. We structure the sessions to spark conversations and heighten clients' consciousness around the following issues:

1. Loss
   - Gender role responses to loss, including death and illness
   - The mediating effects of religion, culture, race, sexual orientation, and immigration status on the experience of loss
2. Gender roles and equity
   - Emotionality, connectedness, isolation, and intimidation
   - Parenting
   - Sexuality
   - Physical affection and physical abuse
   - Exploration of men's movements (e.g., Promise Keepers, men's liberation, masculinities, men's rights, racialized masculinity, gay liberation)
3. Heterosexual privilege and homophobia

4. Economics
5. Immigration and transmigration
6. Colonization and Racism
7. Civil rights movements (from the early men's civil rights movement to the rights of women.)

Clients are shown edited film clips that highlight specific areas to be addressed in social education. We try to keep clips to 20 to 40 minutes so that there is plenty of time for reflection and discussion. Although in the cultural context model social education occurs in a group format, we encourage therapists to routinely experiment with incorporating educational materials into their particular therapeutic format. Clients find the films engaging and useful for punctuating or offering other views regarding issues with which they are struggling.

Films are used in the following manner during sessions.

1. The essence of the movie, and then the specific clip, are described. Therapists should explain the film's relevance to clients' concerns as well as the salient themes emphasized in the clip.

2. Therapists instruct the viewers to assess the film in relation to a corresponding assessment tool, which is created to accompany the film clips (example tools are provided in Tables 2.1A–H, 2.2, and 2.3). While it is helpful to elicit whether or

TABLE 2.1A   Sex, Money, and Laundry

WEEKLY DOMESTIC TASKS (ONCE OR TWICE PER WEEK)	
• take out and bury compost (daily in summer), wash pail	• mow lawn
• wipe off washing machine and dryer	• juggle budget
• wash/dry slipcovers, bathrugs, linens	• sweep front porch
• wash/hang kitchen rugs and dust rags	• pick up trash in front yard
• wash/dry dog bed (winter)	• thoroughly clean wood stove
• drop off/pick up dry cleaning	• run hot water in kitchen sink drain
• do hand laundry	• pay bills/file receipts
• polish kids' shoes	• clean out van
• grocery shopping (store 1 for staples; store 2 for specialty items)	• clean out car
• mend	• maintain garden (hoe, water, tie up plants)
• water plants	• iron
• trip to hardware store	• empty wastebaskets
• clean around dish drainer and compost	• dust
• soak stove tops in bleach	• vacuum
• replenish diaper bag	• clean bathrooms
• rake yard	• scrub kitchen floors
	• polish wood furniture

From *Sex, Money, and Laundry: Sharing Responsibilities in Intimate Relationships* by Marianne Ault-Riché in *Journal of Feminist Family Therapy (1994)* Volume 6, Issue pp. 69–87. Copyright © 1994 Reprinted by permission of the Haworth Press.

TABLE 2.1B

MONTHLY DOMESTIC TASKS

- feed store for dog/cat food
- read/call in gas/electric meter readings
- plan cards and gifts for birthdays
- buy/wrap/send gifts for birthdays
- clean refrigerator
- take pictures
- drop off film
- pick up film
- put photos in album
- get reprints
- send reprints to relatives/friends
- get car washed
- pay mortgage
- refigure budget
- cut kids' hair
- take stuff to recycling center
- pick up bottled water

TABLE 2.1C

QUARTERLY DOMESTIC TASKS

- buy toiletries
- buy cleaning supplies
- attend school functions: orientation/coffees/teacher meetings
- defrost refrigerator
- sort plastic containers
- recirculate kids' wardrobes
- recirculate kids' toys
- clean oven
- vegetation killer on brick sidewalk
- hoe brick sidewalk
- change oil and filters (van)
- change oil and filter (car)
- bathe/dip/dogs/cats
- buy kids' shoes
- disinfect litter box

TABLE 2.1D

BIANNUAL DOMESTIC TASKS

- put up/take down plastic sheeting on sun porch windows
- put up/take down plastic sheeting on second-floor kitchen windows
- put up/take down plastic on air conditioner on first floor
- put up/take down tuff-R on attic windows
- put up/take out air conditioner on second floor
- fix up second-floor bedroom/kitchen
- defrost chest freezer in basement
- organize attic
- clean basement
- buy clean hay
- clean and spray doghouse
- wash curtains
- bring down/take up/clean 4 fans, 3 electric heaters
- bring down/take up winter coats, etc.
- arrange wood delivery
- stack wood
- rototill garden
- plan, shop, and cook for adults' birthdays
- plan, send invitations, shop and cook for kids' birthdays
- spray for bugs
- take van for tune-up
- take car for tune-up
- take stuff to Goodwill
- locate/schedule children's activities—music lessons, sports, etc.

TABLE 2.1E

ANNUAL DOMESTIC TASKS

- update Christmas card list, write and photocopy holiday letter
- address and mail cards (50 French; 150 English)
- file information for updating next year's list
- Christmas gifts—plan, shop, wrap, mail/deliver
- Christmas events—plan shop, prepare, etc
- clean shed
- clean closets and cabinets
- arrange for carpet cleaning
- arrange sand/gravel delivery and shovel
- bleed radiators
- plant garden
- plan, shop, and sew for Halloween

- plan, shop, and sew for July 4th parade
- plan, shop, cook, clean up (Easter, Thanksgiving, Christmas)
- clean gutters
- clean stovepipe
- clean inside kitchen cabinets
- gather tax information
- prepare taxes
- plan vacation
- attend to camping gear, car, packing, reservations
- can tomato sauce for home use
- can fruit jams for gifts
- bake/freeze Christmas breads
- clean windows

TABLE 2.1F

AS-NEEDED DOMESTIC TASKS

- gas/oil/tires–van/car
- house maintenance
- clean toilets, sinks, tub
- change light bulbs
- fill ice trays
- deposit/cash checks
- buy milk and bread
- initiate discussion regarding relationship
- plan and prepare dishes for potlucks
- dinner guests (plan, shop, prepare, cook, clean up)
- house guests (plan, shop, prepare, cook, clean up)
- major projects (e.g., build deck, fence)
- install major appliances (e.g., computer, car stereo)
- minor home repairs (e.g., change washers, rewire electric cords)
- buy, write, and send cards on time (for about 20 friends/relatives for birthdays, major holidays, major events)
- arrange for sitters
- transport sitters
- arrange for substitute daycare when needed

- take off work when child or daycare provider is sick
- take kids for checkups, immunizations, other shots, sick care
- take kids to dentist, pediatrician, orthodontist, optometrist
- take animals to vet for shots, heartworms, stool checks, sick care
- call about errors in billings
- stay home for meter checks, appliance repairs, etc.
- see that appliances, house, vehicles get attention/repair
- arrange for bids for repair work
- take in/pick up/negotiate about small appliance repairs
- keep in touch with friends
- attend school meetings/parent-teacher conferences
- shop for kids' friends birthdays and wrap, gifts
- accompany kids to parties
- initiate contact with other parents regarding kids
- supervising kids/contact with relatives—calls, thank yous

TABLE 2.1G

MISCELLANEOUS TASKS

- paint porch/first-floor exterior trim
- remove and spray paint screen door
- plant grass in bare spots
- remove old hay from doghouse
- pick up 4 hay bales and flea powder
- sort audiotapes
- prepare sun porch for painting
- stain mahogany table/reassemble
- remove mildew from second-floor kitchen
- put up contact paper
- take G's tape player for repair
- get oil filter changed (van)
- de-rust old bed frames in basement
- clean basement
- caulk kitchen sink
- make bed sack for G's bed
- make duvet cover for G's bed
- clean attic; sort holiday stuff
- 5 thank yous, 2 birthday cards,
  4 letters
- kill vegetation/hoe brick sidewalks
- research St. Nicholas
- clean gutter/repair with wood putty
- clean/reassemble 4 box fans
- strip paint from door hardware
- finish beanbag chair
- write, photocopy, and address 50 Christmas
  letters to France in time to send surface mail
- plan Thanksgiving guests/menu
- take tuner/amplifier for repair
- arrange for furnace people to come
- touch-up paint on second-floor kitchen
- 150 domestic Christmas letters
- get pet food at feed store
- bake/freeze Christmas breads
- take cans, glass, plastic to recycling center
- cook green tomatoes after frost

- dismantle garden
- make G's Halloween costume
- mail baby clothes to France
- take unwanted items to Goodwill
- order firewood
- prepare 8 lectures
- prepare 3 conference presentations
- don't think about unfinished book manuscript
- paint second and third-floor exterior trim
- secure hall closet hook
- rewire/hang 2 chandeliers
- remove/replace doghouse
- replace taped window pane
- find/install TV cable barrel
- complete wood trim in G's room
- make hat rack for G
- install electric outlet in front hall
- reassemble baby crib
- diagnose problem with bike
- replace battery in keyboard
- rehang pictures/living room
- clean basement
- replace toilet chain/handle
- cut foam for G's bed
- repair leaky roof
- thank you note to grandfather
- get oil filter changed (car)
- clean/sharpen lawnmower
- stack firewood
- replace knob on dimmer switch
- replace brake light (van)
- polish hardware and put on door
- prepare seminar presentation
- study for exams
- write dissertation proposal

---

not any of the themes in the films are similar to clients' own families or social experiences, we encourage therapists to postpone highlighting the correlations. This is a critical first step in consciousness raising. Leaving client's personal stories aside temporarily helps them to examine power issues on a broader scale first, which circumvents their defensiveness.

TABLE 2.1H

ASSESSING THE ODDS OF YOUR ACHIEVING SHARED LAUNDRY CONSCIOUSNESS (SLC)

	ADD	SUBTRACT
1. If your husband is a woman,	200	
2. If you are very rich or very poor,	15	
3. If you earn more than he,	100	
4. If he comes from an ethnic group in which men do heavy work and/or childcare,	5	
If not,		5
5. If your husband was an adolescent during the Depression,	5	
If during the 60s or 70s,		5
6. If his mother was a feminist,	25	
If not,		50
7. If *he* is an *over*functioner in his family of origin,	5	
8. If *you* are an *under*functioner in your family of origin,	200	
9. If his sibling position is the oldest,	5	
10. If your sibling position is oldest,		25
11. If he has a high energy level,	5	
If he has a low energy level,		50
12. If you are depressed,		25
If he is depressed,		50
13. If he has the DSM-III-R diagnosis of passive-aggressive personality disorder,		15
14. If you have the DSM-III-R diagnosis of histrionic personality disorder,		15
15. If on an *Odd Couple* spectrum, he is Felix (orderly),	10	
If he is Oscar (a slob),		10
16. If you've already divorced a man and had therapy to find/develop yourself,	10	
17. If he had *no* sisters and has lived at least five years collectively with others (e.g., commune, navy, monastery)		10

If you score between 0 and 100, with hard work forever, you have a slight chance of achieving SLC. If you score between 100 and 200, with five years of unceasing hard work, you have a real chance of achieving SLC. If you score over 200, laundry consciousness may be equally shared, but is the laundry getting done?

3. Clients may resist seeing the relationship between the theme of the film clips and their presenting problem. ("This film has nothing to do with me or my problem" is a common response). However, they should be instructed to view the process as receiving pieces of a puzzle relevant to their issues and to reflect between sessions on why the therapist might have selected particular film clips for them. For clients in the cultural context model who receive 6 to 8 sessions of social education, the film clips are sequenced to build critical consciousness. The relationship between the film and clients' life stories becomes evident over time.

TABLE 2.2   Traditional and Expanded Norms of the Male Role

TRADITIONAL NORMS OF MALE ROLE	EXPANDED NORMS OF THE MALE ROLE
1. Avoiding femininity and behaviors traditionally associated with women's role (housework, childcare, gender-nonconforming activities and occupations)	1. Expanded emotionality: the willingness to express the full range of emotions, including exuberance, joy, love, wonder and awe at things beautiful, fear, sadness, remorse, disappointment, and all the rest
2. Restrictive emotionality, suppression of feelings (except for anger), emotional distance, avoidance of affect in self and others	2. Embracing femininity: valuing qualities and activities traditionally considered feminine (household and childcare tasks, cooking, creating art, dancing, composing poetry, human service occupations)
3. Seeking social status and self-esteem via achievement, competition, primacy of work/provider role, earning power	3. Balancing work and family life: seeking pride through contributing both within the world of work and as an active participant in family life
4. Self-reliance, avoidance of dependency on others	4. Embracing relatedness over individualism: valuing interdependence with all other human beings and with the rest of the natural world
5. Aggression (sometimes alternating with avoidance/denial) as a means of conflict resolution	5. Valuing collaboration: using consensus building as a primary means for conflict resolution
6. Toughness and leadership in the face of adversity	6. Maintaining flexibility: when faced with adversity, demonstrating respect for the opinions of others alongside assertiveness regarding one's own ideas, emotional availability, and emotional vulnerability
7. Striving for hierarchical dominance in relationships, patriarchal control over others in the family	7. Valuing shared power of relatedness: striving to create equal partnerships with adults and relationships with children that engender feelings of being loved and respected while also providing appropriate limits and structure
8. Nonrelational attitudes toward sexuality (objectification of women)	8. Relational attitude toward sexuality: participation that affords each partner safety, dignity, and pleasure; respect for others
9. Homophobia (fear/anger at gay men and lesbians, avoidance of emotional closeness and affection with other males)	9. Overcoming heterosexism/homophobia: valuing difference by creating nurturing relationships with gay men, lesbians, bisexuals, and heterosexuals and by borrowing expanded forms of participation in the following dimensions of relationships: nonthreatening behavior; mutual respect; trust and support; honesty and accountability; responsible parenting; household responsibilities; economic partnership; negotiation and fairness in resolving conflicts

Source: Green, R.-J. (1998). Traditional norms of masculinity. In R. Almeida (Ed.), *Transformations of gender and race.* New York: Haworth Press; Font, R., Dolan-Del Vecchio, K., & Almeida, R. (1998). In R. Almeida (Ed.), *Transformations of gender and race.* New York: Haworth Press; Magraw, S. (1993). Feminism and family therapy: An oral history PhD thesis. State University of New York–Binghamton.

TABLE 2.3   Traditional Norms of the Female Role

1. Seeking stereotyped feminine looks: thin, buxom, youthful, like a Barbie doll.
2. Behaving in traditional female roles, such as by choosing to be a nurse, because being a doctor is generally perceived as a male role.
3. Expressing emotions, except anger.
4. Adopting the caretaker role and accepting dependency.
5. Seeking social status and self-esteem vicariously through husband.
6. Seeking co-dependency and hiding independence, competence, and competitiveness.
7. Seeking to be insignificant and invisible.
8. Displaying passivity and martyrdom.
9. Being overly talkative and intensely emotional.
10. Accommodating others in the face of adversity.
11. Experiencing supermom, superwoman syndrome.
12. Accepting of a one-down position.
13. Lacking boundaries between home and work.
14. Accepting sexuality as defined through male attitudes. (Despite 20 to 30 years of the feminist movement, women's roles are still primarily defined by men. The stereotypes are still built into our thinking. Women don't have as many places as men have to go to define themselves as sexual beings. It's all-male defined.)
15. Being accused of betrayal for seeking closeness with or confiding in a woman.
16. Internalizing rigid heterosexuality and homophobia, which leads to devaluing lesbians or men who show feminine tendencies.

Films That May Raise Critical Consciousness

SLEEPING WITH THE ENEMY AND STRAIGHT OUT OF BROOKLYN
    These films should be shown together.

    Themes include gender, violence, race, class, and intergenerational legacies.

    1. *Describe the movies: Sleeping with the Enemy* is a movie about a white, heterosexual couple, Laura and Martin. Martin is extremely abusive to Laura. The couple is of a high socioeconomic class, lives in a beautiful beach house, and has no children. Despite living at the beach, Laura is terrified of the water and cannot swim. Becoming increasingly eager to leave the abusive relationship, Laura secretly learns to swim, stages her own drowning in front of Martin, and swims to safety. She is then able to move away and begin a new life for herself while Martin believes she is dead. Later in the movie, he finds out that Laura is still alive and stalks her until he viciously attacks her. She kills him in self-defense.

    Straight Out of Brooklyn is a movie about an African American couple, Ray and Frankie, living in the inner city with their two teenage children, Dennis and Carolyn. Ray is abusive to his wife, and their children witness much of this violence. Although both partners work outside of the home, the family is poor. The movie shows the many pressures on them as individuals and as a family. Frankie, in an attempt to emotionally support her husband, is protective of him despite his violence toward her. She tries to explain his behavior to her children and people outside of the family.

2. *Describe the clip:* The clip we use from *Sleeping with the Enemy* begins with Martin coming home in a jealous rage because Laura spoke to a man, a physician, who lives nearby. He proceeds to brutalize her physically, then quickly apologizes and attempts to soothe her. He then tells her that he has made arrangements with the doctor for the three of them to go sailing that evening. Knowing that his wife is terrified of the water, Martin tries to quell her fears by saying that he will stay right by her side and that she has nothing to be afraid of. Although it is not shown on this clip, it is during that boat ride that Laura stages her own drowning and temporarily frees herself from Martin's abuse.

The clip we use from *Straight Out of Brooklyn* begins with Ray's physical abuse toward Frankie. During the scene, he yells about all of the pressures he faces. The son, Dennis, comes out of his bedroom, and Ray begins to emotionally abuse him. Frankie sends her son back to the bedroom, and the physical abuse continues. The next scene shows the daughter, Carolyn, questioning the abuse and why her mother tolerates it. Frankie defends and protects Ray and describes the reasons that he acts the way he does. In the last scene, Frankie is meeting with her employment counselor at the Department of Labor. The counselor reports that Frankie's employer is concerned because she comes to work with bruises on her face and tells her she must terminate her employment "until she gets help for her problem." Frankie attempts to explain that losing her job will not help her with her problem.

3. *Instructions:* Ask viewers to examine the power and control wheels Private Context: The Misuse and Abuse of Power within Heterosexual Relationships and White Privilege/Public Context: The Misuse and Abuse of Power toward People of Color (Figure 1.1 and Figure 2.1). Ask them to track any of the dynamics on the wheels that they observed in the film clips.

4. *Questions for reflection, dialogue, and inquiry:* What choices did the two women in the videos have? What are the social class differences between the two women? Do African American women have the same choices as white women? How might the actions of the police differ in response to a call on the white husband as opposed to a call on the black husband? What do you think happened after the black woman was fired from her job? In what ways is the African American husband abused by society? In *Sleeping with the Enemy*, what would have happened if one of Martin's friends had walked in? What would have happened if this friend told people in the office what he had witnessed? Would it have changed Martin's behavior? How might his wealth and power influence the way others respond to the violence? How do you think Laura would have felt if other people were told about the abuse and yet did not help her? Do you think it could make

her feel that she is the problem, and if she just changes, then everything will be okay? From the beginning of the relationship, do you think she was second-guessing herself because of her husband's status, influence, and power? A question for men: If your wife were here, what would she say about you that others would find hard to believe?

STEEL MAGNOLIAS

Themes include gender roles around parenting, illness, and loss, different emotional, and care-giving roles and friendship.

1. *Describe the movie: Steel Magnolias* is a story about a family whose adult daughter, Shelby, dies from chronic kidney disease. The movie illustrates the complex choices that women make around chronic illness, relationships, childbirth, and losses.

2. *Describe the clip:* Our first clip shows the daughter, Shelby, telling her mother, M'Lynn, that she is pregnant. She has previously been medically advised against pregnancy because of her weak kidneys. Our next clip shows M'Lynn's friends, a community of women, responding to Shelby's illness in the beauty shop. A third clip is of a scene in the hospital: Shelby's husband, Jackson, and father, Drum, are in the process of disconnecting Shelby's life support, urging M'Lynn to leave Shelby's bedside and get some rest. The last scene occurs at the funeral and displays the gender rituals surrounding the loss.

3. *Instructions:* Clients are asked to list their experiences of loss. They are encouraged to consider losses by way of death, illness, job loss, moving, immigration, and so on. The Traditional Male Norms handout (see Table 2.2) is examined to help explain the behavior of the men in the film clip. Clients are encouraged to consider how the film is similar to or different from their own families' responses to loss.

4. *Questions for reflection, dialogue, and inquiry:* What are the messages to women and men regarding the need to fulfill oneself through childbearing and childrearing? Can you be an authentic woman and choose to not have children? Or to not bear the pregnancy (e.g., to adopt)? What were the pressures on the daughter that resulted in her "choice" to become pregnant? Do you see it as a freely chosen "choice"? How did the men and women approach care-giving differently in the film? How did you see women helping each other? How did the women deal with their sadness? What did M'Lynn do when Shelby was in the hospital? What was Drum doing in contrast to M'Lynn? What could he have done differently to support his wife and daughter? How did the women take care of each other emotionally? How did the behavior of the men and women differ when they were presented with a problem? (The women shared their feelings of grief; the men were solution oriented.) What do you think about M'Lynn's statement, "Being present when she came into the world and staying with her when she passed on were the most beautiful moments in my life"? What do you think the men were talking

about after the funeral? Why would the men most likely not have been talking about the person who died? In what ways would it help men to be able to better express their emotions? What does it mean for a boy or man to cry?

Questions for men: What were you taught as boys about crying? What are the risks to men in showing their vulnerabilities? What names are men and boys called when they are visibly vulnerable? What does it teach little boys when they are called "sissy" or "fag" when they show emotions? (That unemotional men are better—more manly—than women and queers and that they therefore should keep feelings of pain, love, and tenderness to themselves.) What have you taught or would you teach your children (sons) about crying, showing emotion, and being vulnerable? How do these gender rules regarding emotion affect intimacy within a heterosexual couple? A gay or lesbian couple?

KHUSH

Themes include: loss and race, loss and sexual orientation, loss and immigration, the gay liberation movement, and sexuality.

1. *Describe the documentary.* Khush is a documentary of discussions with Asian Indian gays and lesbians from the United States, the United Kingdom, Canada, and India. It depicts racism and cultural traditions as they impact the "coming out" process for gays and lesbians.

2. *Describe the clip:* The clip we use shows a variety of men and women. The first woman speaks specifically of the overt racism she suffered when her family moved to Canada. She explains that since she was "trying to be as white as possible" to avoid racist attacks, she felt that coming out as a lesbian was something she could not do because it would endanger her further. Other individuals talk about the cultural pressure to marry and the idea that their families view queerness as a "white person's disease."

3. *Instructions:* Viewers are asked to examine power and control wheels including White Privilege/Public Context: The Misuse and Abuse of Power toward People of Color; Public Context: The Misuse and Abuse of Power in Gay, Lesbian, Bisexual, and Transgendered Relationships; and Family Context: The Misuse and Abuse of Power in Gay, Lesbian, Bisexual, and Transgendered Relationships to analyze the interconnectedness of these oppressions (Figures 2.1, 2.2, and 2.3).

4. *Questions for reflection, dialogue, and inquiry:* What were some of the stories of racism told in the film (e.g., violence, eroticization, second-class citizens)? What did the woman mean by "playing it as white as possible"? Why was it important for her to do this? How do you imagine the families of the people in the film taught them to protect themselves from racism? Why do families not teach the same protective strategies regarding homophobia and heterosexism to their children? How does racism influence an Asian Indian family to be less accepting of gays and lesbians and of other families of color? Why might an Asian Indian gay or lesbian be more concerned about a family cut-off than a white American gay or lesbian? What do

you think the woman who talked about joining the white feminist movement, and feeling excluded meant? For those of you who are white, what can you do so that your presence does not silence those of color? For those of you who are heterosexual, what can you do so that your presence does not silence those who are lesbian and gay?

CORRINA, CORRINA

Themes include approaches to loss and grieving that vary according to gender, race, ethnicity, and spiritual tradition. This movie also highlights the impact of race and racism on cross-gender relationships.

1. *Describe the movie:* This is a story of a young woman, Molly, who loses her mother through a sudden death. Her father, Manny, looks for a surrogate mother to help his daughter deal with the loss of her mother and to take care of her. This is a Jewish family turned atheist. The "help" that Manny hires is an African American woman, Corrina. The movie dramatizes the different emotional connections between the female caretaker, Corrina, and Manny, the father, toward Molly. Another theme is depicted in the tension around the spiritual meaning of death and loss.

2. *Describe the clip:* The particular highlights here are the father's role around the loss of his wife and the caretaking of his daughter. We see the hired caretaker, Corrina, embrace and hold Molly's sadness and rage.

3. *Instructions:* Have the viewers identify on the Traditional Male Norms handout (Table 2.2) aspects of male socialization that would make it difficult for this father to express his experience of loss over his wife.

4. *Questions for reflection, dialogue, and inquiry:* Did Manny use any symbols or metaphors to help Molly mourn the loss of her mother? How did he address his sadness and loss? What are your ideas about the differences between religion and spirituality? Do you think it is important that children have a sense of religion or spirituality? What are your views about a white man hiring a black woman to care for his daughter? Did you see any differences in the ways in which the father and the caretaker related to the emotional needs of the child? To their own emotional or spiritual needs?

JOY LUCK CLUB

Themes include loss and race; loss and immigration; and deconstructing gender and culture, class, and masculinities.

1. *Describe the movie:* It is about two generations of four families in China and their immigration to the United States. The women are caught in the trauma of war and patriarchy. The life of one of the protagonists, Ying-Ying is reflected in her story of love for her husband, Li Xiao, who leaves her for another woman. The husband, Lin Xiao, is violent towards Ying-Yang in front of his new lover, and after that, she murders their infant son. While this is a universal story, it is particularly symbolic for Asian cultures, where sons are valued over daughters. It is also a good film to deconstruct the myth that women "batter" as often as their male partners. A close analysis of context of power and control versus interpersonal violence is an important beginning. Ying-Ying then moves to the United States, remarries, and has a daughter, Lena. The daughter's story then unfolds.

2. *Describe the clip:* The clip opens with a scene from China in which a young man, Li Xiao, is pursuing and marrying a young girl, Ying-Ying. It then shows that he engages in extramarital affairs and other forms of abuse. Ying-Ying's response to his abusiveness is also shown. The next scene includes the same woman, Ying-Ying, in the United States when she is older and has a daughter, Lena. This scene shows Ying-Ying's continued depression and the effects this has on her relationship with Lena. The next scene shows Lena when she is grown and is involved in a serious relationship with a man named Harold. While this relationship is not physically abusive, other forms of control are used by the male partner. In the last scene, Ying-Ying is pictured having a discussion with her now-grown daughter about relationships and marriage.

3. *Instructions:* Instruct the viewers to look at Private Context: The Misuse and Abuse of Power within Heterosexual Relationships as well as White Privilege/Public Context: The Misuse and Abuse of Power toward People of Color (Figure 1.1 and Figure 2.1) and track where the various characters fall along the dimensions of power and control.

4. *Questions for reflection, dialogue, and inquiry:* Think about the couple in China. What did you see that fit into the categories on the wheel? Explore each category. What choices did women have at that time in China? What was the role of the concubines? Could Ying-Ying have sought police protection? Or military protection? What are your thoughts about her reasons for drowning her son? Besides revenge, or protecting her son from this lifestyle, what might be some other reasons for this desperate act? Think about the second-generation couple in the United States. What did you see that fit into the categories on the wheel? How do you see immigration, race, and gender play out? Do you think that Harold knew he was patronizing Lena? What other choices could he have made that she would perceive as fair? What could he have done to help her feel less controlled by him? If the men in either generation were to talk their wives to their male friends, would the friends be more or less likely to challenge the man and be supportive of the wife? How do privacy and cultural standards maintain the status quo in these relationships? At the end of the clip, Ying-Ying asks her daughter, "Do you know what you want?" She advises Lena to take a stand. Do you think this would cost her her marriage? What would the cost to Harold be if she took a stand and offered him an invitation to see what a real relationship is all about? Do you think he would leave the marriage? (He is economically independent and does not see or feel an emotional tie). In what ways was Lena blocked from having a 50–50 relationship?

TORCH SONG TRILOGY

Torch Song Trilogy is a story about loss, sexual orientation, heterosexual privilege, and homophobia in a Jewish family.

1. *Describe the movie themes: Torch Song Trilogy* is a story about a Jewish gay man whose lover is murdered in a gay-bashing incident. The movie reflects the intersecting relationships between Arnold; his mother; his lover, Alan; and society. Key issues include death, loss, family tradition, and the familial and cultural oppression of gay lifestyles.

2. *Describe the clip:* This clip begins with Arnold and Alan celebrating their move into their New York City apartment. The younger partner, Alan, decides to pick up some groceries from the neighborhood store. On his way, he witnesses a gang of men beating up a gay youth. He intervenes but is unfortunately killed in the attempt. He is taken away in an ambulance while his lover, Arnold, looks on but is unable to accompany him. The next scene shows Arnold and his mother in the cemetery. She is praying and offering her respects (kadish) to her deceased husband; Arnold joins her to pay his respects to Alan. The mother becomes enraged that her son would share this sacred space of her husband with his lover. She berates him while he expresses his tragedy over the loss of his lover.

3. *Instructions:* Instruct viewers to look at the Public Context of Abuse toward Lesbians and Gays and the Family Context of Abuse towards Lesbians and Gays, (Figures 2.2 and 2.3). Encourage them to discuss the emotional connection between Alan and Arnold, paralleling it with intimate relationships in their own lives.

4. *Questions for reflection, dialogue, and inquiry:* How do you imagine the couple was feeling about moving in together? What might their fears or concerns be about? How do you explain Alan intervening in the gay bashing incident? When he attempted to ask a passerby to call the police, what was the response he received? What happened when Arnold approached the ambulance? In what ways did homophobia impact his ability to be present during his lover's death? How would this ambulance scene be different had this been a heterosexual couple? What would it be like for you to be forced to leave your partner alone, dying in an ambulance? What further oppressions did Arnold's mother inflict on him and his lover? Was this heterosexual privilege or simply her process of bereavement over the death of her husband? How does her lack of compassion towards her son's loss complicate his process of grieving?

The Little Mermaid and *Beauty and the Beast* (to be shown together) Themes include gender and role analysis around love and family connections. Notably, this is a children's film.

THE LITTLE MERMAID

1. *Describe the movie: The Little Mermaid* is a love story about Ariel, a mermaid, and Prince Eric, a human. The dilemma is that they cannot be together because Ariel cannot live on land and Prince Eric cannot live under the sea. Most of the film revolves around Ariel figuring out how she can win Prince Eric's love.

2. *Describe the clip:* The first clip shows Ursula, the sea witch, making a deal with Ariel to allow her to live on land and get Prince Eric to fall in love with her. There is great emphasis on body image, the value of a woman's voice, and the meaning of heterosexual partnering in relation to friends and family. The clip juxtaposes the two women, Ursula and Ariel, with images of evil and innocence, darkness and light, and norms of domination and subordination.

3. *Instructions:* Instruct the viewers to look at the Private Context: The Use and Misuse of Power within Heterosexual Relationships (Figure 1.1), and identify the subtle ways in which women are seduced into accepting dominant descriptions of intimacy and love.

4. *Questions for reflection, dialogue, and inquiry:* What did Ariel have to do in order to be with Prince Eric? (i.e., give up her voice, give up her family and community to have the man of her dreams.) How does this parallel female socialization? How much time did she have to convince Prince Eric to give her "the kiss of true love"? What message does this give women about the urgency of finding a man? What did Prince Eric have to give up to be with Ariel? What does this teach little boys? The evil person in the film was Ursula the sea witch—another woman. She was also the strong woman. What do you think of the depiction of evil women like Ursula—dark skinned, overweight, deep voice, domineering? What message does this give to children? How is Ariel's body image represented? How does this influence little girls' body image? What does this teach both boys and girls of color?

BEAUTY AND THE BEAST

1. *Describe the movie:* This is a Disney film about Belle, the inventor's daughter, who is portrayed as a nontraditional woman. She is more interested in her books and in learning than she is pursuing Gaston—the town's eligible bachelor. The other women in the town disapprove of her position and think she is "crazy" for not marrying Gaston. Belle contends that a person's character is much more important than his or her outside beauty.

2. *Describe the clip:* The first clip is about a marriage proposal. Gaston pursues Belle in the town and then follows her into her home. When he gets to her home, he becomes increasingly abusive. Belle attempts to escape his abuse and rejects his proposal for marriage. Viewers are directed to pay attention to what the townspeople say about Belle in the song they sing and to how they relate to Gaston.

3. *Instructions:* Use the Power and Control Wheel for Heterosexual Relationships (Figure 1.1) to classify the many forms of abuse that Gaston displays toward others. Use the Male and Female Norms (Table 2.2 and Table 2.3) to identify those that are played out by the other characters.

4. *Questions for reflection, dialogue, and inquiry:* Ask clients to point out the categories of control that apply to Gaston. Even though Belle ultimately chooses not to be with Gaston, what messages do you think Gaston's behavior sends to little girls? To little boys? How did the community view Belle? If Belle had a way of being independent, how do you think she would be received by society? Would it be difficult for her to maintain that independence? Why or why not? In what ways does Gaston's behavior define him as masculine or hyper-masculine? How does the community view Gaston?

What do little boys learn about courtship, love, and power?

ORDINARY PEOPLE
Themes include gender constructions of loss around death and illness.

1. *Describe the movie: Ordinary People* is a film about how one family deals with loss and how gender gets constructed and organized around a crisis. The family loses their son, Jarrett, in a boating accident. The other son, Conrad, is left with survivor guilt, attempts to kill himself, and is hospitalized. The mother, Beth, favored Jarrett, and following his death, the conflict between she and Conrad escalates. The father, Calvin, attempts to heal the family with the help of a male psychiatrist, Dr. Tyrone Berger.

2. *Describe the clips:* The first clip opens after Jarretts' death and Conrad's recent hospitalization. The family is in the kitchen, and Beth is making breakfast for Conrad. Calvin asks his wife if she followed up with a phone call to service repairman. Consider the expectations that are placed on Beth compared to the expectations that are placed on Calvin. Later in the clip, Beth and Conrad are embroiled in an argument about his choice to quit the swim team. Calvin supports his son. In another clip, Calvin is in a therapy session with Dr. Berger, who attempts to triangulate Beth around emotional responsibility. Following the therapy session, Calvin returns home and questions his wife about her behavior on the day of Jarrett's funeral.

3. *Instructions:* Instruct the viewers to define the gendered patterns of loss and mourning (for him and for her) using the Private Context: The Misuse and Abuse of Power within Heterosexual Relationships (Figure 1.1).

4. *Questions for reflection, dialogue, and inquiry:* If you have a chalkboard, draw a line down the center and write "expectations of mother" at the top of one column and "expectations of father" at the top of the other. Ask the clients what expectations they saw of each (Note to therapist: Usually the list for the mother is much longer, i.e., expecting her to be nurturing toward her son; visiting him in the hospital; not taking a trip to Europe; making her son a second breakfast; taking care of her husband emotionally at their son's funeral, and not worrying about whether or not her husband's clothes matched; charming the service repairman; knowing everything that her children are doing; not "needing" therapy for her family; etc.). Elicit empathy for Beth. Ask, "Even though Beth appeared cold and abrupt at times, how is this connected to the above expectations and her recent loss?" In what ways do women in general deal with a similar crisis? (i.e., making sure that

things are running smoothly in the family, trying to protect the family image, buffering the pain). How did Beth's concern over Calvin's clothes at the funeral make sense in light of female socialization? After returning from the therapist's office, Calvin accuses Beth of being insensitive on the day of the funeral by worrying about his clothes. He says, "I was crazy that day." In what ways was Beth permitted or not permitted to be crazy on the day of Jarrett's funeral? How could Dr. Berger have helped Calvin take care of Beth while attending to his own loss instead of encouraging him to go home and confront his wife?

BOYZ N THE HOOD
Themes include loss, race, gender, and violence surrounding the lives of urban youth.

1. *Describe the movie:* This film is about African American young boys and girls who survive gang violence. The boy, Tré, a middle-class son of divorced parents, connects to childhood friends who are now gang members. His girlfriend, Brandi, is determined not to become sexually active until she marries after college. On the night that Tré's friends are killed in a shoot-out, he himself is faced with near-death, first by the gangs, and then by a black police officer. He arrives at Brandi's house and breaks down with rage and fear. Under these circumstances, she is overcome with compassion for him and feels compelled to nurture him, ultimately deciding to engage sexually.

2. *Describe the clip:* The first clip highlights the struggle of African American youths to survive the trials of gang violence. Their parents' middle-class status offers little buffering against the insidious violence within community life. The next part of the clip is the struggle of Tré and Brandi negotiating an intimate relationship within the context of urban warfare. The next scene is the gang shoot-out where Tré barely escapes the cross-bullets only to have his life threatened by a black police officer. He appears at Brandi's house and falls apart. She has sex with him, breaking her promises to herself.

3. *Instructions:* Instruct the viewers to view the wheels depicting White Privilege/Public Context: The Misuse and Abuse of Power towards People of Color and the Private Domain of Abuse within Heterosexual Couples (Figure 1.1 and Figure 2.1). Compare and contrast the distinctions between the societal and personal experiences for this couple.

4. *Questions for reflections, dialogue, and inquiry:* How do the struggles over sexuality among black adolescents play out differently from their white counterparts? Could Tré's father have played a different role? What about his mother? How does mourning, loss, and violence get entrapped within expectations in intimate relationships? How does being faced with the death of Tré's close friends, and simultaneously wanting to have him respect her dreams, compromise Brandi's position? What could have happened had Tré brought his sadness and fear to his male friends? What happens when men depend solely on their female partners for emotional support?

THE GREAT SANTINI

Themes include violence, homophobia, definitions within the military and across racial lines, and the rupturing of friendships within white supremacy.

1. *Describe the movie:* This is a film that exemplifies the rigidity of masculinity in the lives of military families. The film portrays the paradox of a successful Colonel, Bill Meecham, who attempts to organize his family like a platoon through hierarchy and violence. Depicted are the gender and race polarities of a white family's experience in the KKK South and the military.

2. *Describe the clip:* The first clip elicits traditional patterns of gender within family life. Awaiting the arrival of her husband Bill, Lillian demands that the children stand to attention. The next highlight is the fathers' challenge of his son, Ben, at basketball and the ensuing abusiveness towards Lillian and Ben when Ben wins. The clip ends with Ben's loss of a dear friend, Toomer, and Toomer's tragic death. The trauma of personal losses colored by the power of race and military are emphasized.

3. *Instructions:* Review Private Context: The Misuse and Abuse of Power within Heterosexual Relationships and White Privilege/Public Context: The Misuse and Abuse of Power toward People of Color (Figure 1.1 and Figure 2.1). Instruct the viewers to first label how the institution of the military creates rigid roles for men and traditional values for women. Have them think of the ways the Great Santini abuses his wife and children.

4. *Questions for reflection, dialogue, and inquiry:*
1. What forms of abuse were displayed in the clip? What are the specific examples?
2. What role did Lillian serve in the family? In what ways was she protective of them?
3. Was Lillian protective of Bill's image in regards to the children and society?
4. How does the military impact family life?
5. What were some of the messages Ben received about how to be a man?
6. What messages did Ben receive about people different from himself? How did his father's definitions of manhood, including the value placed on his son's relationship with a Black man, eviscerate his potential for wellbeing?
7. What are some of the behaviors that were exhibited by the children that suggest their father's emotional unavailability?
8. What "insults" did Bill use toward Ben following the basketball game?
9. How were these insults hurtful toward the daughters?
10. What did the oldest daughter do to get her father's attention? How did she question her status in the family?

REFERENCES

Ault-Riche, M. (1994). Sex, money, and laundry: Sharing responsibilities in intimate relationships. *Journal of Feminist Family Therapy.* 6(1), 69–87.

Font, R., Dolan-Del Vecchio, & Almeida, R. (1998). Finding the words: Instruments for a therapy of liberation. In R. Almeida (Ed.), *Transformations of gender and race.* New York: Haworth Press.

Freire, P. (1971). *Pedagogy of the oppressed.* New York: Herder & Herder.

Freire, A. M., & Macedo, D. (2000). *The Paulo Freire reader.* New York: Continuum.

Green, R.-J. (1998). Traditional norms of masculinity. In R. Almeida (Ed.), *Transformations of gender and race.* New York: Haworth Press.

Green, R.-J., Bettinger, M., & Zacks, E. (1996). Are lesbian couples fused and gay male couples disengaged? In J. Laird & R. J. Green (Eds.), *Lesbians and gays in couples and families* (pp. 185–230). San Francisco: Jossey Bass.

Halevy, J. (1998). A genogram with an attitude. *Journal of Marital and Family Therapy, 24,* 233–242.

Hardy, K., & Laszloffy, T. A. (1995). The cultural genogram: Key to training culturally competent family therapists. *Journal of Marital and Family Therapy, 21,* 227–237.

Hochschild, A. (1990). *The second shift.* New York: Avon Books.

International Forum on Globalization. (2002). *Alternatives to economic globalization: A better world is possible.* San Francisco: Barrett-Koehler.

King, M. L. Address at SCLC Ministers Leadership Training Program. Retrieved on March 17, 2007 from www.quotedb.com/quotes/63

Magraw, S. (1993). *Feminism and family therapy: An oral history.* PhD thesis. State University of New York–Binghamton.

Martin-Baro, I. (1994). *Writings for a liberation psychology.* Cambridge, MA: Harvard University Press.

Patterson, C. (2000). Family relationships of lesbians and gay men. *Journal of Marriage and Family, 62,* 1052–1069.

Roy, A. (2004). *Public power in the age of empire-open media pamphlet series.* Seven Stories Press: New York.

Stacey, J., & Biblarz, T. J. (2001). How does the sexual orientation of parents matter? *American Sociological Review, 66*(2), 159–183.

MOVIE REFERENCES

Achbar, M., & Abbot, J. (Directors). (2004). *The corporation* [Motion picture]. Canada: Big Picture Media.

Arau, S. (Director). (2004). *A day without a Mexican* [Motion picture]. United States/Mexico/Spain: Eye on the Ball Films, Instituto Mexicano de Cinematografia (IMCINE), Jose and Friends Inc., Plural Entertainment Espana S. L., and RTG Productions LLC.

Bogart, P. (Director). (1988). *Torch song trilogy* [Motion picture]. United States: New Line Cinemas and Howard Gottfried/Ronald K. Fierstein Production.

Carlino, L. J. (Director). (1979). *The Great Santini* [Motion picture]. United States: Bing Crosby Productions.

Clements, R., & Musker, J. (Directors). (1989). *The little mermaid* [Motion picture]. United States: Silver Screen Partners IV and Walt Disney Pictures.

Cardoso, P. (Director). (2002). *Real women have curves.* [Motion Picture] United States. HBO Films.

Frears, S. (Director). (2002). *Dirty pretty things* [Motion picture]. United Kingdom: British Broadcasting Corporation (BBS), Celador Films, and Jonescompany Productions.

Glatzer, R., & Westmoreland, W. (Directors). (2006). *Quinceañera* [Motion picture]. United States: Cinetic Media and Kitchen Sink Entertainment LLC.

Greenwold, R. (Producer/Director). (2005). *Wal-Mart: The high cost of low price* [Motion picture]. United States: Brave New Films.

Luketic, R. (Director). (2001). *Legally blonde* [Motion picture]. United States: Marc Platt Productions and Metro-Goldwyn-Mayer (MGM).

Marshall, G. (Director). (1990). *Pretty woman* [Motion picture]. USA: Silver Screen Partners IV and Touchstone Pictures.

Moore, M. (Producer/Director). (1989). *Roger and me* [Motion picture]. United States: Warner Bros.

Nelson, J. (Director). (1994). *Corrina, Corrina* [Motion picture]. United States: New Line Cinema.

Nichols, M. (Director). (1988). *Working girl* [Motion Picture]. United States: 20th Century Fox.

Nichols Parmar, P. (1991). *Khush* [Motion picture]. Women make movies U.K.

Rich, M. (Director). (1991). *Straight out of Brooklyn* [Motion picture]. United States: American Playhouse and Blacks in Progress.

Ross, H. (Director). (1989). *Steel magnolias* [Motion picture]. United States: Rastar Films.

Ruben, J. (Director). (1991). *Sleeping with the enemy* [Motion picture]. United States: 20th Century Fox.

Singleton, J. (Director). (1991). *Boyz n the hood* [Motion picture]. United States: Columbia Pictures Productions.

Tamahori, L. (Director). (1994). *Once were warriors* [Motion picture]. New Zealand: Avalon Studios, Communicado Productions, Fine Line Features, New Zealand Film Commission, and New Zealand on Air.

Trousdale, G., & Wise, K. (Directors). (1991). *Beauty and the beast* [Motion picture]. United States: Silver Screen Partners IV and Walt Disney Pictures.

Wang, W. (Director). (1993). *The joy luck club* [Motion picture]. United States: Hollywood Pictures.

Weitz, P. (Director). (2004). *In good company* [Motion picture]. United States: Universal Studios.

CHAPTER THREE

EXPANDING GENDER IDENTITIES

Male sexual identity is not a "role."
Male sexual identity is not a trait.
Male sexual identity—the belief that one is male, the belief that there is a male
sex, the belief that one belongs to it—is a politically constructed idea.
Male sexual identity is constructed through the choices we make and the
actions we take.

—John Stoltenberg (1989, p. 16)

"Man" and "woman" are fictions, caricatures, cultural constructs. As models
they are reductive, totalitarian, inappropriate to human becoming. As roles
they are static, demeaning to the female, dead-ended for males and females
both. Culture as we know it legislates those fictive roles as normalcy.

—Andrea Dworkin (1974, p. 174)

The structure of mainstream families is built on a blueprint taken from patriarchy, which mandates rigid gender identities designed to preserve male dominance. To help families build relationships based upon social justice rather than male dominance, we must help them transform those gender identities.

This chapter prepares you for this challenge by providing:

- A rationale for placing gender at the center of therapeutic efforts at all stages of the life cycle while also paying attention to other differences.
- An overview of patriarchal male norms and the supporting role of "culture bearer" assigned to women.
- Examples showing how therapists and other helping professionals collude with the patriarchal status quo and contribute to injustice.
- New social justice–based relationship norms for people of all genders.

THE IMPORTANCE OF GENDER, OTHER HUMAN DIFFERENCES, AND HIERARCHIES OF POWER

Patriarchy is based on men's dominance over women and creates a model in which human differences of all kinds—gender, race, sexual orientation, age, and so on—are arranged into hierarchies of dominance. Social justice and patriarchy are mutually exclusive. Although this contradiction is self-evident, the realization recedes in daily experiences within families, work organizations, communities, and societies that function in a context of sexism, racism, homophobia, and classism.

Many people who seek social justice compartmentalize their vision. They confuse working for the empowerment of white, middle-class, heterosexual women with working for the empowerment of all women. They confuse working for the empowerment of heterosexual African American men with working for the empowerment of all people of color. They confuse working for the empowerment of white, middle-class, gay men with working for the empowerment of all queer people.

These patterns show how hard it is to envision inclusive social justice when we have been taught to accept as normal a system based on injustice. It is a challenge for those who seek social justice to keep in mind not only the ways that their own identities make them vulnerable to oppression (as middle-class, white women face oppression by middle-class, white men) but also the ways their identities grant privilege (the white women's movement forgets the plight of women of color, women in poverty, and lesbians). To be effective, professional helpers working to foster social justice must keep the entire matrix of power, privilege, and oppression at the center of their thinking and at the center of therapeutic conversations and interventions.

Gender, as traditionally conceived, cleaves humanity into two classes, one assigned power over the other (which leaves those who do not conform to either class, transgender people, in a predicament). This gendered partitioning of humanity transcends all other differences. All white people experience white privilege, but white men gain additional advantages not granted to white women; all queer people face homophobia, but gay men—unlike lesbians—do not face homophobia compounded by sexism. All poor people experience economic hardship, but men in poverty are privileged relative to women in poverty. Therefore, gender at *all* stages of the life cycle remains this chapter's primary focus, even as we remember the inequities connected to race, ethnicity, sexual orientation, class, and religion.

The Patriarchal Male Code

Each of us constructs a template for male identity that is influenced by our ethnicity, sexual orientation, social class, religious affiliations, regional customs, and family backgrounds. However, when asked to describe the "traditional" rules of American manhood, most of us agree on the major themes, which turn out to be the themes that have historically defined masculinity from the perspective of Northern European, middle-class, heterosexual people—the group whose sensibilities have shaped mainstream American culture.

Boys start learning the male code early in life. Countless interactions with adults and other children teach them subtly but with impressive consistency. They learn the code through the toys that adults hand them and the ones that adults take away. If a boy picks up a toy from his sister's toy box, he may be told to put it back. Adults further imprint and solidify the code through the activities they encourage boys to engage in and those they steer them away from.

Expectations of how boys and men should express themselves reinforce the rules. Remember, "Big boys don't cry!" Before entering kindergarten, most boys know they need to follow the rules of the male code to fit in. Following the rules may even be necessary to avoid physical and emotional assault. Any first grader can tell you that it would be weird for a boy to bring his favorite doll to school for playtime.

Girls endure a complementary pattern of socialization which encourages them to place the interests of others, particularly boys and men, ahead of their own. Girls are often warned not to cry because it will mess up their faces. They are coached to smile and be pleasant and are socialized into the ethic of care and relationship. Marriage and childbearing are pinnacle points for young women. Females learn the role of culture bearer, shouldering the many tasks that support and perpetuate the status quo.

Early socialization damages boys and girls in different ways and leaves females on the down side of the power equation. Caregiving can be fulfilling, but it is also burdensome. A social justice approach to healing relationships recognizes that fairness between the genders provides a cornerstone for love and respect.

The good news is that times have changed, and today's men and women are unlikely to follow traditional role prescriptions with the kind of rigidity typical of previous generations. The 20th century saw major gains achieved by social movements demanding equality for women, people of color, gay men, lesbians, and transgender people.

The movements for social justice that challenged these systems of inequality also began to shake up the rules of manhood. It is important, though, to take a close look at those rules from yesteryear because they continue to significantly influence individual choices, relationship patterns, and institutional behavior.

THE PATRIARCHAL MALE CODE
Rule 1: Don't act like a girl (avoid childcare and other nurturing activities).
Rule 2: Keep your feelings to yourself (showing anger is acceptable).
Rule 3: Work is your first priority.
Rule 4: Be self-reliant.
Rule 5: Solve problems using aggression.
Rule 6: Be dominant and in control.
Rule 7: Women are for sex.
Rule 8: Don't be gay (and avoid emotional closeness with other men).

As you read through the expanded descriptions of these rules, keep in mind that none of us ever operates entirely alone as a completely free agent within any of our relationships. Instead, each of us brings into every relationship strong connections to all the identity groups that contribute to our self-image and social location, such as gender, race, class, and community of faith.

Our lifelong connections to these identity groups profoundly shape the attitudes, feelings, and behaviors we bring to each personal encounter. Therefore, we each face the challenge of identifying how our particular community connections bring with them privileges we take for granted and prejudices we've been indoctrinated into holding. Accepting this challenge marks the beginning of the journey toward critical consciousness, the rewards of which include an increased awareness of the social forces driving interpersonal behavior, a more self-assured understanding of personal accountability, and a lifetime of more satisfying relationships.

Rule 1: Don't act like a girl.   The idea that maleness must be defined in opposition to, and with higher status than, femaleness pervades all aspects of family and community life. "You throw like a girl" is an epithet that male Little Leaguers dread, and its equivalents still strike fear in many areas of life. The underlying rule comes through loud and clear. Real men do not behave like females in any way, shape, or form. The persistent habit some men have of calling women "girls" reflects a biased perspective on the relative status of men and women, as when white slave owners referred to their slaves as "boy" or "girl" regardless of their age.

These patterns contribute to a fundamental imbalance in respect and power that continues to have far-reaching consequences. Boys and men still

- Refuse to learn tasks traditionally performed by women, such as laundry, housekeeping, and child care.
- Lean toward "men only" interests, sports, artistic pursuits, hobbies, and occupations.
- Find it difficult to accept the authority and leadership of women in a variety of life spheres, including family matters, politics, and work.

Rule 1 encourages men to value their own ideas, feelings, rights, needs, property, labor, activities, and time more highly than they value those of women. It has established a social order in which a community of people—comprising only men—unself-consciously assigns itself more significance and power than it does other genders. This pattern of male privilege is so entrenched that many people—men and women—do not see it as a problem.

Rule 2: Keep your feelings to yourself.   When boys and men live their lives in line with axioms like "Big boys don't cry," which equate openness and vulnerability with personal weakness, the result is unfamiliarity with one's own feelings. In relationships, some men follow Rule 2 in a misguided effort to spare their partner emotional pain. In doing so, they presume that they alone should make the decision to shield their partner from their feelings.

Boys and men, taught to equate expression of most feelings with a show of weakness, end up expressing one feeling more strongly than all others. That feeling is anger. Men show anger because its expression connotes power and because experience has taught them that displays of anger often result in compliance from others. In fact, many men have learned to collapse a whole range of feelings—fear, sadness, disappointment, frustration, uncertainty, self-consciousness, embarrassment, and confusion—into anger.

The rule that men must keep their feelings to themselves also fuels men's sense of entitlement to their anger as the one feeling to which the rule allows easy access. Willingness to show anger, coupled with an inability or disinclination to express most other feelings, leads to great difficulty within intimate relationships.

Finally, Rule 2 has grave implications for male physical health and well-being. Many men become so distant from their feelings that they disconnect from their bodies and accumulate numerous health problems such as obesity, heart disease, shortness of breath, fatigue, and recurrent aches and pains. Ignoring one's health has the potential to seriously limit or interrupt aspects of one's life and burdens intimate partners who often feel compelled to assume a parental attitude. Viewed in this light, all people need to make self-care a priority in order to demonstrate responsibility and respect toward themselves and their loved ones.

Rule 3: Work is your first priority.   The ruthless expectation that work takes priority over all other aspects of men's lives continues to be a major theme in our society. In a more humanistic world, we would generate a diagnostic term for this inverted prioritization. *Workaholism* comes close, but our society has co-opted this word in a way that almost makes it a virtue nowadays, despite the lip service many corporations now give to *work–life balance*.

Each of us brings many community connections into everyday interactions. African American men have to deal not only with the male code but also with ongoing racial oppression. In *From Brotherhood to Manhood: How Black Men Rescue Their Relationships and Dreams from the Invisibility Syndrome*, Anderson J. Franklin writes, "Many of us have learned . . . that to get ahead you have to work 'day and night.' That message is also coupled with implicit and explicit messages that we should be prepared, as African American men, to work twice as hard and be twice as good."

The willingness to suffer physical and emotional damage in order to satisfy the demands of employment is not exclusive to any racial or ethnic group. In all of them, Rule 3 contributes to many types of difficulties within family and couple relationships. In addition to painfully distancing parents from their children, this rule allows many men to feel that since they "work all day," they are entitled to refrain from doing the unpaid work of maintaining a home and family connections. This "second shift" includes all the things people do to keep their lives in order: keeping track of food and other household supplies, shopping for groceries and other necessities, preparing meals, and doing housework and laundry.

The second shift also includes child care; supervising homework; managing social connections for the family; and scheduling medical and dental appointments, play dates, birthday parties, scout meetings, and parent/teacher conferences. When men feel entitled to exempt themselves from second-shift responsibilities, enormous pressure falls on their partners and other family members.

Neglect of second-shift tasks also leads to many lost opportunities for men. Tasks such as nurturing and caregiving are often very hard work, but they are instrumental in building human bonds. Bathing, dressing, and feeding our little ones; comforting them when they're not feeling well; tucking them in and reading bedtime stories; sharing mealtimes together as a family—these activities make priceless experiences for parents and children alike. When men decide not to participate, everyone loses.

Finally, Rule 3 increases the pressure on poor and working-class families of all colors. If a man lacks opportunities for reasonably paid employment, it can contribute to an escalation of behavioral patterns through which he hopes to reaffirm his wounded masculinity. Men who are struggling economically sometimes become more domineering toward the women and children in their lives.

Rule 4: Be self-reliant.   This rule encourages boys and men to feel entitled to make decisions based solely on their own perspectives and judgments, regardless of their impact on others. It also teaches males to equate asking for help with failure and weakness, which can be catastrophic for important relationships. Rule 4 makes it a challenge for boys and men to realize that asking for help does not signify weakness and that a willingness to ask for and accept help is a vitally important life skill and the foundation for intimacy.

Rule 5: Solve problems using aggression.   Men learn that it is okay to respond to relationship difficulties with aggression. A certain degree of aggression and toughness is not always a bad thing, but most conflicts or problems can be more constructively approached using a combination of means. When aggression and toughness become the *first and only* tactics used, the results are rarely positive. Imposing this approach, some men run roughshod over the sensibilities and contributions of their partners and other family members and increase emotional distance at a time when all may desperately need togetherness and collaboration.

Rule 6: Be dominant and in control.   This maxim is closely connected to Rule 1 (Don't act like a girl) and Rule 5 (Be aggressive). It assigns men head-of-the-household status within families and positions of ultimate leadership within other organizations. The impact of this rule can be seen worldwide in the enduring pattern of predominantly male leadership in government, business, education, and religious institutions. Rule 6 teaches boys and men that power in relationships means domination and control.

A man's feeling of entitlement to authority within the family often stands in marked contrast to his persona as an employee who would never presume to dictate any course of action to his supervisor and would respectfully defer to his superiors. This difference actually demonstrates a corollary of Rule 6—men generally accept and respect their assigned level within the hierarchy of work and military organizations because it is important to "be a good soldier."

We mentioned earlier that the rules for male behavior reflect mainstream American values—that is, middle and upper middle-class, predominantly white, predominantly heterosexual sensibilities. But while the rules originate from this most influential group, they shape attitudes and behavior across our society, as Alice Walker's novel *The Color Purple* illustrates.

The Color Purple celebrates the survival of African American women who endured incest, other forms of child abuse, domestic violence, and the viciousness of life in the Jim Crow South. The book and the movie that followed ignited a controversy among African American artists. Some writers, primarily men, attacked Walker, arguing that her writing about such issues within a racist social context contributed to the negative picture that mainstream American society already held of African American males. Walker's supporters countered that while the struggle to eradicate racism remains imperative for community members, men and women need to work together toward acknowledging and solving *all* social problems that exist within their communities, including male dominance and the sexual exploitation of women and girls by men.

Rule 7: Women are for sex. Most boys in our society experience their first sexual encounters with pornographic magazines, videotapes, or online images rather than with a real, physically present, human being. Pornography portrays partners as existing solely to gratify them and to be always at their disposal. The airbrushed people in the images are never tired or just plain not interested. If a pornographic image says no, it is always meant as a tease and really means, "I'm just playing hard to get." Once the boy has had his orgasm, he can put the magazine or videotape aside and move on.

Beginning their sexual lives in this way sets men up to experience sex as something they do mostly for themselves. Sex may be enhanced by the physical presence of another person, but that's hardly a requirement. Pornography also teaches that "real men" are ready for sex at all times and that the pursuit of sex is one of life's main preoccupations.

Pornography also promotes racist stereotypes—black women are wanton and insatiable; black men are overly endowed rapists; Asian women are subservient and exotic. Each of these stereotypes reflects the history of white men's sexual exploitation of people of color. White men systematically raped black women in this country for centuries. Stereotyping black women as insatiable and black men as rapists absolves white men of responsibility for their actions through victim blaming. Nonetheless, these pornographic stereotypes continue to shape men's attitudes toward themselves and others.

In keeping with the cultural viewpoint that women are for sex, hip-hop music—the most widely listened to genre among young adults—often promotes contempt for women and homophobia. Young, male hip-hop artists depict women as objects of their desire and define manhood as the sexual conquest of a never-ending parade of young women.

Rule 7 teaches boys and men to feel entitled to receive sex from those whom they find sexually appealing. For gay men, Rule 7 becomes "Men are for sex." The idea that a mutually respectful, loving, and gratifying relationship with another human being is the optimum context for sex mystifies many men, whether straight, bisexual, or gay.

In their real-life intimate relationships, many men try to unlearn the fallacies of their pornographic vision of partnership. But some men continue to separate sex from other aspects of partnership, inviting heartbreak for all involved. They may dismiss regular, extrarelational sexual encounters as having no impact on their "committed" relationships, resulting in devastation when their partner discovers such liaisons.

Rule 8: Don't be gay.   Homophobia—fear and hatred toward gay men, lesbians, and bisexuals—remains one of the hallmarks of traditional masculinity. In fact, some gender theorists argue that mainstream male identity is based most fundamentally on Rules 1 (Don't act like a girl) and 8. "Real" men are supposed to be nothing like girls and 100 percent heterosexual. Rule 8 contributes to hate crimes, including gay bashings that can result in physical abuse and murder, such as the 1998 torture and murder of Matthew Shepherd in Laramie, Wyoming. It also leads to self-hate, as evidenced in the many suicides by gay teens each year. Rule 8 also contributes to the refusal of the federal and most state governments to allow gay and lesbian partners the same legal protections that straight married partners take for granted.

This rule teaches males to be hostile toward gay and bisexual men and to be self-loathing if they are other than heterosexual themselves. It also encourages men to remain emotionally distant from other men lest they be taken for gay or bisexual.

Because none of us can remain entirely isolated from the ways of the world, all men are to some degree impacted by these eight rules and the attitude of entitlement the rules foster. Daily life continues to envelope each of us with society's traditions and expectations no matter how egalitarian the values we received from our parents may have been and no matter how emphatically we vow to resist the roles assigned by gender, race, class, and sexual orientation.

The more closely we examine the patriarchal male code, however, the more we empower ourselves to become critically conscious of long-held beliefs about ourselves and others, which helps us make choices that mean the difference between accepting and resisting patterns that threaten our relationships. We need this fortification because these choices arise every single day.

INTERSECTIONALITY: PATRIARCHY, RACISM, COLONIZATION, AND CAPITALISM

It is critical to keep in mind that patriarchy, racism, colonization, and capitalism are not just internalized norms or even subtly sanctioned attitudes; they are institutionalized at all levels of society. The links to these larger systems must be threaded into the therapy at every stage in order to neutralize the way society pathologizes individuals, families, and marginalized cultures.

It is well known that large-scale prostitution thrives in the euphemistically named rest and recuperation (R&R) zones surrounding American military's forward bases around the world.* When sexual exploitation by enlisted personnel does not take the shape of explicit prostitution, it manifests as convenience marriages between them and local women.

Many women from Korea, Vietnam, and the Philippines have come to the United States with their military husbands. Even when the women are in legitimate marriages, they are frequently stigmatized in their own immigrant communities, which view them as living evidence of their native land's humiliating history of subjugation to foreign powers and sexual exploitation by the occupying forces. Here the norm of dominance at all costs is reflected at the societal level.

The story of Korean comfort women gives us a prism through which to view the intersecting norms of patriarchy, capitalism, and colonization that play out for women across national borders and over the life cycle (Ryu, 2006; Yoshiaki, 2001). Recruited, kidnapped, or sold by their families under the pretense that they would be given respectable jobs in other cities, comfort women were females from poor communities. The Japanese military systematically interned them in brothels integrated into the front-line units and bases. Japanese women were used, but the military also captured women from the foreign lands they occupied, including Korea.

The military established the brothels for several reasons. They hoped that by providing easy access to sex workers, the morale and military effectiveness of Japanese soldiers would be improved. This practice is the ultimate expression of "women are for sex." By institutionalizing brothels and placing them under official scrutiny, officials also hoped to control the spread of STDs and, of course, same-sex relationships. In this way, at the expense of the women, "don't be gay" was reinforced. When the women were no longer useful—that is, became pregnant, bore too many STDs, or were too old—they were often abandoned and left to starve to death. Many of the survivors could not return to their native lands for fear of bringing shame on their families or becoming the victims of honor killings. That women were treated as objects to be used and then discarded aligned with the capitalist value system that commoditizes everything, including human beings.

Organized religion—especially Christianity—played a central role in supporting the comfort women in their ongoing quest to seek apologies and compensation from the Japanese government. At the same time, the individual woman who challenges dehumanizing customs at a personal level, or who struggles to secure safety from a domineering and violent husband, is less likely to be supported by the churches. Patriarchal and nationalistic values are upheld over the fundamental commitment to respect women's rights.

*Nato force "feeds Kosovo sex trade." *The Guardian.* Retrieved on March 1, 2007, from http://www.guardian.co.uk/international/story/0,,1211214,00.html. UN troops cautioned on sex abuse. BBC. Retrieved on March 1, 2007, from http://news.bbc.co.uk/1/hi/world/africa/4313617. stm. War and Sex. *American Chronicle.* Retrieved on March 1, 2007, from http://www.americanchronicle.com/articles/viewArticle.asp?articleID=9947. American Military–Base Prostitution. Paper written by Jennifer Latstetter at College of William and Mary, Williamsburg, VA. Retrieved on March 1, 2007, from http://www.wm.edu/so/monitor/spring2000/paper6.htm.

Less directly, the interwoven threads of racism, capitalism, colonization, and patriarchy construct the identities and interpersonal relationships of men who diverge from the standard norm: white, rich, and heterosexual. In order to fully understand the norm's impact on people's lives, we must examine how these threads intersect with hierarchies of class, race, and sexual identity. In considering men of color, Majors and Billison (1993), McCall (1995; 1998), and Powell (2003) describe the ways that institutional racism limits opportunities for African American men to fulfill the prescription that men prove their masculinity by achieving high incomes and prestigious positions within the world of work. The simultaneous demand for performance and exclusion from opportunity generates frustration, rage, desperation, and an array of other emotions.

According to Gates (1997), men of color feel that they will get little public acknowledgment of their predicament and that expressing their feelings of frustration and rage will bring heightened institutional coercion by the white establishment. The "cool pose" swagger becomes the armor of choice.

Enormous consequences arise from the dissonance between what America expects from adult males and the limitations that racism places on black men's opportunities to fulfill these expectations. The ability to control one's life and accept responsibility is a sign of adult status. For men with little control over their economic landscape, this definition of maturation proves unattainable.

Yet mainstream culture continues to exploit this expectation, for example, in advertising aimed at black men that equates "cool" with consumerism. Images of affluent, virile, sophisticated black men consuming liquor and cigarettes while flirting with affluent, beautiful, sophisticated black women link spending money on substance abuse (alcohol) and self-destruction (smoking) with economic success, attractiveness, and sexual prowess.

Without a critical analysis, African American men, and particularly youth, may respond to their predicament by aspiring to self-defeating images of manhood. Dyson (1997) places gang membership and gangsta rap, both of which support male violence toward female partners, in this category. In the 2005 movie *Crash*, racism and gender expectations collide to create impossible dilemmas for people of color. A middle-class black character, played by Terence Howard, gets stopped by the police and stays cool while the police officer humiliates him by inappropriately touching his wife. She becomes furious at her husband's lack of protection. His lack of response humiliates his wife and him, leaving her assault unchallenged. The assault by the police officer profoundly damages their relationship.

Maduro (1995) describes similar pressures within the Latino community. "We often experience . . . being defined as a *machista* culture, as if male chauvinism were any lesser (rather than different) among Anglos . . . we react at times by rejecting feminism as if it were just an Anglo issue, thus redoubling the frustration of Latinas' voices and struggles for their own specific liberation."

Varón is a Spanish adjective that captures qualities associated with maleness: strong, virile, sexual, aggressive, protective of women and children, often irresponsible, uncontrollable, and *mujeriego* (a womanizer and therefore heterosexual). *Hombre* (man) refers to the essence of being a man: respectful and protective of women, self-absorbed, committed to one's principles, social and politically motivated, willing to risk one's life for the well-being of others, committed to one's family, self-sacrificing, and sexual.

Men, and youth in particular, combine these cultural prescriptions for masculinity with what they learn from colonization and capitalism. Masculinity comes to include pimping women as sex industry workers, controlling people and territory with threats of violence, and committing armed robbery. These patterns reflect the rape of indigenous women and the stealing of land and other resources by white colonists. These realities demand therapeutic interventions to disentangle the positive traditions within *macho*, *varón*, and *hombre* from traditions that value violence and exploitation.

The task of reshaping masculinity depends on individual and institutional work at multiple levels. Some national governments, for example, are taking a leading role in the transformation of masculinity. In April 2005, the Spanish parliament passed a law requiring husbands to "share domestic responsibilities" (Tremlett, 2005). New marriage licenses will require not only housework from men but also partnership in caring for children and dependent adults. Failure to follow through can constitute grounds for divorce.

With other groups, such as Asian or Muslim men, we recommend that social justice–based therapy take into account their culture-specific definitions of masculinity and its intersection with mainstream cultural prescriptions. Within many Asian Indian cultures, for example, the family structure after marriage prioritizes the bond between the husband and his mother and his extended family of origin. Married women, consequently, are expected to find intimacy primarily within relationships with their male children and the families these male children later create. The mothers-in-law in these situations join the male code and frequently abuse their daughters-in-law. This practice differs markedly from contemporary U.S. culture, which encourages men to develop their primary relationships within their work organizations and expects their female partners to provide unreciprocated intimate concern, emotional support, and family maintenance. While Asian men are also required to uphold this economic achievement, they are simultaneously required to be connected to their mothers and extended family.

Asian men often tolerate "effeminate" presentation of self more readily than do their Western counterparts, and they generally affirm men enjoying close friendship bonds and touching one another affectionately. Paradoxically, Asian cultures generally sanction gay and lesbian sexual orientation far more strongly than do Western cultures. The concept of compulsory heterosexuality must be broken down within the context of the Asian diaspora rather than solely within the domestic landscape.

In his book *Racial Castration: Managing Masculinity in Asian America*, Eng (2001) asserts that mainstream America's depiction of Asian Americans as "the model minority" distorts perceptions of this group and sets up the African American and Latino communities to appear economically incompetent. He describes many ways that intersecting mythologies regarding masculinity and communities of color disempower members of those communities.

MASCULINITY, GAY MEN, AND HOMOPHOBIA

With few exceptions, gay men of all backgrounds grow up within families, communities, and institutions that devalue queer people. Like other males, gay men learn to identify with the patriarchal male code. Because that code teaches hatred for people like themselves, survival requires that they also learn to resist the code. A similar challenge faces men of color, as well as all women, because the code undermines the survival and integrity of people from these groups. But a primary difference lies in the individual nature of the challenge, because queer children generally start off with no one but themselves to rely on in making sense of the assault they face regarding their sexual orientation.

Tragically, the assault frequently comes first from their parents and other family members (the challenges for queer children are dealt with further in Chapter 7). Boys of color and girls of all colors, on the other hand, tend to learn about racism and sexism from supportive parents and peers, who often coach them on how to resist and survive these oppressions.

Unless gay men choose to replicate heterosexual patterns, with one partner rigidly enacting masculinity and the other femininity, those who seek partnership in a couple must reject each rule of the patriarchal male code. They must

- Nurture one another.
- Express (and accept the expression of) the full spectrum of feelings and not just anger.
- Offer emotional openness and vulnerability.
- Balance work against relationship priorities.
- Recognize the limits of self-reliance and the value of interdependence.
- Solve problems using negotiation rather than aggression.
- Share leadership.
- Recognize the humanity in their partners rather than exclusively objectifying them.
- Value queer people.

The stretch between patriarchal masculinity and these patterns is challenging, and crossing it may be more an ideal than a lived reality for many couples. But these patterns provide a model for all men, indeed all people, to strive toward.

WOMEN AS CULTURE BEARERS

Patriarchy assigns girls and women a submissive and supporting role and expects them to promote all the traditions of their societies, including those as detrimental to females as the patriarchal male code. We use the term *culture bearer* to describe this assigned role. Every patriarchal rule for males implies a corresponding culture-bearer expectation for females, as shown in Table 3.1.

Girls and women become culture bearers because a myriad of interactions introduce and reinforce this role throughout the life cycle. Those who resist

TABLE 3.1   Patriarchal Gender Rules

PATRIARCHAL RULES FOR MEN	CULTURE-BEARING RULES FOR WOMEN
Rule 1: Don't act like a girl.	Rule 1: Perform but also minimize the value of "women's work" and other human activities and traits traditionally deemed feminine.
Rule 2: Keep your feelings to yourself.	Rule 2: Read, predict, and manage the feelings and desires of boys and men.
Rule 3: Work is your first priority.	Rule 3: Support men's preoccupation with work by sacrificing your own goals and dreams if necessary.
Rule 4: Be self-reliant.	Rule 4: Support the illusion of men's self-reliance while fashioning the illusion of women's dependency.
Rule 5: Solve problems using aggression.	Rule 5: Accept men's aggression, and go along with the story that men's aggression protects families.
Rule 6: Be dominant.	Rule 6: Be submissive. Accept that the head of a household (or other social organization) should rightfully be male.
Rule 7: Women are for sex.	Rule 7: Accept and promote sexual objectification of females.
Rule 8: Don't be gay.	Rule 8: Promote homophobia.

compliance face penalties that include name-calling, ostracism, physical assault, and murder. The culture-bearer role sometimes demands that women perform activities that directly assault their own physical and emotional safety. In societies that practice genital mutilation, for example, women, not men, perform the surgery.

Men, too, participate in and sanction oppressive traditional practices: female genital mutilation, facial scarring of young boys, enforced dowries, the veiling of women, and the valuing of sons over daughters. Men who remain silent about such practices demonstrate that they value tradition over justice.

In Alice Walker's 1998 book *Anything We Love Can Be Saved* (p. 31), she recounts a conversation with Samuel Zan about the facial scarring he was forced to endure in his native Ghana. At the time of the conversation, Zan was the general secretary of Amnesty International in his country.

> **Alice:** How did it happen?
>
> **Samuel:** One day when I was a small boy—maybe five years old—my grandfather came to visit. As he sometimes did without asking my parents, he carried me home with him. While I was there, someone came to the house and did it. I bled a lot . . . I also cried . . . .
>
> **Alice:** Did it hurt very much?
>
> **Samuel:** It did. But it was the surprise of it, the betrayal, that hurt the most.

DISABILITY, AGING AND GENDER

Although men sanction some forms of deliberate mutilation, women's deformities through illness or accident are scorned. In most cultures, women with disabilities, even if facially attractive, are not considered objects of desire and cannot compete with their able-bodied counterparts. In some cultures, females afflicted with disabilities at a young age may be given away to religious communities or murdered.

A strong case can be made that aging socially debilitates women more significantly than it does men. Men of all colors are likely to be honored for their accomplishments and maturity as they age, but older women do not gain respect and deference. Instead, they find themselves moved to the margins of family and community life.

One exception to this is women in south Asian cultures, who tend to gain status during their midlife as they become mothers-in-law, with power over all the younger women and men in the household. They maintain their status by holding on to the role of culture bearer, and as such, they frequently abuse their daughters-in-law.

In Western societies, women collaborate with men in perpetuating female standards of beauty that promote self-starvation and self-mutilation through plastic surgery. Women also do little to celebrate older and disabled women.

Research shows that when women in their mid-40s divorce or are widowed, they are less likely to remarry than are men who face similar losses. Although physically unattractive men often have an array of women, including much younger women, to choose from, an older woman in search of a partner may have to settle for someone much older than herself whom she may have to take care of in the not-so-distant future.

The patriarchal male code and its accompanying culture-bearer role for females is still the foundation within most societies. People frequently view these patterns as having a positive value. They confuse oppressive traditions with other more positive aspects of culture that promote an experience of shared history, connection to an ancestral homeland, group belonging, and communal purpose.

In order for practitioners to help clients make this liberating distinction between culture and oppressive traditions within their own lives, practitioners must keep the distinction firmly in mind. Culture involves the positive transmission of rituals, celebrations, and stories that make the general ordering of life familiar for members of a particular group. Helping professionals need to assert that wife battering is not culture; dowries, wife burning, acid attacks, and female infanticide are not culture; forced veiling for women in Islamic communities is not culture; foot-binding and keeping concubines among the Chinese are not culture. These are traditional patriarchal customs that men have practiced and women have been required to accept for generations. We owe it to our clients to disentangle these dehumanizing traditions from positive cultural practices.

When confronted by varying forms of external oppression, culture can perpetuate connections for families via food, language, particular art forms, and religious practices. When external forces, including racism, colonization, anti-Semitism, and capitalism, weigh down on members of a particular group, that group's positive cultural norms tend to become rigid. But so do the group's oppressive customs. Unfortunately, the attempt to preserve group identity often comes at the expense of women, children, queer people, and others who are most vulnerable.

Families striving to preserve their ethnic identities often exhibit this pattern. A Chinese American woman might say that in her culture, norms of hierarchy and respect based on gender and age are essential to family life. Therefore, to be a good wife and mother requires that she respect her husband and explain his negative behaviors in a positive manner to their older son. In this way, she believes she is teaching her son to value respect and hierarchy.

To help her distinguish between preserving her family's cultural identity and accepting oppressive customs, her therapist can share with her the writing of Chinese feminists and video clips from films such as *The Joy Luck Club* and *The Wedding Banquet*, which depict powerful Chinese women who challenge patriarchy by affirming cultural legacies that do *not* support male domination and female subordination.

A social justice approach to therapy would help the Chinese American woman rethink her acceptance of her husband's domination, while affirming her family's Chinese heritage. Such a conversation would also help white participants in the consciousness-raising discussion examine commonly held myths regarding people of color, such as the idea that all Chinese women are comfortable with subordination or that heterosexuality is the only form of partnering within Chinese culture.

In another case, an African American couple believes that the legacy of slavery requires women to honor the elevated status of all men in order to counter the racism black men encounter daily. They might be asked to view films such as *Warrior Marks* and *Straight Out of Brooklyn*, in which a number of African American women challenge the way in which the civil rights movement obscured their visibility as freedom fighters. ·

Fundamentalist religious communities of all faiths often reinforce the patriarchal male code and the expectation that women will act as culture bearers. For example, most Christian and Hindu fundamentalists stigmatize queer people as sinners who do not follow God's laws. Similarly, some women and men of the Islamic faith argue that religion requires the veiling of adolescent girls. While a young woman may choose to veil because of her own examination of Islamic principles, forced veiling that may be accompanied by threats, beatings, and in some cultures, death, is a fundamental human rights issue.

Social justice–based practitioners raise the conversation about oppressive practices and religion. They bring in voices from within the culture that offer liberating instead of fundamentalist narratives. They may, for example, point to the tenets of liberation theology, which views scriptures from a perspective that asserts the full humanity of all people and refutes the restricting tenets of many fundamentalist approaches.

Practitioners might also show clients videotapes featuring Islamic feminists who challenge patriarchal interpretations of the Koran. These feminists, for example, point out that Mohammed had only daughters and honored every one of them. Clients can be shown *Voices of the Morning*, a movie that depicts the clashes that confront young women of the Muslim faith. These women need all the strength they can muster to survive in a Western-dominated, anti-Muslim world while simultaneously battling their own families and communities to carve identities across new frontiers.

Therapists can begin shifting their approach in the direction of social justice–based practice by simply asking their clients questions that frequently remain unstated:

- In your culture and family, who is expected to educate children regarding the rules of relationships?
- How are children taught to respect elders, fathers, mothers, uncles, and aunts?
- Are your children taught to respect all elders regardless of gender, race, and class?
- Who gets blamed when your children do not follow these rules?
- What are some of the myths about mothers when children behave badly?

These questions initiate a consciousness-raising discussion about patriarchal expectations for males and females. Acknowledging these expectations marks the first step toward transforming them. Your challenge is to create ways of expanding your practice approach so that critical consciousness, accountability, and empowerment—the key elements for social justice–based therapy—become central to your healing efforts.

HELPING PROFESSIONALS AS CULTURE BEARERS

Like everyone else in our society, mental health professionals, physicians, nurses, attorneys, police officers, judges, teachers, college professors, researchers, religious leaders, community leaders, and lawmakers grow up and live their lives within a social system that is saturated by beliefs, expectations, and guidelines for behavior that affirm mainstream values, including the patriarchal male code and its corollary expectation that females act as culture bearers. Consequently, in their work with families and individuals, helping professionals usually reinforce these values and expectations, whether unwittingly or purposely. It should come as no surprise that the majority of schoolteachers and social workers are women who get little social and economic recognition for educating and managing two critical populations of our society. Typically, professional helpers do one or more of the following:

- Treat behavior that is consistent with the patriarchal male code as though it is normal, even "natural," and not a problem despite the negative impact such behavior may wreak on others.

- Expect women to assume more than half of the responsibility for making the changes or accommodations necessary to sustain couple relationships.
- Expect women to shoulder the bulk of responsibility for child care, elder care, and all other family- and community-related responsibilities.
- Minimize the seriousness of abusive behavior committed by all men, particularly by white men.
- Expect female victims of violence, rather than the male perpetrators, to take action to make the violence stop or create safety in some other manner.
- Minimize differences in a way that pretends everybody shares the beliefs, values, access to resources, and expectations generally associated with people who are white, heterosexual, male, without disabilities, and from middle- or upper middle-class backgrounds.
- Ignore the loss of power that women over 40 face.
- Ignore the "power over" choices that men make throughout the life cycle.

Therapists and other helping professionals reinforce these ideas and values to varying degrees. When a heterosexual couple seeks counseling, typically the woman takes the initiative, being more ready than the man to assume responsibility for change. Many therapists go along with this dynamic, asking more of the woman and allowing the man to assume another role, less like a therapy client and more like a cheerleader or supporter for his partner.

The work of psychiatrist Richard Gardner, who concocted parent alienation syndrome (PAS), represents the extreme of collusion with male entitlement, along with the mental health professionals and courts that endorse PAS (Hoult, 2006). This new "diagnosis" is used to prevent battered women from protecting their children from exposure to violent fathers. PAS asserts that children who resist parental visitation are not legitimately seeking protection from their fathers but rather have been "alienated" from their fathers by their mothers. PAS is a bogus diagnosis that has been completely discredited by ethical researchers and practitioners, but it continues to be used by some in the psychological community and sanctioned by the judiciary.*

Most helping professionals do not recognize how much male entitlement, power imbalances, and the traditional male code shape what goes on within couple and family relationships. Instead, they collude with these patterns time after time.

At a recent family therapy conference, a presenter showed a videotaped therapy session in which a white, middle-class man and woman, recently separated and trying to build a solid co-parenting relationship, were meeting with the presenter, a white female therapist. The separated woman, Stephanie, who was the primary custodial parent, voiced doubts about her parenting skills. She worried

---

*The Leadership Council on Child Abuse and Interpersonal Violence is composed of national leaders in psychology, psychiatry, medicine, law, and public policy who are committed to the ethical application of psychological science and countering its misuse by special-interest groups. Members of the Council are dedicated to the health, safety, and well-being of children and other vulnerable populations. More information can be found at http://www.leadershipcouncil.org/

that her busy work schedule prevented her from giving enough time, love, and support to the couple's five-year-old son, Peter. The little boy attended kindergarten and, by all accounts, was adjusting as well as could be expected to the recent changes in his family's structure.

In the videotape, the therapist listened carefully to Stephanie as she described her fears that the father's departure from the home made her son feel insecure and fearful regarding the dependability of both parents. As the dialogue continued, it became evident to conference participants that this mother, from everything the therapist presented, was a thoughtful and loving parent. She put a great deal of time and emotional energy into being considerate, responsive, and thorough in addressing her son's needs.

The father, Joshua, who looked after his son one night each week and every other weekend, experienced no self-doubt regarding his parenting. Instead, he praised himself and his wife as exemplary parents, encouraging her to "give yourself a break and recognize what a great mother you are!"

The therapist had a wonderful opportunity to help both parents examine the gendered pattern they were enacting. The man, who indeed seemed a loving and involved parent, had no difficulty claiming kudos for his fathering. The woman, on the other hand, even though she put in far more parenting time and energy than did the man, found it impossible to rest assured that she was giving enough to their son. By the end of the session, the therapist had characterized the woman's uncertainty as pathological anxiety, hypothesizing the existence of a self-esteem problem.

Some conference attendees challenged the therapist's hypothesis, encouraging her to imagine the way gender socialization, as well as other social pressures connected to race and social class, were contributing to the differences between the experiences of this woman and man.

BEYOND THE PATRIARCHAL MALE CODE

The case descriptions in this chapter show both the complexity of gender issues and the power of cultural norms to shape responses to the problems that clients experience. Often, the cultural norms themselves become the problem. Earlier in this chapter, we described the challenges that confront gay men, who receive the same "training for manhood" as other males, when they strive to build couple partnerships. They struggle with the same notions of equity and shedding internalized norms of dominance. Success depends on reshaping the patriarchal male code into a "partnership code" that supports equality (see Table 3.2). We suggest this new code as a model for people of all genders who are committed to building social justice–based relationships.

We end this chapter by asking you to remember that the patriarchal male code keeps women in the role of culture bearers. Women as culture bearers, with internalized male norms, aggressively compete with other women as foes instead of embracing circles of women toward liberation.

TABLE 3.2 Patriarchal Male Code vs. Partnership Code

PATRIARCHAL MALE CODE	PARTNERSHIP CODE
Rule 1: Don't act like a girl (avoid child care and other nurturing activities).	Nurture one another, and share family caregiving activities such as child care.
Rule 2: Keep your feelings to yourself (showing anger is acceptable).	Express and accept the expression of the full spectrum of feelings, not just anger. Offer emotional openness and vulnerability.
Rule 3: Work is your first priority.	Life is your first priority. Balance work against relationship priorities.
Rule 4: Be self-reliant.	Collaborate. Recognize the limits of self-reliance and the value of interdependence.
Rule 5: Solve problems using aggression.	Solve problems using negotiation rather than aggression.
Rule 6: Be dominant and in control.	Share leadership.
Rule 7: Women are for sex.	Always recognize the humanity in your partners rather than objectifying them.
Rule 8: Don't be gay (and avoid emotional closeness with other men).	Value queer people and people across all dimensions of diversity. Work to replace bias with social justice.

Consider the partnership code as the alternative to the male code. Putting the partnership code firmly in mind, you can make it the center of your therapeutic work as you strive to help clients heal their relationships, families, and communities.

REFERENCES

Dworkin, A. (1974). *Woman hating.* New York: Dutton.

Dyson, M. E. (1997). *Race rules.* New York: Vintage Books.

Eng, D. L. (2001). *Racial Castration: Managing masculinity in Asian America.* Durham, NC: Duke University Press.

Franklin, A. J. (2004). *From brotherhood to manhood: How black men rescue relationships and dreams from the invisibility syndrome.* Hoboken, NJ: John Wiley & Sons.

Gates, H. (1997). *Thirteen ways of looking at a black man.* New York: Random House.

Haggis, P. (Producer/Director). (2005). *Crash* [Motion picture]. North Vancouver, BC: Lions Gate Studios.

Hoult, J. (2006, Spring). The evidentiary admissibility of parental alienation syndrome: Science, law, and policy. *Children's Legal Rights Journal, 26*(1), 1–61.

Lee, A. (Producer/Director). *The wedding banquet* [Motion picture]. Los Angeles: MGM Studios.

Maduro, O. (1995). Directions for a reassessment of Latina/o religion. In A. M. Stevens-Arroyo, Y. Perez, & A. T. Mena (Eds.), *Syncretism with African and indigenous peoples' religions among Latinos.* New York: The Bildner Center for Western Hemisphere Studies.

Majors, R., & Billson, J. M. (1993). *Cool pose: The dilemmas of black manhood in America.* New York: Touchstone Books/Simon & Schuster.

McCall, N. (1995). *Makes me wanna holler: A young black man in America.* New York: Vintage Books.

McCall, N. (1998). *What's going on: Personal essays*. New York: Vintage Books.

Nanji, M. (Director). (1992). *Voices of the morning* [Motion picture]. United States: Women Make Movies.

Powell, K. (2003). *Who's gonna take the weight: Manhood, race, and power in America*. New York: Three Rivers Press.

Rich, M. (Producer/Director). (1991). *Straight out of Brooklyn* [Motion picture]. Los Angeles: Samuel Goldwin Company.

Ryu, E. (2006). Personal communication. Doctoral candidate, Drexel University, Philadelphia, PA.

Stone, O., & Wang, W. (Producer /Director). (1993). *The joy luck club* [Motion picture]. Los Angeles, CA: Hollywood Pictures.

Stoltenberg, J. (1989). *Refusing to be a man: Essays on sex and justice*. New York: Meridian.

Tremlett, G. (2005, April 8). Blow to machismo as Spain forces men to do housework. *The Guardian*.

Walker, A. (1990). *The color purple* [Motion picture]. New York: Pocket Books.

Walker, A. (1998). *Anything we love can be saved*. New York: Ballantine Books.

Walker, A. & Parmar, P. (Producer/Director). (1993). *Warrior marks* [Motion picture]. New York: Women Make Movies.

Yoshiaki, Y. (2001). *Comfort women: Sexual slavery in the Japanese military during World War II*, New York: Columbia University Press.

RECOMMENDED READINGS

Almeida, R. V. (Ed.). (1994). *Expansions of feminist family theory through diversity*. New York: Harrington Park Press.

Almeida, R. V. (Ed.). (1998). *Transformations of gender and race: Family and developmental perspectives*. New York: Hawthorn Press.

Anderson, E. (1990). *Streetwise: Race, class and change in an urban community*. Chicago: University of Chicago Press.

Baldwin, J. A. (1981). Notes on an Africentric theory of black personality. *Western Journal of Black Studies, 5*(3), 172–179.

Beavers, H., (1997). The cool pose. Intersectionality, masculinity, and the quiescence in the comedy and films of Richard Pryor and Eddie Murphy. In H. Stecopoulos and M. Uebel (Eds.), *Race and the subject of masculinities*. Durham, NC: Duke University Press.

Baughman, E. E. (1971). *Black Americans*. New York: Academic Press.

Billingsley, A. (1968). *Black families in white America*. Englewood Cliffs, NJ: Prentice Hall.

Bowman, P. J. (1989). Research perspectives on black men: Role strain and adaptation across the adult life cycle. In R. J. Jones (Ed.), *Black adult development and aging*. Berkeley, CA: Cobbs & Henry.

Boyd-Franklin, N., Franklin, A. J., & Toussaint, P. (2000). *Boys into men: Raising our African American teenage sons*. New York: Penguin Putnam.

Burlew, A. K. H., Banks, W. C., & McAdoo, H. P. (Eds.). (1992). *African American psychology: Theory, research and practice*. Thousand Oaks, CA: Sage.

Caplan, N. (1977). The new ghetto man: A review of recent empirical studies. In D. Y. Wilkinson & R. L. Taylor (Eds.), *The black male in America: Perspectives in contemporary society* (pp. 309–325). Chicago: Nelson-Hall.

Carbado, D. W. (Ed.). (1999). *Black men on race, gender and sexuality: A critical reader*. New York: NYU Press.

Carter, H. A., Walker, W. T., & Jones W. A. (1991). *The African American church: Past, present and future*. New York: Martin Luther King Fellow Press.

Clark, K. (1965). *Dark ghetto*. New York: Harper & Row.

Cone, J. H. (1991). *For my people: Black theology and the black church*. New York: Orbis Books.

Copper, B. (1997). The view from over the hill. In M. Pearsall (Ed.), *The other within us: Feminist explorations of women and aging*. Boulder, CO: Westview Press.

Crenshaw, K. (1999). Introduction. In D. W. Carbado (Ed.), *Black men on race, gender, and sexuality: A critical reader*. New York: NYU Press.

Diener, E., Saptya, J. J., & Suh, E. (1998). Subjective well-being is essential to well-being. *Psychological Inquiry, 9*(1), 33–37.

Dubois, W. E. B. (1989). *The souls of black folk.* New York: Viking Penguin.

Eisler, R. (1995). *The chalice and the blade.* New York: HarperCollins.

Fanon, F. (1963). *The wretched of the earth.* New York: Grove Press.

Ferber, A. L. (1995). Shame of white men: Interracial sexuality and the construction of white masculinity in contemporary white supremacist discourse. *Masculinities, 3*(2), 1–24.

Fine, M., & Weis, L. (1998). Crime stories: A critical look through race, ethnicity, and gender. *Qualitative Studies in Education, 11*(3), 435–459.

Floyd, C. (1996). Achieving despite the odds: A study of resilience among a group of African American high school seniors. *The Journal of Negro Education, 65*(2), 181–189.

Franklin, A. J. (1999). Invisibility syndrome and racial development in psychotherapy and counseling African American men. *Counseling Psychologist, 27*(6), 761–793.

hooks, B. (1990) *Yearning: Race, gender and cultural politics.* Cambridge, MA: South End Press.

Johnson, R., & Leighton, P. S. (1995). Black genocide? Preliminary thoughts on the plight of America's poor black men. *Journal of African American Men, 1*(2), 63–71.

Kimmel, M. S., & Messner, M. A. (1996). *Men's lives* (3rd ed.). Upper Saddle River, NJ: Pearson Education.

Keller, N. O.(1998) *Comfort woman.* London, Penguin.

Kim-Gibson, D. (1999). *Silence broken: Korean comfort women.* Parkersburg, IA: Mid-Prairie Books.

Madhubuti, H. R. (1991). *Black men: Obsolete, single, dangerous?* Chicago, IL: Third World Press.

Noguera, P. A. (1996). Responding to the crisis confronting California's black male youth: Providing support without further marginalization. *The Journal of Negro Education, 65,* 219–236.

Payne, Y. A., & Brown, A. L. (in press). Sites of resiliency: A reconceptualization of resiliency for young black men living in the ghetto. In M. Pierre (Ed.), *A new psychology for African-American men.* Westport, CT: Greenwood.

Pleck, J. H. (1981). *The myth of masculinity.* Cambridge, MA: MIT Press.

Tanaka, Y. (2002). *Japan's comfort women: Sexual slavery and prostitution during World War II and the U.S. occupation.* London: Routledge.

Utsey, S. O., Bolden, M. A., & Brown, A. L. (2001). Visions of revolution from the spirit of Frantz Fanon: A psychology of liberation for counseling African Americans confronting societal racism and oppression. In J. G. Ponterotto, J. G. Casas, L. A. Suzuki, & C. M. Alexander (Eds.), *Handbook of multicultural counseling* (2nd ed.; pp. 311–336). Thousand Oaks, CA: Sage.

Weis, L., Fine, M., Shepard, T., & Foster, K. (1999). We need to come together and raise our kids and our communities right: Black males rewriting social representations. *The Urban Review, 31*(1), 125–152.

Wyatt, G. E. (1999). Beyond invisibility of African American males: The effects on women and families. *Counseling Psychologist, 27,* 802–809.

CHAPTER FOUR

FAMILIES AS SUBSYSTEMS

The master's tools will never dismantle the master's house.
—Audre Lorde (2002, p. 106).

Family therapy literature often overemphasizes the boundary between families and the larger world and overlooks realities that transcend that boundary. For many families, relationships within the workplace loom as large as or larger than relationships at home. Religious doctrines, ethnic patterns, economic pressures, and immigration laws impact the lives of some families both within and outside the home.

In this chapter, we emphasize the permeability of the boundaries between the family and society at large, demonstrating how each family is actually a subsystem of the society within which it resides. We show how gender socialization, race heritage, class legacy, workplace status, and other dimensions of life influence family relationships. We expand familiar family therapy concepts—boundaries, hierarchies, and differentiation—so that therapists can attend to factors outside as well as within family life that contribute to patterns of power, privilege, and injustice within families.

We also discuss family subsystems and strategies for working with them, including practices adapted from a variety of therapeutic models. Topics include

- The impact of sexism, racism, homophobia, and classism on family relationships.
- Subsystems within families.
- Tracking multigenerational patterns with the focus on power, privilege, and oppression.
- Exploring, evaluating, and enhancing alliances and coalitions.
- Letter writing, journaling, oral anthologies, and rituals.

THE IMPACT OF SEXISM, RACISM, HOMOPHOBIA, AND CLASSISM ON FAMILY RELATIONSHIPS

Families share with all other institutions in our society a history colored and textured by patriarchy, which promotes sexism, racism, classism, and homophobia. Accordingly, mainstream family values and social policies prescribe "normal" expectations that are skewed toward privilege for white, heterosexual, middle- and upper-class men, and injustice for women, people of color, queers, and those whose finances are limited. Service delivery and policy do not reflect the range of family forms and diversity of communities (Waldegrave, Tamasese, Tuhuka & Campbell, (2003); Waldegrave, 2005; 2006). For example, inadequate access to health care, the lack of affordable housing, and the absence of socially-subsidized child care impact all families but devastate those in less privileged brackets (Bravo, 2007). Similarly, child welfare, charged with the protection of children, is guided by the same generic, and therefore oppressive, family values. As a prime example of this structural injustice, consider the institution of marriage.

Heterosexual Marriage

Many scholars describe contemporary marriage in the United States as an unjust yet idealized institution (e.g., Coontz, 2005; Ingraham, 1999; Okin, 1989; Silverstein & Goodrich, 2005). Hare-Mustin (1991, p. 40) describes marriage as "a lifelong oppositional play of power masquerading as pleasure." Indeed, on a day-to-day basis, most heterosexual relationships are organized in such as way that women shoulder the bulk of relational and household responsibilities (Haddock, Zimmerman, Current, & Harvey, 2003; Hochschild, 1989; Hooyman & Gonyea, 1995; Zimmerman & Addison, 1997).

The inequitable division of labor occurs not only within family life (housework, child and elder care) but also in exterior contacts with the community. Women, at almost all stages of the life cycle, are largely responsible for connecting with schools, recreation facilities, physicians, dentists, therapists, retirement centers, nursing homes, and social service agencies. They manage and coordinate the needs of individual and extended family members. And in middle- and upper-class families, women are responsible for hiring and managing household and yard workers. Family life, as typically structured in our society, is neither just nor equitable, especially for women (Okin, 1989). Women as single mothers with limited economic resources experience this structuring more harshly. This devastation of inequity is sweeping in poor and disproportionate numbers of families of color.

The accommodations that women make in their work lives to care for others exacerbate the economic disadvantages of females relative to males (Friedman & Greenhaus, 2000; Williams, 2000). The cultural idealization of women as caregivers and nurturers teaches women early on not to expect or demand that men too be caregivers and nurturers in their families. Motherhood, unlike the institution of marriage, is simultaneously exalted and denigrated.

[Heterosexual] women are made vulnerable by constructing their lives around the expectation that they will be primary parents; they become more vulnerable within marriages in which they fulfill this expectation, whether or not they also work for wages; and they are most vulnerable in the event of separation or divorce, when they usually take over responsibility for children without adequate support from their ex-husbands. (Okin, 1989, p. 170)

Women who do not hold paid employment find themselves in a particularly vulnerable position. If they become divorced, they are likely to experience a sharp drop in financial well-being and often must support their children with little or no financial help from the fathers (U.S. Census Bureau, 1999). Financial dependence can restrict their ability to withdraw from a relationship, and economic vulnerability is associated with higher rates of domestic violence. One in four women experiences domestic violence at some time in her life (National Coalition for Domestic Violence, 2005), and nearly three-quarters of family violence victims are female (Department of Justice, 2005). Victims of severe intimate partner violence lose nearly 8 million days of paid work each year—the equivalent of more than 32,000 full-time jobs—and almost 6 million days of household productivity annually (Department of Health and Human Services, Centers for Disease Control, 2003; Wulfhorst, 2006).

The romantic myth of the traditional family has proven especially dangerous for women and children. Accordingly, we must press for national policies that are friendlier to women and children. It is imperative that every adult become economically viable. At the very least, people need the financial means to be able to exit battering relationships. Sweden, for example, has family policies in place that allow both partners to take off work when children are born; and it affords economic and health benefits to divorced women and their children. Because women and men *can* leave, the stress on families is lessened, as are levels of lethality in battering relationships. The ability to leave helps to rebalance power dynamics between partners.

Inequities in power and privilege often are carried over into treatment processes. For example, if the husband of a "depressed" woman engages in treatment—and often he does not—it is likely that his therapist will ask very little of him. The therapist is more likely to placate him and even congratulate him for supporting his partner, "support" in this case being defined in purely emotional or physical, but not functional, terms. Male and female therapists rarely define support in relationships in functional terms such as taking responsibility for chores related to other family members or the home. Therapists often neglect to explore the respective roles partners carry or how couples manage financial arrangements.

Conversely, therapists working from a social justice perspective explore money, child care, household chores, and relationship care with couples. They view issues of inequity as central to the distressed partner's experience. Often, when a woman must take responsibility for the bulk of household and people care duties, the man also ends up miserable because his female partner is often angry and/or critical of him for not doing his fair share. Certainly sex may be put on the back burner if one partner is constantly cleaning up for the other. Doing another's household chores is not sexy to most people.

From a social justice perspective, therapeutic efforts to help heal a depressed wife must include assessing the practical responsibilities that tend to fall on the person with less power and privilege in a relationship. Therapists can challenge the other partner to stop using his or her privilege to avoid such tasks and to take on a more equal share of child care, housework, and all the other efforts required to maintain extended family and community connections.

As part of the overall effort to build more justice into couples' relationships, both members are provided skills to help them become equal partners in the responsibilities of family life and are expected and encouraged to use these skills. Similarly, a depressed man may be carrying too much of the financial burden, or may require assistance in advocating for better benefits and opportunities at work. For there to be equity in relationships, both partners need to assume responsibility and learn the skills needed to generate income and perform people and house-care tasks.

In fact, efforts toward equity have been shown to be helpful to both partners. Papp (2000) suggests that both female and male depression is abated when a man offers emotional and functional help to his partner. Gottman's (1994) research indicates that "men who do housework and child care have better sex lives and happier marriages" (p. 157). Gottman also found a direct correlation between how much housework a man does and his physical health. They speculated that "resolving this major marital issue means there is less conflict at home, so the man experiences less stress over the years," which improves his overall health (p. 158). This assertion was consistent with Schmaling, Goldman, and Sher's (2000) research on couples and illness, which suggested that negative interactions in intimate relationships are stressful and are linked to long-term harmful health outcomes.

On the global level, Spain, which gave the world the word *macho*, is trying to remedy its historically poor grade on sexual equality. Spanish inventor Pepe Torres has introduced a washing machine that forces husbands to do the laundry themselves half the time. For the prototype, he attached an inexpensive biometric sensor that reads fingerprints. If the prints don't alternate between the husband's and wife's from wash to wash, the machine won't work. "This isn't a gimmick, but a message to change this machista society," says the 40-year-old inventor, writer, composer, and public-relations man. He calls his creation the *lavadora paritaria*, or the "equal-rights washing machine," which is a play on a favorite government buzzword: *paridad* ("equality") (Tremlett, 2005, p. 2).

SOCIAL CLASS AND THE WORKPLACE

Upper- and middle-class men, the people who design the structure of modern workplaces, have created political, educational, and social institutions that further their own interests at the expense of others. Williams (2000) describes the "ideal worker" as a person who "works full time and overtime and takes little or no time off for childbearing or childrearing." Those who provide caregiving are marginalized and cut off "from most of the social roles that offer responsibility and authority" (p. 3). Williams challenges us to "persuade women [and men] to think about their own lives in a different way, not as expressions of personal priorities [choices] that occur within their heads but as a clash between the way a society tells women [and men] that children should be raised and the way it chooses to organize market work" (p. 271). The current conception of the ideal worker discriminates against women and families. Changes are needed in the language we use and social policies regarding the workforce (Williams, 2000, p. 14).

Therapists can encourage all family members to look at how they contribute to earning money, to caregiving and household tasks, to relationship building and maintenance, and to maintaining contact with the community (e.g., agencies, friends, recreation). Additionally, they might be invited to examine how they contribute to community life. Betty Carter (1995) and others (Putnam, 2000) have written about the extent to which today's families in American society have lost their connections to community. What was viewed an idyllic flight into suburban bliss has now been shown to exact its toll on families in terms of isolation, heightened stress, and limited quality of life. Structuring justice into the lives of the working poor and other disenfrachised families requires major shifts in social policies and therapeutic resistance to the institutional fracturing of family life.

THE COSTS OF HOMOPHOBIA

The belief that marriage is reserved exclusively for male–female couples is another example of imposing a "traditional" standard to define "normal" family structure and interaction patterns.

The "marriage movement," which gained momentum in the United States under President George W. Bush, seeks to codify heterosexual marriage as the only legally protected option for adult partnership. This movement validates heterosexual privilege and marginalizes alternative family forms that are gaining growing acceptance elsewhere (Canada and Spain, for example).

In reality, gay families can teach the mainstream a great deal about equality in couple and family life. Research on men who became fathers after coming out suggests that gay men positively transform traditional cultural norms for fathers, families, and masculinity. Their "de-gendered" parenting styles, reconceptualization of family, and reworking of masculine gender roles offer useful alternative models for all families (Schacter, Auerbach, & Silverstein, 2005).

Family therapists who fail to recognize and acknowledge the variety of family forms, sexual orientations, and identities may not see indications that a marital problem stems from a husband's (or wife's) questioning of his (her) sexual identity or orientation. The therapist may miss that an adolescent's suicide attempt followed an act of discrimination based on sexual orientation. Heterosexism and homophobia determine which groups receive support, such as federal funds to preserve heterosexual marriage. They influence which groups get privileges such as tax breaks, the right to a partner's inheritance, the right to be affectionate in public, and the right to be treated fairly and courteously.

In the United States today, men in general have more privilege than women, and heterosexual white men and women have more privilege than gay men, lesbians, and people of color. Social class also matters with regard to these hierarchies.

The interaction of social location and relative privilege is an important determinant of our freedoms and responsibilities. The following questions bring this reality into therapeutic conversations.

- Who has access to meaningful and lucrative work?
- Who has access to health insurance?
- Who is not a target of racial, sexist, and homophobic slurs and discrimination?
- Whose relationship is socially sanctioned and rewarded?
- Who carries more household and child and elder care responsibilities; who cuts back their work, if needed, to care for family members?
- Who earns the most?
- Who tends to make the major family decisions?
- Who is responsible for socializing children into their racial and cultural heritage?
- Whose name is bestowed on children and partners?

A social justice–based approach to family therapy takes these realities into account and strives to rebalance families toward fairness for all. Neutrality on matters of justice and oppression is not a virtue in social justice–based work.

SUBSYSTEMS WITHIN FAMILIES

Just as families are subsystems of the broader social order, they also contain subsystems of their own. Working with family subsystems—mothers, fathers, uncles, siblings, partners, children, grandparents, other extended kin, and friends—greatly expands the helping model, providing the resources and accountability necessary for effecting just changes within families.

Meetings might be held with siblings to strengthen or repair relationships between them. A parent and adult child might work out an unresolved issue together. Inviting someone from outside the family system to witness or participate in the conversation is especially useful to support as well as empower change and to hold parties accountable for the commitments they have made. For example, an adolescent who is negotiating for additional privileges may be coached with other siblings present and may be provided an adolescent sponsor or mentor to help negotiate with his or her parents.

Years ago, Jay Haley, (1963) father of strategic family therapy, pointed out that when things are stuck, it's a good idea to bring in more people. Privacy exacerbates problems. It does not prevent them. The message throughout this book encourages you to think bigger, go beyond your comfort zones to create liberating change. At all levels, this process empowers family members to respect each other, encouraging them to bring reason and thoughtfulness, along with collaborative decision-making skills, to family and social events. When witnesses are included in the process, they strengthen accountability and empowerment. Witnesses will remember particulars of the family's emotional process, historical patterns of disappointment and harm, promises made, and conclusions reached to change family life. Witnesses can hold participants to their word as well as support the change process.

Case 4.1 shows the value of witnesses—in this case, participants within a shared culture circle. The South Asian American family comprises a mother, father, their two daughters, and a son.

Tracking Multigenerational Patterns with a Focus on Power, Privilege, and Oppression

Multigenerational theory posits that patterns of behavior and beliefs about ourselves and others tend to travel down the generations and be replicated or reacted

■ ■ ■ ■ ■

CASE 4.1
LEAVING HOME

Shortly after Anu turned 15, her family experienced numerous conflicts related to her autonomy and the family's values of collectivity. Anu's desire to spend more time with her peers, extend her curfew, and monopolize the family's phone sparked numerous arguments between her and her parents. Her father, Anil, and mother, Sareeta, viewed Anu's need for greater autonomy as disrespectful. It signalled a break with the family's cohesion. They feared that Anu, their oldest daughter, would soon begin dating, a prospect that increased family anxiety because theirs was the first generation of family members who would not be following the tradition of arranged marriages. These matters brought the family to therapy.

Anil and Sareeta were supported and challenged in therapy by their culture circle peers. They were helped to replace blind fear over cultural disintegration with opportunities to effectively parent their adolescent child. The other adults helped Anu's parents evaluate their worst fears about her eminent emancipation and they proposed options to help Anu experiment safely with independence while

honoring relevant legacies of her culture. They encouraged Anil and Sareeta to have Anu plan museum visits, outings to local movie theaters, and other activities such as bowling and miniature golf with her peers. Anu's participation in these activities would provide her parents with opportunities to evaluate her judgment and get to know her friends.

Anu took part in her own culture circle of adolescent peers. The therapeutic team and her fellow culture circle members coached her, sharing specific ways she might demonstrate to her parents that she was able to navigate the freedoms she desired. On many occasions throughout her family's treatment, Anu's rebellion was mitigated by having a therapeutic circle of her own peers to call when faced with what she felt were unreasonable demands from her parents. Polarizations of a first generation immigrant family were mitigated.

This subsystem work facilitated healthy new pathways for leaving home and for effectively parenting adolescents against the backdrop of the family's long-held cultural traditions.

to in other parts of our lives. Families have prominent stories, myths, and rituals that they live by. They are like little communities (organizations) with rules, roles (heroes, villains, tricksters, etc.), hierarchies, strengths, and diseases. Families can be open or closed systems. Members are more or less differentiated, range from enmeshed (tightly interconnected with little independence from other family members) to disengaged (isolated, cut off). There are gender and cultural distinctions along these trajectories.

Genograms allow all of these issues to be mapped, offering a visual view of the family in context and helping its members see the systemic connections between people and issues. The process of developing a genogram with clients broadens therapeutic focus from individual issues to a view of "self-with-others" (McGoldrick & Carter, 2001, p. 287). The map becomes a pictorial multigenerational family tree usually depicting at least three generations. Genograms are useful for assessing and tracking the transmission of cultural and family messages, attitudes, issues, and patterns. They not only convey who the members of the extended family are but also give details such as names, ages, sibling positions, relationship status, divorces, births, deaths, geographical locations, religious affiliations, occupations, ethnic and cultural origins, socioeconomic status, illnesses, sexual orientation and identity, strengths, and resources (see McGoldrick, Gerson, & Shellenberger, 1999, for more on genograms).

Although Murray Bowen, (1978), the theory's founder, did not situate his analysis of families within a social, political, or gender context, the feminist critique of the 1970s and 1980s began to significantly influence many of his students, such as Betty Carter, Monica McGoldrick, and Harriet Lerner (1988). For example, *The Invisible Web* (Walters, Carter, Papp, & Silverstein, 1988) challenged and empowered women in families. The authors offered guidelines for feminist practice that altered the previously revered stance of therapeutic neutrality.

Other feminist writers then began to integrate feminist theory into practice (Avis, 1989; Hare-Mustin, 1989 and 1991; Goldner, 1988; Braverman, 1988a; Bograd, 1986; Ault-Riché 1986). They brought women's experiences into the picture by arguing for the existence of views of reality that differ from that of western, bourgeois, heterosexual, white males.

Feminist theory, however, all too often had as its subject western, bourgeois, heterosexual, white women, which was correctly challenged by feminist women of color. hooks, (1984); Almeida, (1994); Pinderhuges, (1986); and Boyd-Franklin (1989, 2000) offered a needed analysis of the simultaneous and multiple oppressions of black women. Unfortunately, much of this scholarship was not incorporated into the white feminist literature in a way that moved the scholarship forward. Consequently, multiculturalism and feminism developed along mostly separate paths. The work of Silverstein and Goodrich (2002) moved to bridge this gap.

When postmodern theory—with its emphasis on the subjectivity of "accepted truth" and the need to examine a subject within its cultural context—entered the scene, it offered needed critiques of both multiculturalism and feminism, which tended to reduce the complexity of the experiences of women, men, and people of color. Joined by critical race and liberation theorists, the feminist postmodernists then sought to unearth the missing voices, the hosts of women and men living within unmarked networks of class, race, culture, and sexual orientation (Harding, 1986). Social justice theorists added another dimension to this landscape (Waldegrave, Tamasese, Tuhuka, & Camphell, 2003). This work introduced the uses and misuses of power, privilege, and oppression onto the landscape of assessment and treatment.

We share this brief history to help you contrast our social justice approach to other theoretical models. Although we incorporate much from other models, we keep issues of power, privilege, and oppression at the center of therapeutic planning and intervention. Accordingly, in constructing multigenerational legacies from a social justice perspective, it is important to acknowledge that historical patterns look very different when situated in legacies of oppression and liberation.

Concepts such as differentiation and triangulation are regarded through a cultural and feminist lens to incorporate issues of power, privilege, and oppression both within the family system and from without, something Bowen's original theory omitted. We suggest that therapists include in their map influences from outside the family, such as culture, race, affiliation, work communities, friendship circles, kinship-like relationships (e.g., foster families and godparents), and migration history. Tracing these issues with clients early in the therapeutic process is useful in highlighting the vast and often rich heritage that frames current experience. Also, it helps clients consider the subjectivity of their own perspectives.

Genograms used alongside the power and control wheels help to gather information regarding clients' diverse backgrounds, including legacies of oppression and experiences of loss and resilience. These instruments also provide a graphic representation of ways in which families are embedded in contexts of power, privilege, and oppression.

The following questions can be used to integrate social justice considerations into the assessment process when evaluating a couple's life:

MONEY

- How much money do you each earn, and how many hours do you each work?
- If one partner has cut back on work to raise children or care for the home, how did you as a couple decide on that arrangement? (Heterosexual couples often fall into prescribed gender role behaviors when a baby is born, with the woman cutting back her work hours to care for the child and the man assuming more financial responsibility. Caretaking is idealized as a role more suited to females, but single male parents and gay parents have been found to function as well as females do. Caretaking decisions are often made unconsciously, without considering both partners' needs, wants, and hopes for their family. Many men would like a closer relationship with children, and many women enjoy the fulfillment they get from their work lives.

Dealing with all these needs consciously, and looking at the repercussions of decisions, helps to keep equity alive).

■ Can you each support yourself and your children should you want or need to? (Here we try to assess whether both partners are economically viable. Again, we raise these issues to a conscious level showing that they are decisions to be made rather than roles to be assumed). We may pose other questions as well. How do resources get allocated in the family? Who makes the major decisions about spending or saving? Who tends to accommodate more? Who pays the bills? These same questions may be asked of single-parent and immigrant families, revealing often times the lack of choices regarding money and income.

LABOR AND RESPONSIBILITY

■ How are household chores and care taking responsibilities handled?

■ Who provides for, or arranges, the child care in the family? Who stays home if your child is sick and can't go to child care or your child care worker is sick and doesn't show up? [In this category, we also question responsibility for housework (cleaning, shopping, cooking, laundry), child and elder care, and who is responsible for the family's contacts with the outside world—(connecting with children's schools, recreation facilities, physicians' offices, retirement centers, nursing homes, and social service agencies). One partner (usually the female in heterosexual couples) often tends to be the manager and coordinator for individual and extended family members' needs even when both partners work full time. That partner also tends to be the one responsible for hiring, arranging, and managing household and yard workers. These same questions may be used for single-parent and immigrant families where the load on women is tripled].

SEX

■ How do you define sexuality and sensuality?

■ How is your sex life organized?

■ What does your sexual repertoire consist of? Who decides what sexual and sensual activities you engage in? What is the frequency of sensual and sexual contact?

■ Who initiates more or less? Is one partner's pleasure given more importance than the other's?

■ Is pornography used? If so, what effect does it have on each partner's desires or sense of self?

It is important for therapists to understand that sexuality has been largely defined by males. And the ease of access to pornography since the advent of the Internet has exponentially increased pornography's place as a contentious issue in couples' sexual relationships. It is up to therapists to shine a light on sexist or racist ideologies and behaviors that give priority to one partner's pleasure over the other's.

Race and Ethnicity

We encourage you to explore racism, sexism, and homophobia with *all* clients to change the fabric of discrimination throughout family and community life. Killian (2001) provides examples of how to do so:

> Which aspects of your racial/ethic [cultural] heritage are important to you/are a source of pride? Which have you rejected/are a source of shame? Did you or your family experience racism or stereotyping as a member of a racial group? Do you have ancestors who were persecuted or who persecuted others? How has your family dealt with these painful memories? Whom could you "bring home to dinner" and whom could you not? . . . What parts of your heritage and history do you want to pass on to your children? (p. 40)

Patriarchy, white supremacy, homophobia, and other oppressions must be addressed simultaneously so that the safety of women, children, gay men, men of color, and poverty-stricken men of all colors is never given less emphasis and priority than the safety of middle- and upper-middle-class, heterosexual, white men.

Hardy and Laszloffy's (1995) cultural genogram and Halevy's (1998) "genogram with an attitude" provide a method of using the genogram to track cultural and racial legacies. Pinderhughes (1998) and Colon (1998) provide illustrations of each author's own mutigenerational explorations. Watts-Jones's (2004) work shows the importance of investigating internalized norms of racism with all families of color. The genogram is just one tool to elicit these silenced legacies. The power and control wheels are additional tools designed to locate and identify the sources of power, privilege, and oppression that can resurrect these ghosts from the past so that families can begin conversations of equity and justice.

Questions alone are insufficient for developing a critical consciousness. The experience of having a group watch and then discuss a film that addresses white supremacy (for example, *American History X*, Carraro & Kay, 1998) is a good way to get to the heart of the subject. Watching and discussing a film is especially effective when coupled with experiential exercises such as those described within Kivel's *Uprooting Racism* (2002).

Exploitation and domination do not occur in a vacuum. They are part of our national, ethnic, and cultural legacies. A male Irish employer's domination of his African American employee can be placed alongside 500 years of British colonization in Ireland and numerous other countries. The invitation of the Irish into the category of "whiteness" in the United States in order to prevent their alliance with blacks and First Nations Peoples is another important reference point. The shameful ghost of slavery still makes itself felt in the United States and in the psyche of most African Americans.

In the therapeutic setting, raising these historical realities in a matter-of-fact manner provides a framework for making sense of clients' present-day issues. Seeing the connection between individual problems and the broader context helps clients recognize that they are part of a network of privilege and domination. This knowledge frees clients from the burden of individual pathology and empowers them toward change through social action. Truth-telling, bringing voice to the voiceless, is a powerful strategy for empowerment. By telling their stories, African Americans have succeeded in creating large pockets of resistance and resilience, as evidenced by their contributions to American society. When the silence of whites is broken regarding the perpetuation of white privilege and power, true healing and liberation can occur.

Other oppressed groups also have ghosts lurking in their histories. Our task is to help make these ghosts visible and to create safety for those who have been silenced so they are empowered to speak up. We therapists must work on our own baggage as well. If we have not carefully unpacked the issues relating to our own families of origin, we will bring our own unconscious and unrecognized patterns into the work we do with clients. If we have not grappled with issues of power, privilege, and oppression within our own lives, we are more likely to be blind to them in our clients' lives.

If I protected my father's feelings in my family of origin, I will have a tendency to do the same with men with whom I work. If I have not confronted my own heterosexism and homophobia, I may silence clients who are questioning their own sexual orientations and identities. If I have not examined the ghosts of my past, I will have difficulty recognizing the possible ghosts in clients' legacies. We invite you to let your readings not only prepare you to work more effectively with others but also to raise your own consciousness about issues you need to face in your own life so that you are mindful in your work with others.

Exploring, Evaluating, and Enhancing Family Alliances and Coalitions

Meeting with smaller subsystems within families allows the therapist to explore and enhance alliances between members. It also allows therapists to break up harmful coalitions. While these types of interventions are well documented in the family therapy literature (for example, structural family therapy), they tend to be aimed at dissolving family problems and are less often concerned with how to dismantle accepted power injustices.

We suggest that when therapists meet with smaller groups within the family, sponsors (which we discuss more extensively in Chapter 5) or others who can serve as witnesses be included, especially in the early stages of the process. Providing witnesses facilitates the handling of sensitive issues, especially when hidden issues of power and privilege require confrontation.

Parent–child negotiations are also much more effective when accomplished in the presence of supportive others because their presence often recalibrates the power dynamics. Accordingly, therapists without a collective treatment format should think creatively about who can be invited as witnesses or resources, as well as who is available to help family members incorporate elements of empowerment and accountability into their process of change, both inside and outside the therapeutic context.

Others have written about the value of witnesses in the therapeutic context. Examples include "reflecting teams" (e.g., Hoffman, 1992) and "definitional ceremonies" using outsider witnesses (White, 1999), although these practices are often one-time events in the course of the described therapy. The advantage of an ongoing therapeutic community is that the witnesses are present week after week to maintain an environment for empowerment and to hold family members accountable for promises made. This process begins to create new structural maps for equity. The result is a community that can challenge misuses of power and privilege empowering those with less power and privilege, while simultaneously giving voice to experiences that might otherwise remain silenced.

Such a process is especially critical for the empowerment of women, glbts, and racial minorities because it can hold clients and staff, and particularly those wielding more power and privilege, accountable over time to the new critical consciousness. Without this structure, often there is no built-in mechanism to hold clients accountable for maintaining attitudinal and behavioral changes over time, particularly clients with more power and privilege—men, whites, and nonimmigrants.

When a therapist meets alone in her office with a man to discuss the challenges he faces negotiating a reasonable hour to leave work so that he can still have time and energy for the relationship with his wife and children, too often the struggle is understood to be his alone, or perhaps his family's struggle. But when a therapist invites this man to meet with three other men from diverse backgrounds to discuss the pressures of life within a world driven by family-unfriendly corporate values, the problem can be approached and understood differently. This process takes the conflict from a personal level to the collective level, and while individual choices remain to be made, the collective experiences and vision afford this man a much more complex and expanded perspective.

We cannot overemphasize the utility of linking clients into collectives. Traditional therapeutic structures, such as individual, couples, and even family therapy, limit the experience of change to the interior of family or individual life, reinforcing the notion of change as a force driven by individual action. The changes mostly leave untouched the status quo within hierarchies of power and privilege. In contrast, therapists working from a social justice perspective challenge themselves to expand the therapeutic context by working with collectives of individuals and families when possible. They may also invite relevant others into sessions to serve as witnesses to the work being done. The witnesses are available to provide feedback and to act as voices of empowerment and accountability for the changes family members are attempting to make. In order to heal families, therapists must address the ways in which institutionalized, daily realities connected to race, gender, class, and sexual orientation shape family life.

HOW LETTER WRITING, JOURNALING, AND ORAL ANTHOLOGIES LEAD TO HEALING

> Hating is like drinking poison and expecting the other person to die.
> It's not going to kill them; it's going to kill you.
> —Barasch, 2005, p. 243

> To forgive is the highest form of self-interest. I need to forgive you so that
> my anger and resentment and lust for revenge don't corrode my being.
> —Archbishop Desmond Tutu, quoted in Barasch, 2005, p. 208

Freedman and Combs (1996) say that a letter is worth many sessions of good therapy. Letters make quite an impact on both the sender and the receiver. Narrative therapy (Epston, 2001) has made good use of letter writing and is responsible for it being more widely integrated into therapeutic work. Though the process is notably cognitive, often individually focused, and of course inaccessible to clients who are illiterate, it can be a powerful tool in the process of empowerment.

Letter writing and journaling are linked to longevity and positive, emotional, and health outcomes. The continuity of retrieving and disclosing memories reduces traumatic stress and integrates therapeutic experiences (Pennebaker, 1993) Letters may be written from therapists to clients, from family members to each other, and from clients to each other when working in a collective therapeutic format.

Letter writing serves a variety of purposes:

- It brings legacies of power, privilege, and oppression to the center of family-of-origin work.
- It creates new boundaries for truth telling.
- It summarizes or extends work accomplished in sessions.
- It invites reluctant family members to be part of the therapeutic process.
- It provides closure and offers beginnings to new relationships.
- It requests accountability for offenses done to others.
- It apologizes for misdeeds or regrets in relationships.
- It acknowledges accomplishments and strengths.
- It invites critical feedback.
- It offers reparations (a plan or actions that begin to repair past offenses, including lack of consideration or generosity of spirit with others).
- It offers rituals to define boundaries, create closure, and open up new life spaces.

Letter writing may accompany a client's individual journaling. Keeping a journal helps clients gain perspective on thoughts, feelings, attitudes, behaviors, and relationships to others and work. Taking quiet time to reflect on one's own responsibility in relational situations can be very clarifying and can help to avert reactive and defensive postures in relationships.

Within the cultural context model, clients in culture circles are encouraged to communicate between group sessions by telephone and e-mail to maintain the systems of empowerment and accountability in their day-to-day living. All clients are on a list-serve and are encouraged to communicate regularly. When clients are preparing to write a letter to their partner, children, or other significant person, they submit the letter to their culture circle via e-mail for feedback. A letter may go through many revisions and include contributions from others before a final draft is ready to send. Clients who are unable to read or write share their stories with other clients and sponsors who record their oral anthologies.

In Case 4.2, in his men's culture circle, Sam first broke down the issues for which he came to therapy. Genogram work paired with journaling and social education was pivotal for Sam to be able to see his part clearly in his failed relationships. The subsystem work with other family members was stalled until Sam could

■ ■ ■ ■ ■

CASE 4.2

LETTER WRITING TO MAKE AMENDS

After participating in therapeutic and consciousness-raising work in his men's culture circle for many months, Sam, a 52-year-old African American man, was ready to make amends for past abusive behavior toward his two former wives and children and his current wife and three children. His genogram documented a long history of violence toward his partners and nine children for whom he had never accepted responsibility. Three of his children dropped out of school before high school, and two had extensive drug histories.

To prepare for the session during which he would read his letter to his entire family, Sam first worked on recognizing and taking responsibility for his abuses of power and privilege. The next step was to acknowledge his behavior with his family members. Letter writing was chosen as the vehicle. As is often the case, many of the initial letters Sam wrote laid blame and included little self-reflection, which is where coaching from other men was important. After writing several drafts, Sam began to authentically own up to his part in his troubled relationships and to responsibly communicate the role he played in the family's distress. Accountability letters detail and take responsibility for abuses of power and privilege.

Because Sam was part of a men's culture circle, he was able to share several drafts of his letter with his fellow group members for feedback and thoughtful reflection. Team members and culture circle members coached him so that his words reflected compassion while assuming responsibility in an effort to be received authentically by family members.

For example, Sam worked to stop blaming others as he took responsibility for the specific ways he violated family members' trust. Finally, after all the preparatory work, he was invited to read his letter to his current wife and their three children. His past wives and their children were also present for the reading, which occurred within the public forum of Sam's men's culture circle. Several female sponsors were also present to support his wives. His letter detailed his abusive behavior toward family members and offered to make reparations and develop new ways to be in their lives. Reading the letter was a step toward repairing the relationship damage he had caused. The circle of men provided support to both Sam and his family members in this difficult truth telling. Accountability was addressed through the other men's commitment to hold Sam responsible for following through on the reparations that were offered and for doing no further harm to his family.

The mothers and children involved in the session expressed contradictory feelings of anger, suspicion, and thankfulness that he had finally acknowledged the years of harm he had brought to family members. Having confidence that the other men would press Sam to honor his commitments to them and to sustain nonviolent behavior toward family members contributed to their sense of feeling physically and psychologically safe. They told the group that they had never previously experienced a community of men and women committed to bringing justice to family life. One important positive outcome was that two of Sam's older sons (15 and 17 years old) entered drug treatment programs, and one stopped participating in a gang in which he was about to be initiated.

authentically begin to grasp his place as a black male raised in a racist society and as a heterosexual male partner raised in a sexist and patriarchal society. Both of these public personas deeply influenced who he was in his personal relationships.

As he began to see the connections between these various social locations, he could start to take responsibility for his abuses of power and privilege with people he cared most about. Once clients attain a level of consciousness regarding their own responsibility for problems, this form of subsystem work—engaging other relevant people such as family members—opens the possibility for making amends and ultimately healing.

We end this chapter with brief descriptions of two other strategies for working with families as subsystems: oral anthologies and rituals.

Oral Anthologies

Oral anthologies originated from a tradition practiced for centuries among cultures around the world, including African Americans and Native Americans. An example of an oral anthology is the Iroquois Constitution, which was preserved through oral anthology and much of which was incorporated into the United States Constitution. The tradition of oral anthologies transferred knowledge across generations through storytelling. It allowed the fundamental traditions and knowledge of the culture to be passed on through narration. This tradition served people for whom the written word or textual knowledge was not possible or significant, and the practice offers an alternative to letter writing in therapy today. Clients who are not literate are empowered in this process of remembering and being able to pass on significant events of the present and past by recording these events on audio or videotape.

Rituals

Rituals are described in the family therapy literature for use in facilitating systemic change (Imber-Black Roberts, & Whiting, 2003). They are tailored for particular personal, family, and group circumstances, often serving to punctuate or celebrate a transition or an identity redefinition or to heal a past hurt or injustice. We use rituals for these purposes and to define boundaries, open up new life spaces, mark pivotal changes, create celebrations, and mourn past losses. Clients create their own rituals around various dimensions of power, privilege, and oppression. For example, a woman shedding years of oppressive domesticity might create a ritual of pampering herself by buying a bouquet of flowers, getting a massage, or taking a trip with a friend. A man who is being held accountable by his therapeutic team for years of escaping domestic responsibilities might create a healing ritual by which he celebrates his family by cooking one or two meals a week and enrolling the children in age-appropriate afterschool activities. A couple with a history of contentious arguments creates a ritual to bury their past behavior via accountability letters. Then with their support community, they engage in actions that display their respect and love for one another. Rituals emerge from the relational context, creating new meanings intended to guide future behavior.

■ ■ ■ ■ ■

CASE 4.3
EXERCISE

We invite you to take a moment to personally reflect on a pertinent issue in your own family of origin. For example, how was (is) loss or death handled in your family of origin? Think about a recent or past loss, someone who was significant to you. Did family members openly share and discuss the facts of the death? Was the event of death openly discussed while the circumstances surrounding the death were kept secret? Was there an untold story?

Storytelling is compelling. Storytelling is compounded by the inclusion of significant intersectionalities. Consider this story. A young Italian American mother (Ariana), with two sons ages 11 and 8, is recently divorced from her Uruguayan partner. Her older son engages in sexually harassing comments and behavior toward girls his age, especially girls from marginal cultures, and has been repeatedly suspended from school for these acts. The untold family story is that in the prime of her adolescent love and sexual trajectory, Ariana's Jamaican (black) lover was murdered. He was killed by her cousin on her father's side for refusing to end his relationship with Ariana. It was his punishment for not abiding by the rules of white supremacy.

The cousin served a minimal sentence for the brutal murder. The story of Ariana and her lover remain untold. Her rage toward and betrayal by her family was silenced. Her rage against white supremacy remained untold. Her son engenders the same disregard for women and peers of color that the men in her family harbor. Yet her son is biracial. Ariana relives her rage toward her family through her son. She unleashes her rage toward his choices, particularly his choice to harass innocent girls of all races. She brings justice to the death of her lover by demanding a different moral code from her son. She challenges the oppressive legacy of her family by refusing to tolerate her son's choices. She is empowered to forge a new legacy in a more compassionate way.

■ ■ ■ ■ ■

CASE 4.4
EXERCISE

Storytelling is a powerful medium to integrating the intersectionalities of loss. What stories might your family like to revisit? What are your beliefs about life, death, and mourning within your cultural, ethnic, and religious communities? What about mourning rituals? Have there been accidental deaths, torture, or murder in your family of origin? What are your family's beliefs about what happens after death? Are these beliefs about life and death influenced by religion, war, or economic survival? Do gender roles determine the emotional expression of grief or funeral arrangements?

Are there stories of colonization, war, or religious oppression? What about immigration to escape poverty or political persecution? Notice that these questions help you to trace loss through the complex intersections of your multigenerational family.

Now, reflect more broadly. Do historical, racial, cultural, or religious experiences shape your relationship to loss? For example, are certain deaths, such as by suicide or AIDS, stigmatized within your cultural background or considered exceptionally traumatic? What are the legacies of oppression (e.g. racism, slavery, genocide) or privilege (e.g., suburban or private schools, inherited family money, accumulation of wealth from federal government policies, direct slave owning)? These legacies are often unexamined, so they require careful and gentle questioning. Journaling and/or oral tradition can elucidate these histories and transform experience when spoken in collective gatherings.

REFERENCES

Almeida, R. (1994). *Expansions of feminist family theory through diversity*. Haworth Press, New York.

Ault-Riche, M. (Ed.), (1986). *Women and family therapy*. Rockville, MD: Aspen Systems.

Avis, J. M. (1989). Integrating gender into the family therapy curriculum. *Journal of Feminist Family Therapy, 1*, 3–24.

Barasch, M. I. (2005). *Field notes on the compassionate life: A search for the soul of kindness*. New York: Rodale (distributed by Holtzbrinck Publishers).

Bograd, M. (1986). A feminist examination of family therapy. What is women's place? *Women and Therapy, 5*, 95–106.

Bowen, M. (1978). *Family therapy in clinical practice*. New York: Jason Aroson.

Boyd-Franklin, N. (1989). *Black families in therapy: A multisystems approach*. New York: Guilford.

Boyd-Franklin, N., Franklin, A. J., & Toussaint, P. (2000). *Boys into men: Raising our African American teenage sons*. New York: Dutton.

Braverman, L. (Ed.) (1988a). A guide to feminist family therapy. New York: Hamington Park Press.

Bravo, E. (2007). Taking on the bigboys. On why feminism is good for families, business and the nation. New York: Feminist Press.

Carraro, B. (Producer), Kay, T. (Director). (1998). *American history X* [Motion picture]. Canada: Newline Cinema & Turman Morrisey Co.

Carter, B. (1995). Focusing your wide-angle lens. *Family Therapy Networker, 19*(6), 31–35.

Colon, F. (1998). The discovery of my multicultural identity. In M. McGoldrick (Ed.), *Revisioning family therapy: Race, class, gender* (pp. 200–214). New York: Guilford.

Coontz, S. (2005). *Marriage, a history: From obedience to intimacy, or how love conquered marriage*. New York: Viking.

Department of Health and Human Services, Centers for Disease Control and Prevention. (2006). Intimate partner violence fact sheet. Retrieved April 10, 2006 from http://www.cdc.gov/ncipc/factsheets/ipvfacts.htm.

Department of Justice, Bureau of Justice Statistics. (2005 June). *Family violence statistics*. Retrieved February 21, 2006 from http://www.ojp.usdoj.gov/bjs/pub/pdf/fvs.pdf.

Epston, D. (2001). Notes from workshop at the 2001 Adelaide narrative therapy and community work conference. Adelaide, Australia.

Freedman, J., & Combs, G. (1996). *Narrative therapy*. New York: W.W. Norton.

Friedman, S., & Greenhaus, S. (2000). *Work and family: Allies or enemies?* New York: Oxford.

Goldner, V. (1988). Generation and gender: Normative and covert hierarchies. *Family Process, 27*, 17–31.

Gottman, J. M. (1994). *Why marriages succeed or fail*. New York: Simon & Schuster.

Haddock, S. A., Zimmerman, T. S., Current, L. R., & Harvey, A. (2003). Parenting practices of dual-earner couples who successfully balance family and work. *Journal of Feminist Family Therapy, 14*, 37–56.

Haley, J. (1963). *Strategies of psychotherapy*. New York: Grune & Stratton.

Halevy, J. (1998). A genogram with an attitude. *Journal of Marital and Family Therapy, 24*, 233–242.

Harding, S. (1986). The instability of the analytical categories of feminist theory. In M. R. Malson, J. F. O'Bar, S. Wetphal-Wihl, & M. Wyer (Eds.), *Feminist theory in practice and process*. Chicago: University of Chicago Press.

Hardy, K., & Laszloffy, T. A. (1995). The cultural genogram: Key to training culturally competent family thera-pists. *Journal of Marital and Family Therapy, 21*, 227–237.

Hare-Mustin, R. (1986). Autonomy and gender: Some questions for therapists. *Psychotherapy, 23*, 205–212.

Hare-Mustin, R. (1989) The problem of gender in family therapy theory. *Family Process, 26*, 15–27.

Hare-Mustin, R. (1991). Sex, lies, and headaches: The problem is power. *Journal of Feminist Family Therapy, 3*, 39–61.

Hochschild, A. (1989). *The second shift: Working parents and the revolution at home*. New York: Viking Penguin.

Hoffman, L. (1992). A reflective stance for family therapy. In S. McNamee & K. Gergan (Eds.), *Therapy as social construction* (pp. 7–24). London: Sage.

hooks, B. (1984). *Feminist theory from margin to center*. Boston: South End Press.

Hooyman, N. R., & Gonyea, J. (1995). *Feminist perspectives on family care*. Thousand Oaks, CA: Sage.

Imber-Black E., Roberts, J., & Whiting, R. (2003). *Rituals for our times: Celebrating, healing, and changing our Lives and our relationships*. New York: W.W. Norton.

Ingraham, C. (1999). *White weddings: Romancing heterosexuality in popular culture*. New York: Routledge.

Killian, K. D. (2001). Reconstituting racial histories and identities. *Journal of Marital and Family Therapy, 27*(1), 27–42.

Kivel, P. (2002). *Uprooting racism: How white people can work for racial justice*. Gabriola Island, BC Canada: New Society Publishers.

Lerner, H. (1988). Is family systems theory really systemic? A feminist communication. In L. Braverman (Ed.), *A guide to feminist family therapy* (pp. 47–63). New York: Hammington Park Press.

Lorde, A. (2002). The master's tools will never dismantle the master's house. In C. Moraga & G. Anzaldua (Eds.), *This bridge called my back: Writings by radical women of color*. Freedom, CA: Third Women Press. Comments at The Personal and the Political Panel (Second sex conference, October 29, Michigan).

McGoldrick, M., Gerson, R., & Shellenberger, S. (1999). *Genograms, assessment and intervention*. New York: W.W. Norton.

McGoldrick, M., & Carter, B. (2001). Advances in coaching: Family therapy with one person. *Journal of Marital and Family Therapy, 27*, 281–300.

National Coalition for Domestic Violence. (2005). *Domestic violence statistics*. Retrieved February 23, 2006 from www.ncadv.org/resources/statistics_170.html.

Okin, S. M. (1989). *Justice, gender, and the family*. Basic Books: New York.

Papp, P. (2000). *Couples on the fault line: New directions for therapists*. New York: Guilford.

Pennebaker, J. W. (1993). Putting stress into words: Health, linguistic, therapeutic implications. *Behavior Research and Therapy, 31*, 539–548.

Pinderhughes, E. (1986) *Understanding race, ethnicity and power: The key to efficacy in clinical practice*. New York: Free Press.

Pinderhughes, E. (1998). Black genealogy revisited: Restorying an African American family. In M. McGoldrick (Ed.), *Revisioning family therapy: Race, class, gender* (pp. 179–199). New York: Guilford.

Putnam, R. D. (2000). *Bowling Alone*. New York: Simon & Schuster.

Schacher, S. J., Auerbach, C. F., & Silverstein, L. S. (2005). Gay fathers extending the possibilities for us all. *Journal of GLBT Family Studies*. New York: Haworth Press.

Schmaling, K. B., & Goldman Sher, T. (Eds.). (2000). *The psychology of couples and illness: Theory*. Washington, DC: American Psychological Association.

Silverstein, L., & Goodrich, T. J. (Eds.). *Feminist family therapy: Empowerment and social context*. New York: American Psychological Association Press.

Tamasese, K., & Waldegrave, C. (1993). Culture and gender accountability in the "just therapy" approach. *Journal of Feminist Family Therapy, 5*(2), 29–45.

Tremlett, G. (2005). Blow to machismo as Spain forces men to do housework. *The Guardian*. Retrieved from http://www.guardian.co.uk/spain/article/0,2763,1454802,00.html.

U.S. Census Bureau. (1999). *Custodial mothers and fathers and their child support*. Department of Commerce, Economics, and Statistics Administration. Retrieved January 16, 2006 from http://www.census.gov/prod/2002pubs/p60-217.pdf.

Waldegrave, C., Tamasese, K., Tuhaka, F., & Camphell, W. (2003). *Just therapy—a journal: A collection of papers from the Just Therapy Team*, New Zealand, Dulwich Centre Publications, Adelaide.

Waldegrave, C. (2005). 'Just therapy' with families on low income. *Child welfare, 84*(2), March/April, p. 265–276.

Waldegrave, C. (2006). *Cultural, gender and socio-economic contexts in therapeutic and social policy work.* A paper given to the National and Paverting Institute 'Parent Child Conference 2006, London, UK.

Walters, M., Carter, B., Papp, P., & Silverstein, O. (1988). *The invisible web.* New York: Guilford Press.

Watts-Jones, D. (2004). When should a therapist confront racist language in the consulting room? *Psychotherapy Networker, 28,* 27–28.

White, M. (1999). Reflecting: Team work as definitional ceremony revisited. *Gecko, 2,* 55–82.

Williams, J. (2000). *Unbending gender: Why family and work conflict and what to do about it.* New York: Oxford University Press.

Wulfhorst, E. (2006, Aug. 18). Domestic violence takes toll in workplace: study. Reuters. Retrieved September 9, 2006 from http://today.reuters.com/news/articlenews.aspx?type=domesticNews&storyID=2006-08-18T133856Z_01_N18434966_RTRUKOC_0_US-LIFE-WORK.xml.

Zimmerman, T., & Addison, C. (1997). Division of labor and child care among dual-career couples: A qualitative analysis. *Journal of Feminist Family Therapy, 9*(1), 47–72.

CHAPTER FIVE

HEALING AS A COMMUNITY EFFORT: CULTURE CIRCLES

Silence from and about the subject was the order of the day. Some of the silences were broken, and some were maintained by authors who lived with and within the policing strategies. What I am interested in are the strategies for breaking it.

—Toni Morrison, *Playing in the Dark: Whiteness and the Literary Imagination* (1993, p. 16).

In Chapters 1 and 2, we challenge therapists to always bear in mind that people have multiple identities. We exhort therapists to consider what it is like to live in and cross between intersecting and compartmentalized worlds. A person might be gay and Latino; disabled, male, and Chinese American; female, African American, and poor. The intersecting aspects of a person's identity cause that person to interact differently in various cultural contexts. A white man who has developed a critical consciousness may have trouble bridging his world of work, where he is an advocate for unions and worker's rights, and his suburban neighborhood, where complacency and compartmentalized lifestyles are the order of the day.

Therefore, we take care to examine the larger picture. We deal not only with family of origin issues but also with legacies of colonialism, racism, homophobia, sexism, and other limiting ideologies. This broader focus diverges radically from seeing the solitary individual or even families as isolated, self-sustaining systems. It pushes therapists to think more broadly about how they can empower clients to make transformative change in their lives, change that goes beyond the boundaries of the individual and the family to alter hierarchies of power, privilege, and oppression.

In this chapter, we make the case for redefining and expanding the therapeutic context. We invite therapists to create, where possible, circles of healing rather than rely on traditional couples or family counseling. Such circles should contain a cross section of people of diverse backgrounds—social classes, races, cultures, religions, and sexual orientations—who are seeking therapy for a variety of problems.

If you practice in a community where there is little or no diversity, strive to bring it in through film, popular media, and literary writings.

Because the circles contain a varied pool of people, they disrupt some of the structural obstacles that normally separate members of a community. Those who live in wealthy, segregated communities generally are not in contact with people who live in inner cities; people who can afford medical insurance do not interact with those who cannot; the wealthy do not cross paths with the working poor; people dealing with addictions have different concerns from those dealing with violence and failed marriages; those addressing work and school issues do not have the same priorities as others confronted by the challenges of the criminal justice system. Culture circles work to connect families across differences (Figure 5.1).

Achieving substantive behavior change requires critical consciousness strengthened by empowerment and accountability. Insuring that people remain accountable can be especially difficult in more traditional delivery systems because it remains largely the responsibility of the therapist and, perhaps, family members.

To accomplish behavior change, we suggest that therapists break through perceived walls surrounding the nuclear family and create therapeutic communities that directly link individuals and families to one another. This means we have to move beyond our own preference for privacy in order to persuade our clients do the same.

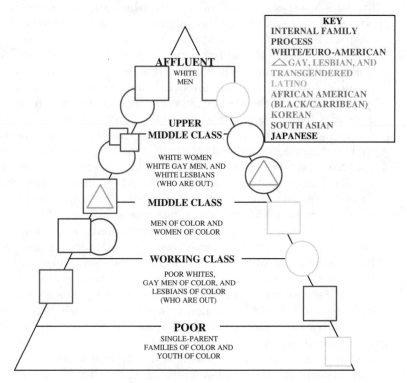

FIGURE 5.1   **Hierarchy and the Culture Circle**

Because they are receiving coaching and feedback from nonfamily members and other invited consultants—including community and religious leaders—clients operating within a multifamily or community milieu can more fully examine gender, class, race, and other systemic patterns that contribute to their behavior. Empowerment and accountability are fundamental to a social justice model in a public (versus private) context.

This approach is very different from psychotherapy as we usually practice it, which most often is conducted within a single-therapist and single-client (individual, couple, or family) system. The change process typically focuses on the individual psyche or the internal dynamics of family life, thereby privatizing and isolating personal and family concerns from the larger context.

Salvador Minuchin recently mused over his ideas from 30 years ago (The Top 10, 2006), when *Families of the Slums* (a well-known book by Minuchin, Montalvo, Guerny, Rosman, Schumer, 1967) suggested that oppressed families empower themselves! But these families clearly needed a system of advocacy that would confront the institutions that oppressed them. Three decades later, families with multiple problems are still simply referred to a range of agencies and left to try to garner services for themselves. When group therapy is employed, rarely are multiple family members included, except in groups that encompass a number of families addressing similar life circumstances, thereby creating a community organized on the basis of a specific problem or dysfunction (e.g., schizophrenia, loss, substance abuse, eating disorder, parents of children with attention deficit hyperactive disorder [ADHD] or Asperger syndrome).

In contrast, a social justice approach works to develop collective, nonhierarchal healing communities in which diverse groups of individuals and families with multiple and differing issues join with teams of therapists and sponsors to consider varying concerns. Therapeutic intervention, then, is not compartmentalized on the basis of a presenting problem, ability to pay, or research interest. When therapists are not familiar with a particular problem area, they invite experts into the culture circle to educate members so everyone learns about a particular family's dilemma, such as cancer, obesity, depression, addiction, and domestic violence.

Building a culture circle is sometimes difficult in Western society, where family life is viewed as private and autonomous. Psychotherapeutic interventions and reimbursement requirements typically mirror society's views and establish different payment schemes for individual, family, group, and community therapy. This discrepancy perpetuates the split between private actions and public accountability. Treatment is geared toward shifting power imbalances within the confines of the family unit without any accompanying social support.

We addressed contributions of a liberation-based approach to family therapy in Chapter 4. It is worth mentioning some other widely used interventions. Structural and strategic family therapy, for example, focuses on defining the covert and overt boundaries that exist within a family. They strive to realign hierarchy and power between generations to enable members of a family to experience the emotions appropriate to their place in the life cycle. Parents are empowered to take an executive (parental) role so that children are better able to rely on them for nurturing and setting boundaries and rules. Cross-generational coalitions, such as a grandparent siding with a child against the child's parent, are blocked, and care is taken so that the therapist does not inadvertently form coalitions with family members.

Clinicians working from the perspective of Murray Bowen may concentrate on investigating and reconstructing generational lineages of a client's psychological traumas, such as loss or other legacies. While these interventions are historic, they do not go far enough. Not only are they focused mostly within the family system but they fail to incorporate gender, race, and sexual orientation in their analysis of the family. In the case of a young heterosexual couple experiencing difficulty having their marriage accepted by the wife's family, particularly her father, a standard Bowenian approach would coach the adult child of this family to negotiate this system on her own: in other words, to differentiate herself.

In a social justice approach, the male partner would be encouraged to provide support by strategically engaging with the significant in-law family members around shared interests. The couple would be further coached on keeping the situation with this part of their family light and embracing. The power of a collaborative system is greater than the self in these situations.

The feminist critique, heralded by Hare-Mustin (1978), challenged neutrality in family theory and practice because that stance colluded with patriarchy to maintain the oppression of women in families. This challenge was followed by an explosion of feminist writings and practices that defined gender and age as equally relevant hierarchies.

Linking the presenting problem to the larger forces of power, privilege, and oppression keeps the analysis honest across diverse couples and families. Take the example of parenting. A scarcity of jobs, inadequate access to child and elder care, lack of medical care, and exposure to environmental hazards all impact what is considered to be effective parenting. Parents in suburban communities may be better able to work with their schools to improve the academic success and emotional well-being of their children than are parents in working-class and inner-city communities or single mothers.

Accordingly, it is imperative that therapists consciously connect presenting problems with the social realities that maintain and exacerbate those problems. When appropriate, therapists may help parents connect their child's birth defect to environmental hazards or the lack of adequate medical insurance. Adolescent violence may be connected to social and economic realities in disadvantaged communities that limit access to safe schools, meaningful relationships between adolescents and parents in the home after school, decent housing, and jobs, all of which are essential for the healthy functioning of families.

Raising critical consciousness as it relates to presenting problems is essential to a social justice perspective. It can be accomplished more readily when others are included in the therapeutic context.

The cultural context model's method of including others in every aspect of the treatment process establishes an ongoing therapeutic community that supports *collective* problem solving and solution discovery. Feminist and postcolonial scholars, critical race theorists, and liberation theologians argue that collective knowledge, dialogue, inquiry, and action are needed to dismantle networks of power, privilege, and oppression and to create just solutions.

As you read about the specifics of creating communities of change, think about how you might apply the process, even in small ways, to your own unique therapeutic context. The model presented here can challenge you to find ways to expand your work. Bear in mind that empowerment and accountability are less likely to be accomplished within an interiorized or private process.

Without the participation of external others, no one is there to hold clients (or ourselves) accountable for the changes that need to be made. Likewise, there are no witnesses to help us recognize and celebrate our victories. You can begin by inviting one or two members of your community (college students majoring in gender or race studies; people doing activist work in your community; progressive members of a church, temple, or synagogue) to participate in a few sessions with three or four families with whom you are working. Invite the group to watch some film clips, and then engage the members in a discussion about the struggle of families to live fair and balanced lives. Encourage them to think in terms of healing circles.

CREATING HEALING COMMUNITIES

A major objective of the cultural context model and a social justice approach is to create a collective experience that can transform individuals within those systems. A guiding premise is that the liberation of women is intrinsically tied to the accountability of men, the liberation of people of color is intrinsically tied to the accountability of white privilege, and the liberation of the poor is intrinsically tied to the accountability of the wealthy (Lui, Robles, Leondar-Wright, Brewer, & Adamson, 2006; United for a Fair Economy, 2006).

Therefore, dismantling and restructuring the power imbalances that exist between people is a critical aspect of therapeutic change. Reshaping relationships through social action is key to liberation. The cultural context model strives to disrupt power and privilege on a number of levels—between therapists and clients, between therapists, between clients, between family members, and in society. We also focus in this chapter specifically on culture circles. Notice that at every level, more voices are brought into the conversation.

Leveling Power and Privilege between Therapists and Clients

We suggest that a team, rather than a single therapist, should conduct the therapy whenever possible. In Chapter 6, you will learn about the inclusion of volunteer sponsors who are often themselves graduates of therapy. Sponsors can be available as resources even in initial intake sessions to expand the therapeutic context from the start. The use of a team of therapists and sponsors aims to equalize power differentials and therefore reduce dependency between clients and therapists. Therapeutic influence, responsibility, and accountability for maintaining

■ ■ ■ ■ ■ ▬▬▬▬▬▬▬▬▬▬▬▬▬▬▬▬▬▬▬▬▬▬▬▬▬▬

CASE 5.1

A CORPORATE EXECUTIVE ENCOUNTERS THE MEANING
OF PUBLIC CONTEXT IN PRIVATE AFFAIRS

"When I began coming to the group here," says Frank, a white, middle-class corporate executive, "I slowly realized that I had a lot in common with these other men. I realized that these sponsors are here for a purpose, that they are much farther down the road than I am. I could relate to them—not all of them—but there were some who had a history very similar to mine. There was Stan [another white man in his late fifties, a physician's assistant]. He asked me detailed questions about my financial situation and the role that my wife played in the economic management of our lives.

"Even more surprising to me, Stan then offered details of his own and his family's financial life. I never imagined talking to anyone about my finances in such detail and most certainly not to a stranger I had known for just a few weeks. Our conversations and his respectful suggestions gave me a small window into the possibilities here.

"Well, Stan was much farther along in his therapeutic process, but it was clear that we were similar in many ways."

change are expanded because clients look to the sponsors as well as to their therapeutic team for support and assistance, as Frank's comments in Case 5.1 demonstrate. This process teaches clients to transfer to their lives the learning that occurs in therapy.

LEVELING POWER AND PRIVILEGE
BETWEEN THERAPISTS

Therapists, too, need a system to monitor themselves and each other for sexism, racism, and homophobia. We suggest that therapists create a team with others who are committed to consciousness-raising and who will be available to observe sessions from behind a one-way mirror or on a television monitor. Team involvement provides accountability for therapists in session and empowers their consciousness-raising. They are empowered to work with a group of clients across multiple divides, unlike therapeutic settings that focus on a particular population of interest (e.g., depression, substance abuse, couples, children with ADHD, etc.) or where therapists work with their own particular racial or ethnic group.

Social education is not just for clients. We suggest that all clinical staff members be trained in this approach and then "sign on" for a clinical environment that rigorously applies these principles. Students in training, too, participate in this process. Developing critical consciousness in tandem creates a context for power-sharing between students and clients and therapist and clients.

The transformation and liberation of clients—those with less power and privilege—is dependent on the continuing transformation and openness of clinical staff and trainees—those with more power and privilege. Sometimes clinical staff members, like their clients, are reticent to examine their own misuses of power and privilege. Such staff members need to be coached, just as the clients are coached, with gentle and good-natured reminders when they fall back on patriarchal or internalized dominant thinking or behavior patterns. There should be no assumption that clinical staff members are less immersed in dominant culture behavior than their clients. Accordingly, reminders and coaching are an integral, and mostly welcomed, part of the cultural context model.

We must acknowledge, however, that men—especially white, heterosexual men—are the most challenged as therapists and trainees by this model. In our culture, many men are accustomed to holding positions of greater power and privilege, and they understandably resist accepting a program that asks them to decrease their "power over" in favor of "power with." An additional challenge is that the program also asks them to share their privileged positions with others. It means, for example, accepting training from professionals outside the mainstream and from lay sponsors. It also means having their therapeutic work observed and critiqued for sexism, racism, and homophobia, and having to work collaboratively (power with) rather than remaining *the* expert. We have found that white male *sponsors* more readily participate in this transformation than do white male therapists.

Leveling Power and Privilege between Clients

We suggest that whenever possible, therapy be primarily conducted within some form of healing community. The cultural context model conducts therapy within culture circles, which replace individual, couple, or family counseling. The culture circles expand existing therapeutic models to include nonrelated persons in the change process. The term *culture circle* is borrowed from Freire's (1971) model for building critical consciousness and is tied to Spivak's (1987) postcolonial analysis.

Our culture circles include a team of therapists and sponsors in addition to a heterogeneous helping community of various families who come for treatment. The structure and function of culture circles employ action and reflection to help clients understand how domination and oppression operate in their lives. These healing circles become transformative communities that engage in forms of social activism. Employing culture circles as a primary mode of intervention interrupts the usual therapeutic obsession with what is "private" in personal, family, and community life but that could, in fact, often benefit from being more public.

The diagram in Figure 5.2 depicts the hierarchy of power privilege and oppression discussed earlier. Juxtaposed within it are the community (mixed-gender) circle members. The members are placed according to their relative positions on the hierarchy. Squares are male members; circles are female members; the triangle depicts gay, lesbian, bisexual, or transgendered (GLBT) persons.

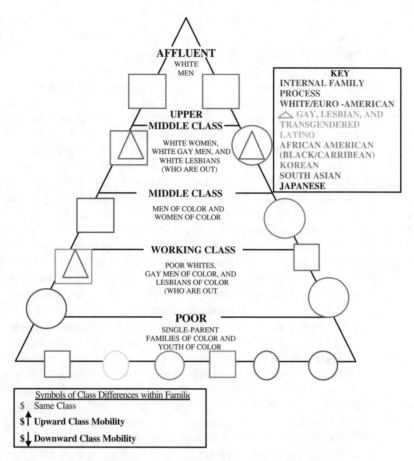

FIGURE 5.2 Depiction of the Composition of One Culture Circle Including Individuals from Many Social Locations

The results of a community healing process are

1. An expansion of family boundaries that empowers clients to take advantage of diverse forms of advocacy, resources, and critical support made available when multiple families' lives become connected.
2. An awakening of social consciousness that occurs when social patterns common to many families are critically examined.
3. An experience of satisfaction with members' connectedness, which quickly alters the depression or angst they bring to therapy and moves them forward with a range of social action projects.

The process opens an ever-expanding window, allowing individuals to recognize the ways in which their particular dilemmas are fundamentally linked to prevailing societal patterns. By becoming aware of the common themes across families and the variations on these themes represented by families of diverse structures and backgrounds, many clients are able to move forward and make needed changes. The culture circle experience moves people beyond the limits imposed by conventional notions of personal dysfunction and toward a broader range of options.

In the cultural context model, there are community culture circles for women, men, children, adolescents, couples, and community. They are made up of persons of mixed ages, social classes, races, sexual orientations, and life problems. By compartmentalizing a person's sense of identity and emphasizing his or her experience in terms of the presenting problem, we not only pathologize the person, but we fail to take into account all of the person's resilience and adaptation.

On the other hand, working in a multiproblem (and multisolution) context brings to the fore alternate and more liberating life stories, thereby truly expanding the possibilities for an individual's identity. In addition, by dividing family members among larger gatherings of men and women who create a community together, we emphasize the notion of family as an open unit: open to resources, input, and relationships. Organizing the culture circles by gender makes it easier to examine the different ways in which the dominant patriarchal, racist, and class-related discourses affect women and men. It also acknowledges the different pace at which women and men develop critical consciousness, empowerment, and accountability. The culture circle structure takes apart notions of what is private in personal and family life and emphasizes that some things could benefit all by being more public. It also levels the power hierarchies between diverse client populations, thereby liberating, or providing a legitimate forum for, the perspectives of traditionally subjugated groups.

Along the trajectory of empowerment and accountability, people learn to recognize the voices and actions of those who uphold dominance. The trajectory of dominance and subjugation evolves differently *within* nodal experiences of oppression. In Case 5.2, both women are Latina and oppressed in different ways within the larger Latino/a culture. One is light skinned and can pass, but her accent subjugates her. The other woman is darker skinned with an acculturded accent that provides her access to the dominant culture. They celebrate their Latina heritage. However, within these histories, experiences of power and privilege get elevated over those of oppression. Although both women are oppressed within the larger culture, their histories related to Judaism (Israel) and Islam (Palestinian) were unexamined.

After an initial intake session, all clients in the cultural context model join a same-gender, 6- to 8-week social education orientation circle. As described in Chapter 2, clients in this circle examine the many factors that contribute to the problems that brought them to therapy, and the problems are contextualized within the larger social order. Video clips of popular movies and documentaries provide vivid, engaging examples of how issues of power, privilege, and oppression play out in personal dilemmas of families and society.

Some clients question the usefulness of developing critical consciousness and watching movies. But most are engaged and quickly let go of their rigid preconceptions. After the orientation period, clients join an ongoing culture circle, which may vary in size from 12 to 20 people. Within their circle, clients continue to examine and break down their problems and work out solutions.

By this stage, clients have some foundation in the connection between their issues and broader social dynamics and issues. Meetings of the men's and women's

CASE 5.2

TWO LATINA WOMEN ENCOUNTER PRIDE AND PRIVILEGE

Isabelle, of Chilean, upper-class, and Jewish origin, is in the same circle as Sabrina, who is of Venezuelan-Palestinian and middle class origin. Sabrina was raised Catholic but identifies as Latina and Muslim. Isabelle and Sabrina came to the center because of marital difficulties but developed a staunch connection around their Latina identities. Isabelle was light-skinned, and Sabrina dark. The Jewish–Palestinian and social class identities were mostly ignored. At the celebration of a Jewish holiday, where many of the community members were present, Isabelle remembered the Holocaust and deferred to Israel as the savior of the Jewish people.

While remembering the Holocaust seemed fitting to Sabrina, the honoring of Israel went too far. She responded with her own narrative of Palestinian relatives dying because one of them was refused treatment in an Israeli hospital, and the other was killed when Israelis targeted Palestinian civilians. Their opposing views made for a strained evening. What their differences did telegraph, however, was the tragedy of these women's lives and identities that were truncated because of social and political circumstance.

Isabelle was committed to shedding her naïveté about Israel's policies, while Sabrina wanted to continue to share her intimate space with Isabelle. Over a period of about 6 months, Isabelle delved into readings about the Israeli–Palestinian conflict and talked with Jewish members of the circle who helped her

differentiate the state from the many people of Israel who have opposed and continue to oppose the imperialist policies of Israel. She attended numerous Palestinian and Jewish activist progressive events. She came to better understand, the rage and dehumanization of the Palestinian people. She learned about the deeply scarred psyches of the Israeli soldiers. Most importantly, she came to understand her internalized norms of dominance, something she had attributed only to the men in her life.

With the help of others in the community she prepared a letter of accountability and offered reparations to Sabrina in the form of ongoing activist work against the genocide perpetrated by the state of Israel against the Palestinian people. She joined two organizations: Women in Black,[1] an organization of women "for justice, against war" that originated in Israel, and a Palestinian women's organization.[2] Isabelle read her letter of accountability for the therapeutic community to witness and participate in. They celebrated with a ritual of eating Palestinian and Jewish food and with poetry readings to mark this new boundary. Sabrina and Isabelle share a deep friendship today.

[1] http://www.womeninblack.org/history.html

[2] Palestinian Women in Struggle for National Liberation, available at http://www.newjerseysolidarity.org/resources/palestinianwomen.html, offers information on the central role of women in the Palestinian movement for liberation.

circles and the mixed-gender community meetings alternate. The separate male and female circles often take place at the same time, which is convenient for family members who may be participating in several circles. Intermittent family or couple sessions take place in the broader community circle, where there is regular feedback.

Many of the tools for liberation that were introduced in Chapters 1 and 2 and in the figures are used in the culture circles to assist clients in keeping alive their awareness of how power, privilege, and oppression shape family, work, and other arenas of their life. Clients learn to use these tools in conjunction with viewing many of the film clips we identified in Chapter 2 to raise their critical consciousness.

■ ■ ■ ■ ■

CASE 5.3

BEYOND THE 12-STEP: A RECOVERING ADDICT FACES POWER, PRIVILEGE, AND OPPRESSION

The following example is about Jonathon, a 52-year-old African American man who is a recovering addict seeking to save his marriage. Throughout the course of his addiction, Jonathon enrolled in numerous treatment programs. While some programs addressed his family of origin issues, none integrated how power, privilege, and oppression affected his life in ways that competed with philosophies of 12-step recovery.

Figure 5.3 is Jonathon's genogram situated within the hierarchy of power, privilege, and oppression. The emphasis of his 12-step program is on his powerlessness to substances and addiction, conflicted with his social location as a man, a husband, and a father. Accountability as a healing endeavor was absent from his past therapies.

Jonathon wrote an accountability letter to his deceased father, which he read to his culture circle. Jonathon brought along his father's portrait. Their physical resemblance was striking. After reading the letter, Jonathon burned it and placed the ashes in a container he planned to take to his father's grave. Such rituals helped him separate parts of his own masculinity from those of his father, leading to more mature and expanded ways of being a man. This process was pivotal in redefining Jonathon's marriage. Not only was the intergenerational legacy interrupted, but it was done with the help of other men who shared their masculinity with him in very different and caring ways. They called on him to create a more equitable relationship with his partner.

It was important for Jonathon to grapple with issues connected to his black masculinity and his fluctuating position on the power hierarchy, with no legacy of financial assets. It enabled him to acknowledge ways in which he continued to have adequate housing, medical care, and lucrative work. This case highlights the complexity of a community healing context in which members can be empowered and held accountable to each other as well as to the treatment team. His letter demonstrates his therapeutic work that connects the nuances of his social location.

Jonathon's Letter: An Attempt to Redistribute Justice

Dad,

I was going to begin this letter as any correspondence with you might start, but the truth is it's an assignment, and I'm sure it wouldn't get written otherwise. I was thinking recently about how often or how seldom I think about you; and it wasn't that I felt I didn't think about you often enough, I just wondered if there was actually a right amount of time I should spend thinking about you. I don't sweat it too much anymore. I couldn't escape having you cross my mind even if I wanted to. Plus, in the different forms of treatment I've been through in the last years in my recovery, I've had to at least think about you. We did a genogram in group, and the parallels in our lives are amazing—the women we marry, our ways of making a living, the underdeveloped artistic talents. I was pretty shocked at the similarity between you and me. I used to spend a lot of energy thinking of what you did and didn't do with me as far as growing up, but I don't sweat that much either. I guess you did what you knew how to do. I look at my life, and sometimes I do the math to see how it compares to your life. And when I do that, I seem to find some tolerance and forgiveness. When you were 35, which is 15 years younger than I am now, you were feeding five kids; and you were doing it armed with more hustle than education, and at a time that was less hospitable to a black man than my time is. I see now how the fact that you worked every day, and as far as I know, you were home every night, was more than the fathers of most of my friends could say. If I had to feed and shelter five kids at 35, I don't now if I could do it. So, I

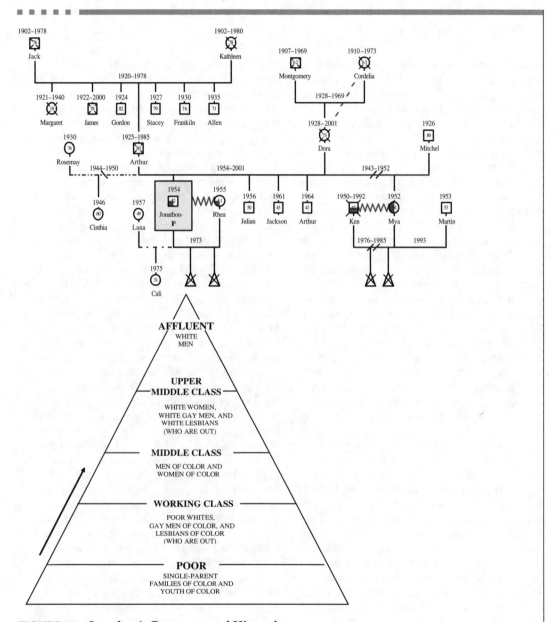

FIGURE 5.3   Jonathon's Genogram and Hierarchy

need to give you your props in that area. I know now too that things about you that I saw as subservient or cowardly were, for a man born in Mississippi in 1925, actually survival skills. I grew up in the northeast in the 60s and 70s, when at least the ideas of rebellion or revolution could be said out loud. So, in hindsight, and in the big picture, I love you. But

(continued)

■ ■ ■ ■ ■

CASE 5.3   CONTINUED

don't get it twisted. There was a bunch of stuff about you that I hated. You were aloof around us kids at best and ignored us at worst. You came from a school that said that if your kids ate dinner tonight and there are shoes on your feet, then you've done your job. Well, we needed more than that. That fact pissed me off even more when I started to gain some recognition for athletics, and all of a sudden, somehow you thought you had something to do with it. I hated the condescending way you treated mom sometimes. I hated how she would make herself small for the sake of your ego. When I got old enough to run the streets and figured it out that you were somewhat of a womanizer, I hated you for that. I hated the way that you spoke about, and at times to, Jimmy about his lack of what you saw as manliness, or in your words, for acting like a faggot. I'm feeling now that I've spent so much of my life in reaction to you. I think the big thing in trying to piece together our bond is how hard it is to figure out how I became you. It's uncomfortable being in a place where neither logic nor intuition seems to give me any answers. Before I even begin to figure out how I became you, I have trouble even identifying the specific ways that I am you. One of the things about you that I hated was how condescending you could be. And I've tried so hard to avoid that in myself that it's bordered on my being patronized sometimes, which ironically is condescending. I guess the big thing we share in common is that we both married "up," as they say. We married women from somewhat of the bourgeoisie black community. And when we come across any rough patches in our relationships with them, we hold it against them like a weapon. Another thing we have in common is a certain smugness and a cynicism toward the world in general and to our loved ones in particular. We believe that the other person has no clue what is right or fair or equitable, so why should we even bother trying to explain, or more impor-

tantly to listen to, what they feel or think. I see other similarities, but I'm not sure what to make of them. We both seem to put a little too much stock in that useless currency that so many black men trade in, which is the idea of being cool, which is a beautiful thing in us when it comes out as far as art or music or style or just a confident way to be in the world. And it comes out despicably when it shows up at the expense of other people or as a mask to hide and frighten little boys. I remember the paradox of not liking so much about you yet basking in (your) approval when my name or my picture was in the paper or on television or when some fly girl came by to pick me up—or when I took an interest in your Ellington or Coltrane records. I remember how weird it was when I came back home from California, kicked off the basketball team and out of school, and started selling a lot of dope in the streets. Because you were running cabs and limos, you would see me and you seemed to take some perverse pride in me being a hustler. I'm not sure what of you I want to keep or share. I don't blame you for anything. My feelings for you mellowed greatly when I watched the spirit with which you spent your last years fighting cancer. Though you were frighteningly bitter at times, there were times when you carried the pain like a warrior, and I remember bringing you pot to make you eat. You needed this to ease the chemo symptoms. We talked with nowhere near total honesty but with much more than we would otherwise. I got to tell you that I love you and I hate you, and I'm grateful for that. Trying to get that kind of feeling from you growing up was like trying to pick up a penny with boxing gloves on. It took so much effort. It is like you could lift up one side of the coin only to feel it drop just when you thought you had it in your hands. And, even if you did pick it up, it was only a fucking penny.

Jonathon

Family genograms are constructed to explore multigenerational legacies, gendered and racial norms, and immigration and diaspora patterns throughout time. Genograms are located within the hierarchy map of power, privilege, and oppression (Chapter 1, Figure 1.4). This process links power and oppression within the family to similar systems within the larger social context. We want to keep alive the notion of families as subsystems of the broader society.

Traditional treatment formats featuring one therapist and one individual, couple, or family simply do not afford the possibilities of empowerment and accountability offered by the collective treatment formats. As a result, they cannot and do not affect justice issues. Creative processes like community healing are very difficult to sustain within the confines of single-client treatment.

The cultural context model's active advocacy projects work to dismantle power, privilege, and oppression on a broader societal level. Clients who have participated extensively in this model often express a wish to "give back" what they learned, which is a concrete measure of effective treatment.

To that end, several male clients established the first NOMAS (National Organization of Men Against Sexism) group in New Jersey. Another group of EuroAmerican clients established a white privilege circle to raise their own consciousnesses regarding their white privilege and to develop social action projects. Among their projects is a program established to monitor and evaluate racial, gender, and cultural bias in the family courts.

SAFEGUARDING SOCIAL JUSTICE: THE COLLABORATION PROCESS

Case 5.4 presents one client's comments regarding her participation in a white privilege circle and her social action work.

Other clients speak to schools and churches on violence prevention, sexism, white privilege, and racism. Many serve as sponsors to newer clients. As we point out in Chapter 6, the sponsors are not therapists but supporting 'lay' persons who serve in a variety of roles. They serve as mentors to those struggling with issues of equity around gender, race and class, and nonviolence in relationships. They help to expand notions of masculinity to encompass traits such as nurturing, gentleness, and empathy and to expand concepts of femininity to include financial viability and empowerment. Across diverse cultures, they foster respect for women, children, people of color, sexual minorities, and others who are different from them. Moreover, they may serve as a special resource to a client of the same cultural or religious background or may provide needed and missing information on a particular culture circle topic.

Case 5.5 illustrates how a culture circle offered diverse experience and knowledge to empower Juan, a Mexican immigrant, to pursue options he otherwise may not have learned were open to him. Juan's genogram and hierarchy are shown in Figure 5.4.

The structure of the therapy within the cultural context model (i.e., culture circles, sponsors, and social education) and its liberation framework suggest to

■ ■ ■ ■ ■

CASE 5.4
WHEN WHITENESS TRUMPS GLBT

"I was always interested in civic and social justice issues," says Sally. "However, before getting involved in this white privilege circle, I thought that as a white person I had the power to say what I had to say and effect change. I would speak up in isolation on issues of social justice. I did not have the skills or consciousness to know that I would need supportive collaborators in this process. As a result, I tended to alienate the people I most wanted to influence and also put those I was trying to support at risk. For example, when I was advisor to the GLBT group at a local college, I was about to approve a 'Coming Out' booth for National Coming Out Day.

"With the support of my circle colleagues and friends, I was able to help the GLBT group assess the climate at the school as well as the safety concerns of those who were looking at coming out publicly so that they could proceed much more effectively. After processing these concerns and collaborating with campus police and the student activities office, we decided to put together an information booth that was very successful and included students and professional staff. I was able to achieve this while safeguarding the vulnerability of the students."

■ ■ ■ ■ ■

CASE 5.5
COLLECTIVE POWER AND ACCOUNTABILITY: BECOMING MIDDLE CLASS

Juan, a Mexican immigrant, was referred for treatment because of violence toward his son. During the course of his treatment with his family, it became apparent that he was being exploited at his workplace, a food store, where he was required to work long hours and received no benefits. Because of his undocumented citizenship status, he believed he had no rights. Juan's culture circle, a diverse group of men, first supported him by suggesting different options to navigate fairness at work (addressing accountability in repressive work contexts).

When this approach did not work, they explored with him financial avenues toward opening his own store, and they provided him with legal options. The exploration (empowerment and accountability) on his behalf was critical because Juan did not have the language or educational skills to pursue this path. Many of the men in his circle who had this access shared their knowledge and skills with him, which enabled him to obtain a small business loan and open his own store.

The day his store opened, Juan came to the center with a huge basket of fruit and flowers, crying. He was crying over a dream he never thought he could reach as an immigrant with no resources. Through the efforts of collective empowerment and accountability, he was able to move up in class.

clients that (a) issues related to power, privilege, and oppression are central to all relationships; (b) problems have social roots and (c) problems are better solved in a diverse community, particularly one that shares a critical consciousness. Likewise, broader social values that isolate family life from community life are problematic.

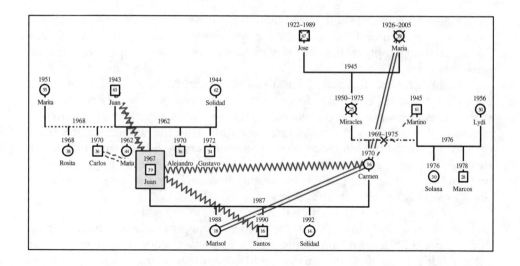

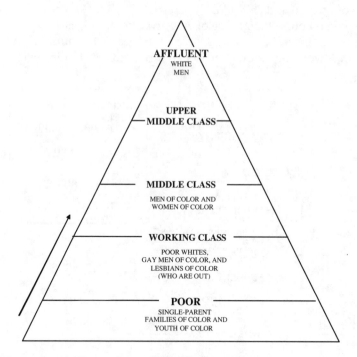

FIGURE 5.4   Juan's Genogram and Hierarchy

Culture Circles: A Glimpse at a Culture Circle

What might an evening in a culture circle be like? The following description (see Case 5.6) of members in a circle reflects the diversity of social location and presenting issues.

Figure 5.5 gives a visual representation of the relative power and privilege of members of a community culture circle containing both male and female clients. Remember that people on the upper levels have more power and privilege than do those on the lower levels.

Within each culture circle, there are men, women, adolescents, and sometimes even children, at different trajectories in their treatment. Individuals and families with different presenting problems join together to develop stronger and more complex identities as they become better able to face adversity and suffering in their lives.

Women's culture circles can empower members by helping them prioritize their needs, dreams, and desires at a level that females have been taught to reserve only for others. They are further encouraged to experience the full range of emotions, especially anger, in healthy ways.

Various forms of social action that serve to mobilize women in their families and communities help to empower the women. Examples include women helping one another with legal actions, pressing for improved work conditions, sharing the daily dilemmas of raising children, and generally working as a community to better the lives of women and children.

As these women build their sense of empowerment, they also expect greater accountability from others. For instance, help with legal action around child support not only empowers the mother and her children but also holds the father and

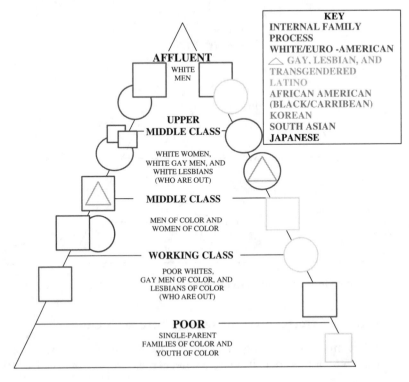

FIGURE 5.5   Hierarchy and Culture Circle at a Glimpse

■ ■ ■ ■ ■ ▬▬▬▬▬▬▬▬▬▬▬▬▬▬▬▬▬▬▬▬

CASE 5.6

A GLIMPSE AT INTEGRATION THROUGH CRITICAL CONSCIOUSNESS

A single female parent (white Irish) brings her sons into the circle to be supported and challenged regarding their increasing lack of respect for her.

A biracial man (Mexican and white) reads his letter of accountability detailing his lack of responsibility to his ex-wife (Colombian) and their adult children.

A young professional couple (German and Puerto Rican) seeks parenting tools for dealing with their overly precocious 3-year-old son while also trying to balance high-powered careers.

An adult African American woman with a drug problem describes that she has relapsed for the eighth time and that her parents are frantic because they have already lost a son to a drug overdose.

Parents of a 23-year-old South Asian daughter celebrate that the daughter has finally, after numerous failed attempts moved out of the family house and found a job.

A male teenager (Cuban) requests the men's circle's help with his school situation, where he is in trouble.

A divorced and remarried couple (of French, Irish, and German descents) struggle to reign in their adolescent daughters from drugs and dating violence.

A divorced gay white man struggles to remain connected with his two young adult daughters after his coming out.

A lesbian Latina woman faces challenges of how to embrace a "femme" partner.

A 60-year-old woman (Uruguayan, dark skinned) has just been diagnosed with cancer. She discusses alternative medicine options along with customary approaches.

An African American single father of three children seeks help in advocating for his children in the school system, seeking empowerment and accountability.

courts responsible for doing the right thing. A mother who is empowered to get medical tests for her daughter instead of succumbing to the school pressure to put the child on medication for ADHD finds out that her child has hyperthyroid disease. When the child is treated for this disorder, all of her ADHD symptoms disappear, and the physicians and the school are held accountable.

Women are also challenged to recognize and address their own personal and collective misuses of power and privilege over other women and men in the community. A sponsor's circle for racial and economic justice grew out of these and other challenges.

For men, culture circles generally get participants to focus on their relationship responsibilities rather than on self-serving initiatives. Women and men need to be coached out of traditional gender-prescribed behaviors. Male participants are encouraged to embrace and experience the full range of emotions, particularly emotions like fear, sadness, insecurity, and vulnerability that men frequently avoid because of their traditional commitment to stoicism and control. In terms of behavior, they are encouraged to participate in activities like doing housework and taking care of children, extended family, and the elderly.

Women, in turn, are encouraged to embrace assertiveness and self-definition. They are supported in their multiple roles as mothers, wage earners, and caretakers of extended family and are offered structural sabbaticals from this overload.

Many men report that their work has benefited from using these expanded forms of masculinity. A 45-year-old school principal stated that, to his horror, his mostly female staff saw a huge change in his attitude toward them once he stopped making unreasonable demands for their participation at work. They, in turn, were much less resistant to working with him on important school policy projects.

More broadly, within the context of the culture circles, men are encouraged to address their gender, race, and class privileges over other men and women. These circles can also evolve into social action networks aimed at ending war, racism, domestic and dating abuse, homophobia, and other forms of violence and encouraging civic participation by youth from oppressed communities.

Social education is an ongoing part of the therapeutic process within the circles. News articles about the myths and realities of men's lives (See Article 5.1 for an example) might be used in a men's culture circle to further social education. Articles might also be used in an individual or couples counseling session to break through stereotypes and spur conversation and reflection regarding gender roles in relationships.

■ ■ ■ ■ ■ ▬▬▬▬▬▬▬▬▬▬▬▬▬▬▬▬▬▬▬▬▬▬▬▬▬▬▬▬▬▬▬▬

ARTICLE 5.1

NEW TRUTHS ABOUT REAL MEN BY ROSALIND BARNETT AND CARYL RIVERS[3]

The news about men in the year just past was dismal. A high-profile court case saw a husband (Scott Peterson) convicted of murdering his pregnant wife. CEOs at Enron and World.com stand accused of defrauding employees and investors. NBA players waded into a crowd, fists flying. Then, to put the icing on this poisonous cake, the Department of Labor reported that the working woman spends twice as much time, on average, as the working man on household chores and care of children.

It gets worse. At home men are seen as lazy slugs and at work are viewed as old-fashioned, kick-butt bosses. In school, boys' verbal abilities lag far behind those of girls. As parents, males are thought to lack parenting abilities. Expanding paternity leave is pointless, since males are programmed to have little emotional attachment to their kids. Males lack empathy with others. If a friend approaches them to talk about problems, they change the subject or make a joke. In relationships they don't have a clue. They are faithless wretches "hard-wired" by their genes to be promiscuous.

Is this picture accurate? Happily, new research shows that it is not. Indeed, real men manage to escape the stereotypes much of the time. For example:

■ The lazy slug label is unfair. In fact, in dual-earner couples, the dominant family form in the United States, men's housework chores and childcare have increased steadily since 1977, says the 2003 National Study of the Changing Workforce. The "gender gap" in hours declined by more than 70 percent, from

2.4 hours per day in 1977 to one hour a day in 2002. Men are also doing more childcare. Between 1977 and 2003, employed fathers in dual-earner couples narrowed the gap by 57 percent.

- Are men really "command-and-control" types in management style? The most effective manager, it's now believed, is "transformational," one who gains the trust of followers and empowers them to reach their full potential. Psychologist Alice Eagly of Northwestern University found that women managers were indeed more "transformational" than men. But the difference was very small: 52.5 percent of females and 47.5 percent of males.
- Do boys lack the "natural" verbal skills of girls? An analysis by psychologists Janet Hyde of the University of Wisconsin and Marcia Linn of the University of California at Berkeley found the difference between boys and girls was trivial. Boys overall don't suffer from an inability to speak and write.
- Do men lack a natural ability to parent young children the way women do? No. And when men are the primary caretakers of young children, they "mother" in the same way women do, reports North Carolina State sociologist Barbara Risman. And for the first time, fathers now spend more time with their kids than on their own pursuits and pleasures, reported the U.S. National Study of the Changing Workplace in 2002.
- Do men duck and run when others approach them with problems? In fact, a 2004 study of "troubles talk" finds that both men and women largely provide support by giving advice and expressing sympathy.
- Are men impelled by their genes to be natural rovers? Psychologists Kay Bussey of Macquarie University and Albert Bandura of Stanford found that most males mate monogamously. "If prolific, uncommitted sexuality is a male biological imperative," the researchers write, "it must be a fairly infirm one that can be easily overridden by psychosocial forces."

In terms of fidelity, men and women are quite similar. In 2002, the National Opinion Research Center at the University of Chicago reports 15 percent of women said they cheated, while the number for men was 22 percent.

It's time to jettison the idea that males are clueless oafs who come from the planet Mars. Men, like women, are perfectly able to be people-oriented leaders, caring parents, good listeners, and true friends in time of need.

[3]Rosalind C. Barnett is director of the Community, Families and Work program at Brandeis University. Caryl Rivers is a professor of journalism at Boston University. They are the authors of *Same Difference: How Gender Myths Are Hurting Our Relationships, Our Children, and Our Jobs.*

Source: "New Truths About Real Men" by Rosalind Chait Barnett and Caryl Rivers *The Boston Globe,* January 1, 2005, Copyright © 2005. Reprinted by permission of the authors.

After reading the article, participants can be invited to talk about gender roles they came in contact with in their multigenerational families and from role models in school, the workplace, the media, sports, and the like. Social education lets families understand the insidiousness of patriarchy within families and community and work life. It also teaches them to become consumers of good journalism and research on families.

Those of us who practice in more traditional therapeutic formats are challenged to find ways to incorporate sources for holding clients accountable for maintaining attitudinal and behavioral changes over time. This is a particular problem for those who hold more power and privilege—men, whites, people with wealth, and many parents (over children).

Case 5.7 focuses on Gina and Tom, a couple who have tried a range of couple's therapy without satisfaction. Gina and Tom's genogram and hierarchy are shown in Figure 5.6.

■ ■ ■ ■ ■

CASE 5.7

GINA AND TOM FIND COMMON GROUND

Gina and Tom are Jewish of Polish and Russian descent. Tom, 48, is the oldest of three children, two boys and a girl. Gina, 49, is the youngest of four: a girl, then two boys, then Gina. She contends that her sense of self has been ruptured at many levels within the confines of her marriage. Tom reports that he is misunderstood and that Gina consistently hurts his feelings. They have two children, a boy, 4, and a girl, 6.

Gina and Tom went through a range of couple's therapy with some of the most distinguished therapists in the Northeast. Tom's pattern was to leave therapy when the therapist suggested something uncomfortable to him, such as that he become aware of how he treated his wife or that he take on some of the second shift responsibilities (home, relationship, and house care).

Gina decided to try the social justice approach. Although Tom accompanied her, he was suspicious and resentful toward the process and toward therapists in general. After Gina enrolled, Tom grudgingly agreed to come in for one session to express his disillusionment with his past therapy. The team and Gina's culture circle let him present his concerns in the community circle, which included the men's and women's circles.

Tom explained to the circle of clients that their previous therapist damaged his relationship with Gina by not supporting the marriage. His entire reaction was based solely on his own feelings. He said he worried that the current therapy, with its separate gender circles for husbands and wives, would further damage the relationship and requested that he and Gina sit together and face each other's hurts and challenges.

Tom and Gina met within the community circle. In the room were men and women at different stages in their treatment process, along with a few sponsors and two college-age sons of one of the other couples who participated in this circle.

During the session, many of the men attempted to put Tom's unease with nontraditional couples' therapy in context and explain that it was a normal reaction. For example, John (a community member) told Tom: "At first I too was confused and angry that my wife and I were separated. I thought we were coming to therapy to get together, and then they ask us to be in separate circles. But now, having been here for six months, I realize that as a couple we were unable to get enough distance from our problems to see that power and control was destroying our relationship.

"Now I see," John continued, "how all of the prior therapies that asked me whether I loved Pat, and of course I love Pat, didn't explore how my power and control over her was slowly and successfully eroding her love for me. What's hard is, we men like our marriages to be a private thing. I mean, we men created the institution of marriage. We like it the way it is. And we don't want it to change."

Here's what Mike (another circle member) told Tom: "I too thought I had a great marriage. But according to Marian, she felt like she was in a prison. The reason that my boys (19 and 21) are here today is that I want to read my letter of accountability to Marian and to them as well.

"All these years, I would tell them how their mother should be happy to have me as her husband and their father. And I just controlled everything she did, including the amount of money she used for gas, food, and so on. But, we were not poor, and Marian worked!

"So, I just thought I had the right to be the chief and decide what everyone in the family needed and deserved. I am glad that Marian has given me another chance to get this right, and I want my boys to never do this to anyone they love.

"I think you should consider the possibility that perhaps even though you think you are being a great partner, unless you hear this from Gina, I don't think you can count on your own assessment. I also hear you saying that it does not feel safe. But our feelings are often notoriously unreliable!"

Ahmed explained: "Before your partner had the support of a women's circle, she was probably too afraid to tell you all of the ways in which you were oppressing her. Here she has a great circle of support, and she can clearly say how and when you are oppressing her. That is why you are unhappy. You feel left out, but that can change if you choose to make it different."

Even though many of the men attempted to explain the value of the culture circle format, Tom remained upset and was not convinced. It took him another 6 months to renegotiate with Gina and engage in the process. He told Gina and the team that he would try this therapy for 6 months, and if nothing changed, he would go on to try yet another form of therapy.

Gina calmly told him that he was free to use these options, but she had finally found a therapy that addressed all of the complexities in her life and was not about to go forum shopping. In past therapies, without the buttressing support from other men and women, she would rapidly regress into guilt and moral responsibility for the marriage.

After Tom heard the letter of empowerment that Gina had been working on in her women's culture circle, he agreed to continue therapy. Gina read her letter to Tom in the surround of the community circle. The letter explained the ways in which he infantilized and controlled her during her pregnancies; how he insisted on making all the big decisions about what type of car to buy, where to live, the type and cost of the house they bought. She told him that although he let her manage the checkbook, he did not keep her informed about their larger financial situation. He made big purchases without mutual discussion or consent. Finally, he also undermined her authority with the children.

After listening to Gina read her letter, Tom took an important first step in soliciting the men's assistance in helping him begin to repair his marriage. In Tom's men's circle, it became clear that he had adopted the worst of his father's male legacies to carry forward in his own family. His father demanded a traditional marriage even though his wife worked outside of the home. With all of the responsibilities that Tom's mother carried, his father remained the centerpiece of the household.

The team invited Tom to write a number of letters. The first was to his mother, offering compassion for her position and choice in her marriage. Then he wrote one to his father, detailing all of the ways in which he honored him and the positive things he learned from him. In addition, he was coaxed to address his father's patterns of rage, control, and self-centeredness.

Tom's preoccupation with completing numerous jobs he had ignored in the home led him to put off completing his letters. The male sponsors in his circle signed up to help him complete his labor-intensive tasks, such as painting the house and getting rid of old

(continued)

■ ■ ■ ■ ■

CASE 5.7   CONTINUED

furniture in the basement to make it a welcome place for the kids. His male sponsors also scheduled regular cooking classes with him to get him to do his share of the household chores.

It is significant that within the cultural context model, the other men and sponsors in Tom's culture circle kept urging him to finish the letter to his father and to increase his participation in family responsibilities. With persistent encouragement, including listening to other men's letters to their fathers, and practical support from the men in his culture circle, Tom finally began to write the initial letter. The whole process of writing and revising the letter, with feedback from the other men and the team at each stage, took about 4 months. Through feedback, Tom was encouraged to challenge his father over the ways his mother was oppressed and to express his sadness that his father had always been preoccupied with work and never enjoyed family life or the achievements of his children.

When the letter was complete, Tom read it to the community culture circle, and he detailed the ways in which he intended to be a different man, partner, father, and son. Afterwards, he was encouraged to read the letter at his father's grave with his sponsor and daugh-

ter present, along with friends and community members. Such rituals can strengthen family relationships and create new paths for connections between family members.

Three months later, Tom read his accountability letter to Gina and offered reparations to her family and their close friends. These were all relationships that he had interfered with and blocked over the course of their marriage. A year later, Tom became a sponsor to other men to give back what he had learned.

In the process of letter writing, Tom underwent numerous changes. He had to come to terms with his having fully absorbed a traditional male code even though he thought of himself as a great, liberal guy. He needed to see how his hidden rage toward his deceased father kept him in a pseudo-connection that left little room for compassion toward his mother. He also developed real friendships with other men, which were different than the superficial connections he once had.

Certainly, Gina did her own work addressing how she had colluded with Tom's assertion of privilege, and she saw the need to create a new generational legacy of empowerment for their daughter.

The advantage of the cultural context model is that the structure of sponsors, culture circle members, and a team approach heighten this accountability. In Chapter 4, we discussed the value of ongoing witnesses versus one-time appearances in the therapeutic context. Reflecting teams and definitional ceremonies using outsider witnesses (White, 1999) are examples of ways community members can participate in the healing endeavor. These approaches are designed to elevate subjugated voices, creating systems of empowerment. Accountability of the oppressors is not a parallel treatment process, however, and these forms of community participation in treatment tend to be one-time events. The witnesses often do not return in following weeks to create a foundation of empowerment and accountability. The cultural context model affords an ongoing community of empowerment and accountability. Sponsors who have gained a critical consciousness are able to

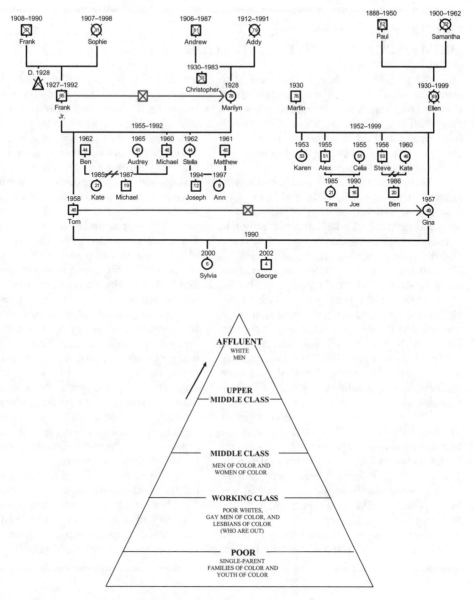

FIGURE 5.6   Tom and Gina's Genogram and Hierarchy

challenge misuses and abuses of power and privilege directly within an ongoing system of therapeutic justice.

Case 5.8 illustrates how a culture circle's discussion of a couple's presenting problem led to the empowerment of another circle member to stop seeing herself as a victim and to recognize her potential for growth and self-determination.

CASE 5.8

FROM MELTING POT TO EXPANDED IDENTITIES

Liu, who is Chinese, and her partner Jack, who is Irish, face a challenge as they move from their internal conflicts to coming to grips with race, ethnicity, and colonization. In their culture circle, they told of a recent fight they had over Jack's refusal to participate in the care of their two young children.

During the fight, Liu's mother, who was helping them with child care, told Liu in Chinese that she should be more of a traditional wife and forgive Jack's lack of participation in household tasks. Jack does not speak Chinese and did not understand what was being said. He continued to argue with Liu about how much he should have to do around the house.

As they told this story in the culture circle, a white woman, Gertrude, took issue with the fact that Liu did not translate her conversation with her mother for her husband. Gertrude maintained that Liu's not translating for Jack was rude and that she and her military family practiced the use of foreign languages differently.

Other members of the circle disagreed. They said that it placed an undue burden on Liu to always be responsible for creating a bridge between Jack and his biracial family. They argued that Gertrude was falling into the gender expectation that the women, Liu and her mother, should speak English, not that Jack should learn Chinese.

Gertrude responded that she was raised to believe that the United States is a melting pot and that when immigrants come to this country, they should be willing to forego their language, heritage, and customs for the privilege of being American. Many of the circle members, who were white and who had developed a critical consciousness, responded that white people pay a price when they give up their culture. The people of color in the circle embraced this conversation as validating for them and for Liu.

This prolonged discussion had an impact on Gertrude, who came from a working-class background and felt that many people of color in this circle were better educated and had more class privilege than she did. For several weeks, she held on to her self-definition as a victim and could not understand why the melting pot theory was a bad one for whites and people of color. She was, however, willing to keep discussing it because she was connected to many members in the community. Through numerous conversations and readings, she came to better understand the multiple layers of social location as it pertains to language, colonization, gender, and class. Months later, she even signed up to attend a white privilege conference.

Gertrude's embrace of Liu also opened up the possibility of revisiting her relationship with her own parents and their military connection with many of the countries they lived in. In this way, the possibilities for growth and self-determination are endless.

We hope to challenge you to find ways in your practice to create these circles of healing. You can, for example, invite others into sessions for feedback and reflection. You can establish witness circles of people who can be available to sit in on sessions. You can identify cultural consultants who can be included in a session. You can find reasons to organize your clients as communities and begin the process to create culture circles yourself.

How Are Culture Circles Different from Most Group Therapies?

Like our group-work colleagues, we are great believers in the value of a collective experience. There are, however, some differences between culture circles as we conceive them and some forms of group work.

Groups are often formed around a specific presenting problem (drugs, alcohol, loss, eating disorders, etc.). But culture circles include clients who come for therapy around a gamut of issues. Culture circles strive to enhance healing by viewing a person's identity as something more than his or her problems. This approach is similar to narrative approaches that externalize the problem or work to separate the problem from the person. But in the culture circles approach, there is more focus on empowerment and accountability than on the presenting problem (externalized or not). As people become responsible for their lives, they repair the damage they have done in relationships and begin to experience themselves in new and empowered (that is, power with versus power over) ways. The problems for which they sought therapy begin to disappear.

With help from the team, sponsors, and other culture circle members, clients find ways to creatively solve their problems. We find that multiproblem circles or groups offer greater diversity in resources to clients and help them to discover solutions in many arenas of their lives. When insurance monies are depleted, members can continue to participate at a reduced cost, or as sponsors who often pay nothing. The culture circle provides a foundation of critical consciousness that buttresses the experiences of new clients. These factors, together with the economics of reimbursement, make this approach a sustainable model.

IS THE PERSONAL POLITICAL? IF SO, ARE POLITICAL ISSUES APPROPRIATE FOR THERAPY?

Group therapy often bolsters the status quo. Therapists, whose exclusive focus is the presenting problem, often help clients adapt to—rather than change or resist—normative familial, cultural, and institutional practices.

Consciousness raising is seldom part of the therapy. To be sure, there are group workers who pioneered the notion that the personal is in fact political and that social action is a necessary component of transformational change. Feminist work, for example, has, at its core, women's and men's consciousness-raising groups. Community organization has a history of activist work. But little of this pedagogy of critical consciousness and social action has been incorporated into the therapeutic streams.

By now you are well aware that consciousness raising and social education is a central component of culture circles. Liberation and accountability—not adaptation—fuel the mandate that therapy be proactive and political in ways that ultimately benefit all. There is a constant interplay between social education and a personal and relational focus in the treatment format.

For example, a therapist might ask, "What does the fact that you are a white man (or a Latina woman) have to do with the problem you are struggling with?" The model attempts to treat clients' intersecting identities (gender, race, social class, sexual orientation and identity, physical ability, religion, etc.) as sites of resilience and vulnerabilities. Problems are dismantled and redefined within that mosaic. Remember the hierarchy figure (Chapter 1, Figure 1.4) and the family depicting these nodal point experiences?

Group Membership: Permeable or Rigid?

Within the cultural context model, membership in the circles is fluid, which allows family members, cultural consultants, friends, and coworkers to be invited in to participate as needed and when helpful to the process. Group membership is not static. Participants can come and stay for as long as they need to. Others may be invited in to offer a particular perspective. Clients become aware that the treatment philosophy values multiple perspectives and does not elevate therapists as the only experts. Rules for operating as open systems are discussed within both families and communities for liberation.

While confidentiality is always respected where there are issues of safety—for example, with battered women—there is no emphasis on the secrecy that accompanies many therapies. Rather, there is an emphasis on openness and a commitment to deprivatizing all information.

Privacy Versus Ongoing Connection and Support

Some group therapies prohibit members from having contact with each other outside of the therapy group. Culture circles encourage group members to connect and see that connection as part of the ongoing healing long after members have left therapy. Often, therapies fail because there is no built-in source for holding clients, particularly those with more power and privilege, accountable for maintaining attitudinal and behavioral changes over time.

Within the cultural context model, this accountability is facilitated by the circle structure, the sponsors, and a team approach. Clients call and e-mail each other to reinforce and support agreements made in session and to coach each other in the life changes they are seeking. The ongoing support of others in the circle is fundamental to the work. That support can be in the form of empowerment or accountability, or both.

REFERENCES

Barnett, R. C., & Rivers, C. (2005, January 1). New truths about real men. *Boston Globe.*
Figueroa-McDonough, J., Netting, F. E., & Nichols-Caseboult, A. (2001). Subjugated knowledge in gender integrated social work education: Call for dialogue. *Affilia 16,* 411–431.
Freedman, J. (1975). *The politics of women's liberation.* New York: David McKay Co.

Freire, P. (1971). *Pedagogy of the oppressed*. New York: Herder & Herder.

Hare-Mustin, R. T. (1978). A feminist approach to family therapy. *Family Process, 17,* 181–194.

Hoffman, L. (1992). A reflective stance for family therapy. In S. McNamee, & K. Gergan (Eds.), *Therapy as social construction* (pp. 7–24). London: Sage.

Krestan, J., & Bepko, C. S. (1980). The problem of fusion in the lesbian relationship. *Family Process, 19,* 277–289.

Lui, M., Robles, B., Leondar-Wright, B., Brewer, R., & Adamson, R. with united for a fair economy (2006). *The color of wealth: The story behind the U.S. racial wealth divide*. New York: W.W. Norton.

Minuchin, S., Montalvo, B., Guerny, B., Rosman, B. L., & Schumer, F. (1967). *Families of the slums: An exploration of their structure and treatment*. New York: Basic Books.

Momson, T. (1993). *Playing in the dark: Whiteness and the literacy imagination* New York: Vintage Books.

Silverstein, L. B., & Goodrich, T. T. (2002). *Feminist family therapy. Empowerment in social context*. American Psychological Association, Washington, D.C.

Spivak, G. (1987). *In other worlds: Essays in cultural politics*. New York and London: Methuen.

The top 10: The most influential therapists of the past quarter-century. (2006). *Psychotherapy Networker*. Retrieved on March 8, 2006, from http://www.psychotherapynetworker.org

White, M. (1999). Reflecting-team work as definitional ceremony revisited. *Gecko, 2,* 55–82.

CHAPTER SIX

CREATING COMMUNITIES OF RESISTANCE AND SUPPORT: SPONSORS AND CULTURAL CONSULTANTS

A human being is part of a whole, called by us the Universe, a part limited in time and space. He experiences himself, his thoughts and feelings, as something separated from the rest, a kind of optical delusion of consciousness. This delusion is a kind of prison for us, restricting us to our personal desires and to affection for a few persons nearest us. Our task must be to free ourselves from this prison by widening our circles of compassion to embrace all living creatures and the whole of nature in its beauty. Nobody is able to achieve this completely, but the striving for such achievement is, in itself, a part of the liberation and foundation for inner security.

—Albert Einstein (1954)

A social justice–based approach to therapy challenges clients to change patterns of understanding and interaction that are continuously reinforced within family and social networks. Implementing change at such a fundamental level requires clients to establish communities of resistance, networks that help them challenge and resist the oppressive norms and messages that exist everywhere in our society. Sponsors and cultural consultants to the therapeutic process provide the foundation and support for these new networks.

This chapter

- Identifies the roles that sponsors and cultural consultants play in mentoring clients into lives of equity and nonviolence.
- Offers strategies for training and recruiting sponsors.

- Offers examples of sponsors and cultural consultants in action within the therapeutic process.
- Describes the differences between social justice sponsors and those active within 12-step programs.
- Distinguishes the role of cultural consultants.

THE ROLE OF SOCIAL JUSTICE SPONSORS

Sponsors are volunteer participants and clients who partner with clinicians in the therapeutic process. Their presence changes the structure of the therapeutic encounter, replacing the isolation that characterizes most psychotherapy with an enhanced experience of connection and support. Within therapeutic sessions, sponsors are invited to describe life experiences that are similar to those of clients, as well as their own process of change.

When a young, Latina, Catholic woman, who is pregnant with her first child and is part of her African American husband's second family, shares in therapy that it is okay for her husband to "party with the boys" two or three times a week as long as he comes home at a reasonable time, her diverse group of female sponsors in the session—including Latinas—provides ready feedback and challenges her regarding a woman's automatic acquiescence to her husband's desires and behavior. The peer sponsors suggest alternatives that offer more dignity for her and equity in the relationship, including that her partner participate in the building of their home life and be actively involved in preparations for their new child. They also encourage her to learn about their joint finances and to expect her partner to share in making plans for child care and to create activities to strengthen their relationship.

His sponsors, on the other hand, want to understand the arrangements of his last relationship, offering their analysis on why it failed and giving strong support for alternative ways of being a partner to a young pregnant woman. They suggest that he participate equally in their second-shift responsibilities by accompanying her to the doctor's office for prenatal checkups and that he celebrate the coming of their new baby by actively participating in all that it takes to bring a baby into a home. Central to the marital conflict is the male client's absence as a father. Consequently, a male sponsor might help him to understand that fathering includes changing diapers, getting up in the middle of the night to care for a colicky baby, deciding when his child's behavior warrants an appointment with the pediatrician, and arranging for play dates. The sponsor emphasizes that these responsibilities should not automatically fall to the child's mother.

This sharing between men normalizes the experience of fathering as well as deconstructs traditional gender-role training, which often does not prepare men to be equal partners. It also offers a supportive framework in which human dilemmas and solutions become a shared effort. The resulting social education around the possibility of expanded gender roles in creating these solutions becomes more palatable because it is offered by peers.

Sponsors, recruited by therapists, become a community of mentors and role models who demonstrate versions of manhood and womanhood in which equity for all is the guiding value. They acknowledge the constraints of both male and female gender-role socialization across cultures. Male sponsors model an expanded masculinity characterized by vulnerability, nurturing, gentleness, empathy, and compassion for others. They demonstrate critical consciousness by supporting other men in a manner that consistently values, and more importantly *remembers*, to carry out relationship responsibilities.

The support offered by male sponsors links empowerment to accountability. As described in the example on equitable partnering, sponsors help a man balance his strivings for career advancement—our society's accepted venue for male empowerment—against his responsibilities to his partner, children, and extended family. All family members benefit when male empowerment is redefined in terms that honor, rather than conflict with, relationship priorities. Male sponsors are able to offer the needed support because they have redefined male norms, fundamentally refuting prevailing social norms in the following ways.

MALE SPONSORS

- Help other men take into consideration their partners, children, and families when considering their problems and choices. They teach other men to evaluate the impact their choices have on others and to embrace values traditionally associated with women.
- Break down the barriers of privacy and autonomy that maintain male domination and isolation of women and children by becoming a presence in their intimate lives. Sponsors also help clients to examine and break down the barriers of race and class segregation.
- Partner with men who engage in violence with the goal of mentoring them into lives of nonviolence.
- Exhibit a model of masculinity that includes vulnerability, nurturing, gentleness, empathy, and an understanding of others. They also show respect for women, children, people of color, sexual minorities, and others who are different from them.

Female sponsors demonstrate critical consciousness by promoting life options and a femininity that affirms the complete range of human possibilities across differences in family structure, occupational choice, and other life priorities. Female sponsors also encourage women to express their full range of emotions, including anger. They encourage women to seek independence, assertiveness, and balance in their home, work, and community relationships. They accept all sexual orientations and encourage women to define their sexuality on their own terms and to maintain friendships with women who are gay, bisexual, and heterosexual.

FEMALE SPONSORS

- Acknowledge patterns of female subordination but also challenge the ways that women participate in class and race privilege.

- Assist other women to gain clarity about their relationship intersections (e.g., working, parenting, coupling, friendships) and move away from traditional and stalled connections toward more progressive options and actions.
- Form partnerships with victims of domestic violence that help to empower them toward a violence-free life.
- Participate in action coalitions to assist women, men, and children in challenging oppression in schools, workplaces, and the courts.
- Embrace the use of traditionally associated male behaviors like assertiveness, self-determination, and anger to foster truth telling and liberation.
- Reject internalized norms of competition and dominance that erode women's relations and coalitions of support.

SPONSORS OF ALL GENDERS

- Promote critical consciousness by sharing stories from their own experiences that emphasize connections between empowerment, accountability, and liberation.
- Emphasize the communal nature of liberation, noting that freedom gained at the expense of others is exploitation rather than liberation.
- Partner with therapists and members of culture circles to model expanded gender identities that affirm equality as a guiding value.
- Mentor clients into safe, nonviolent lives by promoting equity across dimensions of gender, race, class, and culture.
- Help clients differentiate positive aspects of culture from oppressive traditions. For example, a man connects to male sponsors from the same faith who affirm gender equality and empower him to rethink his belief that his faith requires male domination. With sponsors of the same ethnicity, a woman rethinks her belief that her ethnic community requires women to be subservient. Her connection with sponsors of the same ethnicity empowers the woman to reexamine her role in her community.
- Support nonviolence in all relationships.
- Break through the secrecy surrounding violence toward women, gays, lesbians, bisexuals, transgendered people, and children.
- Break the silence toward oppression based on race, gender, class, and sexual orientation.
- Expand therapy into a community process of empowerment and accountability, transcending the isolation and compartmentalization in which men and women often make their choices in their relationships.

RECRUITING SPONSORS

The cultural context model's first sponsors were volunteers recruited by staff members from various civic organizations, including Rotary Clubs, chapters of the National Association for the Advancement of Colored People (NAACP), churches, the local police, and colleges. These volunteers received 12 weeks of social-education training regarding power, privilege, and oppression before participating in therapeutic sessions.

At this point, most sponsors are men and women who have undergone therapy themselves and decided at the conclusion of their own therapeutic work to continue their involvement as volunteers. Often, these people are interested in staying on as sponsors because it keeps their own consciousness raising fresh in a society that mitigates against it, and it is an opportunity to give back what they have learned.

In 1995, Robert Jay Green, a researcher at the California School of Applied Psychology, interviewed our sponsors. He was interested in why men choose to be sponsors. Their responses reflect much of what we describe here. Men who had never used violence were quite surprised to see that they misused power and privilege just as did men who used violence, though not to the same extreme. Men who were never violent learned that they had devalued women's life experiences and had refused to accept equity in their personal lives, reflecting the same rigid norms as men who were violence prone. They saw sponsorship as a means to challenge a range of men's behaviors and an experience that forced them to actively strive to bring equity into women's lives. They also discovered the sweet benefits of domestic partnership and an increased sense of intimacy and sexuality with their partners. All of these benefits make a social justice approach to mental health an economically and socially sustainable model.

Sponsorship can be adapted to fit your practice setting. One of our authors works in a corporation-based employee-assistance program. He enlists his previous clients as well as people who are part of his current clients' professional networks to become sponsors. While sponsors need to be coached regarding their role with clients, during and between sessions, many people welcome the opportunity to help others, and they readily offer assistance when the expectations and time requirements are clearly defined.

TRAINING SPONSORS

The notion of recruiting clients to assist in the work of therapy may startle some readers. "What about appropriate boundaries?" you may ask. We respond that social justice–based practice cuts through boundaries that create a rigid hierarchy and perpetuate the isolation of client families. Moreover, the traditional boundaries do not empower the very families we seek to liberate.

Recruiting former clients as sponsors acknowledges their ongoing development and welcomes their partnership in creating change that benefits all members of a therapeutic community. Sponsorship can be thought of as the final stage of therapy in which the most civic-minded clients expand their personal development by assuming the role of community change agent.

Whatever path has led people to volunteer, we suggest that therapists complete the following steps with sponsors-in-training:

1. Explore the candidate's multigenerational family patterns (genogram), paying particular attention to their experiences and attitudes regarding violence, white privilege and racism, male privilege and sexism, heterosexism and homophobia, spirituality and religion, and ethnicity.

2. With permission from clients, allow the candidate sponsors to sit in on therapeutic sessions, particularly sessions that include the use of social-education tools such as movie clips.

3. Take time to process sessions with candidates to help them make connections that link critical consciousness, accountability, empowerment, and liberation with the issues for which clients have come to therapy.

4. Encourage candidates to participate in projects and gatherings involving your practice's established group of sponsors. We recommend that you occasionally bring together your sponsors for joint reflection, social education, and social action projects.

5. Increasingly call upon candidates to share their experiences and reflections during therapeutic sessions.

6. Encourage candidates to function as sponsors outside of therapeutic sessions. This participation includes making themselves available to support clients and other sponsors on the phone, via e-mail, or in person. Make time to go over these extra-therapeutic contacts with the sponsor-in-training.

WHO SHOULD NOT BE CONSIDERED FOR SPONSORSHIP?

Some candidates, despite their best intentions, should not assume the role of sponsor. These include individuals who

- Demonstrate unreliability. They make commitments to attend sessions or make phone calls but do not follow through.
- Will not relinquish oppressive beliefs. They adhere to racist, sexist, or homophobic bias.
- Relentlessly lecture instead of sharing personal vulnerabilities when relating their stories of lessons learned and strength gained.
- Do not learn from feedback they receive regarding the value of change.
- Are not good team players towards equity and justice, declining to share with the therapist (or team of therapists) and with the community of sponsors the content of their communication with clients.
- Impose their religious values on others.

We have found that effective sponsors must be truly committed to a life of equity and liberation for all families. They have chosen to participate with others who struggle to embrace difference, nonviolence, and equity in all aspects of their lives. They are men and women who continue to work to expand their gender roles at work, at home, and in the community. They are willing to be open about their own struggles with intimates, others at work, in their social contexts, and those whom they are sponsoring. They model equitable relational patterns that new clients witness.

As you assemble your team of sponsors, having regular meetings with them fosters their development as a network. You might host a quarterly covered-dish dinner or screen a recently released movie and discuss themes related to gender, race, sexual orientation, and class. You may plan discussions regarding the sponsors' personal and collective concerns or particularly vexing client situations. Since the culture circles are gender specific, with periodic meetings of the entire sponsorship community, the cultural context model encourages male and female sponsors to meet separately.

Ideally, sponsors coalesce into a community of men and women who support your clients and each other. They support one another by becoming friends in the truest sense, willing to point out patterns that they see undermining important relationships, something most friends are afraid to confront for fear of loosening the connection. They celebrate each other's family milestones such as birthdays, anniversaries, graduations, and promotions and support each other around family losses, death, and illness. They attend community events together, such as gay pride celebrations, ethnic pride marches, and antiwar protests.

Sponsors can work to advance social justice in a variety of ways. They may partner with groups and institutions on community development efforts, develop projects that raise consciousness within their peer group and culture circles, and participate in highly individualized support initiatives for client families. For example, the Institute for Family Services and local shelters for battered women launched a program in which male sponsors attend family court hearings and introduce themselves to men who have just been ordered into batterers' intervention programs. The sponsors act as resources, providing support and information about the program the men are about to enter.

Many empowering programs exist for battered women, but there are virtually none for batterers. Men who take a strong public stand against violence can be alternative role models for young people and their families.

In another project, white female sponsors and some male sponsors, together with a white therapist, initiated a circle to deepen their understanding of white privilege, working to end white supremacy. In one project, members teamed up with teenagers of color, mostly African American and Latino boys who had been placed in a program for juvenile offenders, and together they carried out a very successful door-to-door voter registration drive in a primarily African American working-class neighborhood. The boys' parents worked on the project as well.

Sponsors have also initiated projects that help single parents with monitoring their children's schoolwork, help people cope with all of the tasks associated with maintaining a home, buying life insurance, and discussing financial planning and security (asset building), and help develop protocols for expanding equity in the workplace.

CASE 6.1

DISMANTLING RIGID GENDER NORMS THROUGH SPONSORSHIP

Dear Fellow Sponsors and Team,

Roger, Rob, Ian, and I met on Friday at Ian's home to plan our exercise for Tuesday's Men's Circle, focusing on the relationship between anger and violence and the lessons men are taught through sports. We decided we would begin by having the sponsors role-play a discussion about a basketball game we had just played. To illustrate the kinds of messages that contribute to anger and violence, each of us will make comments about the game, our opponents, and ourselves that are typical of things we have heard ourselves and other men say.

On Tuesday, we'll touch on the following points with one person leading the role-play and discussion:

1. The importance of sports in men's lives (Ian).
2. Put downs in men's banter with one another (Gary).
3. Aggression (Roger).
4. How awful it is to be chosen last (Rob).
5. How men typically deal with pain (Gary).
6. How we tend to see disputes as black or white (open for volunteers).
7. How men believe that winning is good; dominating is even better (open).

After the role-play, we'll ask the men in the group what they feel about what they saw and heard and then to relate it to their own experiences. This could lead to a discussion of the following questions, and we could record responses on the white board:

1. While growing up, what messages did you get from your coaches, fathers, and teammates about violence, anger, and pain in your sports activities? What form did these messages take?
2. How did these messages make you feel and act?
3. How do these messages impact your legacy in how you compete with others, how you coach and teach your children, what you value in athletics, and attitudes toward fitness, strength, prowess?
4. What do we want to pass on to our children, partners, friends, and families regarding competition, violence, anger, pain, and athletics? How can we do this?

We are open to suggestions and comments from all sponsors and the team.

Thanks,
Gary

Expanding Masculinity

The e-mail in Case 6.1, from a group of sponsors to the team of therapists, describes the social educational project the sponsors were planning for a culture circle within the cultural context model. They wanted to emphasize how sports can fuel anger and violence in men's lives. Notice that the sponsor group is taking responsibility for furthering social education with the client group.

This process of raising critical consciousness about sports was very useful to many clients, including women. For the first time, some of the women expressed concern about their sons becoming engaged in brutal sports. Others were surprised that sports had anything to do with masculinity and the way men behave in families. Many men were shocked to confront the link between sports, aggression, lack of intimacy, and the socialization of "harmful" (their word) gender roles.

■ ■ ■ ■ ■

CASE 6.2

DEMANDING JUSTICE: YVETTE AND HER SPONSORS CHALLENGE THE RACIST STATUS QUO OF THE SCHOOL DISTRICT, DELIBERATING ON THE CORNERSTONES OF JUSTICE FOR *ALL* YOUTH

Yvette's most recent ordeal began when a white boy on her son's basketball team accused her 17-year-old, Peter, of stealing his cell phone. Peter was confronted by his coach, then arrested by police and detained in a juvenile detention center. (It turned out that Peter had done nothing wrong, and the only phone in his possession was his own.)

Contrary to school district policy, neither the principal nor Yvette was initially informed of Peter's arrest and incarceration. Peter ended up being held in the juvenile detention center for several months. Yvette had to get an attorney and challenge the school on its own policy.

Yvette decided to seek redress from the school board. At the school board meeting, the superintendent refused to listen to Yvette. Instead, he told her to submit her concerns in writing. But his demeanor changed from dismissive to attentive when three of Yvette's white female sponsors made their presence known and asked why the school had not followed its own policy requiring immediate parental notification after such an event. The superintendent apologized and offered to do what he could to secure Peter's release. With the support of the white sponsors, Yvette decided to file charges against the school and the arresting officer.

A LETTER OF THANKS: PRACTITIONERS LINKING WITH SOCIAL ACTIVIST COMMUNITIES

Please pass along this note of thanks to the women sponsors for the support they give to our women and boys, and specifically for helping Yvette through this extremely difficult situation. Greta and Marion stood by Yvette tonight at the Board of Education meeting, and their presence was invaluable.

Yvette entered the meeting feeling dejected, carrying the pain of her son's depression about being incarcerated. After demanding to be heard (even though none of her questions were answered), she experienced validation through the actions of the women standing beside her. By the end of the meeting, Yvette looked and sounded rejuvenated, even with all of the work that lies ahead.

The purpose, value, and meaning behind "community" were so alive tonight when your group of sponsors and our group came together to expose the privilege that most often goes unquestioned within our political system. We witnessed women empowering one another when, alone, they might feel dismissed, wrong, and without hope. White women and women of color joined together to expose the game of patriarchy and white supremacy, demanding justice instead of business as usual.

Case 6.2 shows how a community of sponsors helped Yvette, an African American single mother, and her four sons. While her two older sons had managed to stay out of the juvenile justice system, her younger sons were repeatedly arrested and charged with minor infractions (see Figure 6.1).

Lisa Dressner, founder and director of Affinity Counseling Group, a social justice–based practice in New Brunswick, New Jersey, that works primarily with court-mandated youth, sent the e-mail in Case 6.2 to Rhea Almeida, her colleagues, and the sponsors after the sponsors attended the school board hearing with Yvette.

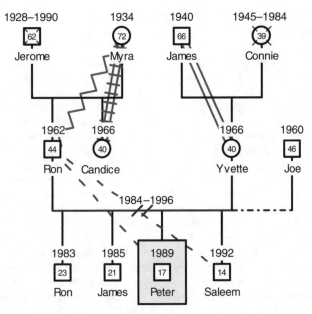

FIGURE 6.1   Yvette's Genogram

■ ■ ■ ■ ■

CASE 6.3

SOCIAL CAPITAL OUTCOMES FROM A SOCIAL JUSTICE PERSPECTIVE: THE CASE OF MEL

In another case, Mel, an African American sponsor-in-training, sought the advice and help of his community of male sponsors about how to address a workplace dilemma. Mel was the sole man of color holding a leadership position in his district, and he encountered discriminatory treatment from his direct superior. Mel received crucial feedback from a number of men, including one working in labor relations. With the support of his peers, Mel ultimately got a promotion and a substantial raise in salary, and he moved into a different department. The e-mails in Case 6.3 highlight Mel's exchanges with two members of his community of sponsors. Mel carefully followed the suggestions from the sponsors and documented his actions at work. With this strategic feedback and empowering support, Mel was able to hold his employers accountable and was promoted with no backlash.

Mel Writes to His Sponsors: Garnering Affirmative Action through Linking with Politically Situated Sponsors

Hi Guys

I need to get some feedback from all of you about a problem I'm having at work. First of all, I work for a major discount retail store as a regional meat manager. I supervise and train all the managers who are in my district. I am accountable to one of four regional VPs. To give you a better understanding of what I'm going through, I'll say this: I work in an environment that's predominately white. In fact, I'm one of only four people of color in my district, and the only one who holds a management job. The others work as meat cutters.

My boss, Bill, never supports me and never acknowledges my contributions. He takes

(continued)

■ ■ ■ ■ ■

CASE 6.3   CONTINUED

my suggestions/ideas and uses them as his own. I often hear him tell others that it was hard fixing a certain problem he was having, when in fact it was me who fixed the problem. I didn't have a problem with it at that point, but I did have a problem hearing him tell some of his cronies that he was going to promote them for one reason or another, even though I knew they weren't qualified.

Two weeks ago, a manager in my district was having a quality control issue that kept resulting in bad inventories and lost bottom-line profits. I was called to fix the problem because Bill couldn't solve it. My first instinct told me to say I couldn't figure it out, either. Then, I decided to fix the problem as a way to show my value, knowing all too well that Bill would take the credit for it, which he did.

Recently, a posting was put up for a job that would be a promotion for me. I knew Bill didn't want me to have that job because it would make me his equal. He recommended one of his friends, a guy I trained, and who is at the organizational level below mine.

My anxiety level when in contact with my boss is off the radar. I need some feedback on how to best address this stressful situation.

Thanks!
Mel

Hi Mel,

This sounds awful. I'm wondering if you can document the things that you do and/or copy others on your memos and correspondence to make sure that the credit for your hard work and knowledge goes to you, as it should. It certainly seems unfair, at best, that you are not getting acknowledged for what you do. Can you go to human resources for help?

Kevin [works in a pharmaceutical corporation]

Hi Mel

Can we map out *who* in the organization hired you and *who* remains helpful to you at this time? Can you begin to keep a paper trail of all of the discussions between you and your boss? Every time he asks you to do something verbally, send an e-mail back stating that you will be glad to do it, or you need some time, etc. Just put it in writing. Most importantly, do NOT confront your boss because confrontations usually go nowhere. There are some other strategies to challenge him without compromising your job stability. Lastly, contact the person who hired you, and share some of your concerns with him; get his positioning on the matter.

Jason [works as an employment law specialist at a university]

The next example of sponsoring (Case 6.4) relates to gender accountability: a man's accountability to his wife. Many sponsors weigh in on different aspects of accountability. These e-mails show the guidance that Ed received from sponsors on drafts of his accountability letter to his partner, Ellen, whom he had emotionally abused. His accountability letter is not shown here, but the coaching he received from the male sponsors regarding the letter is shown.

Case 6.4 illustrates how sponsors engage in a multilevel effort of dialogue, inquiry, reflection, and social action to create social justice. The sponsor community that you initiate increasingly takes on a life of its own, generating great benefits for your clients and the larger community, creating a growing pool of social capital (complex exchange of resources and time contributions) that helps to make this approach a sustainable model of healing.

CASE 6.4

ED WRITES AN ACCOUNTABILITY LETTER TO HIS WIFE: RETHREADING THE STRANDS OF GENDER OPPRESSION TOWARD EMPOWERMENT

Hi everyone,

Please let me know what you think about this draft. It was harder to write than the first. Also, Kevin, thanks for letting me know about your experience. Sometimes I'm embarrassed writing this stuff. It helps to know I'm not the only one. Thanks to everyone for helping me out.

Ed

Hi Ed,

I think the letter continues to improve. A couple of things you may want to consider:

1. Could you leave out the part about how you never learned to deal with conflict as an adolescent? It comes across as justification to me.

2. In the fourth paragraph, you use the word "at times" when you refer to your intimidation of Ellen. How would deleting "at times" change the meaning of this sentence?

3. Can you write more about the events that evening leading up to you throwing the bowl? For my partner Sue, my escalation of anger during arguments and my volatility were very frightening. What did you say and do in the moments and hours before you threw the bowl?

4. Can you give some more examples about other times you were abusive before the night you were arrested? You mention in the letter that there were "occasions prior to this event." It may be helpful to include some of these as well to illustrate your understanding of your history/patterns of abuse in the relationship.

Hope this helps,
Gene

Ed,

I agree with the feedback you've gotten so far. I think it would be good to add more specifics and details, keep the focus on Ellen, and don't include things about your process like not knowing how to handle conflict.

Recheck the "Power and Control" wheel and see if anything else shows up for you in your history. As Larry said, we all have a history and usually behave with patterns. Finding them is what helps us to be most accountable.

Peace,
Chad

Ed,

There are a lot of great parts in the letter. I think you did a good job of capturing some of the events and taking responsibility. I have a couple of comments: When you start the letter, you talk about taking accountability for July 24th. However, the letter really talks about a whole history of events. Can you expand that beginning and, perhaps, bring other examples of the power you used in similar ways in the beginning of your relationship with Ellen?

I think it may be helpful for you to consider some form of reparations to Ellen for your actions to help build a bridge for growth for you and your relationship. Outside of the letter, what is the current status? Are you and Ellen living together? Do you have visitation rights with your children?

Hope this helps,
Larry

Thanks Guys,

I appreciate all the feedback and will recheck the wheel. Several of you mentioned that I should include specific examples. Do you mean the exact nature of the argument? Also, can you let me know what you mean by

(continued)

■ ■ ■ ■ ■

CASE 6.4   CONTINUED

reparations? Is this something to be included in the letter?

Larry, regarding your last point, Ellen and I live together. There was a brief period of separation after the abusive incident. We went into couples counseling twice a week after the incident, and individual therapy too! We started at the center around one month later. Fortunately, the children were not present during the incident and I think it has not affected them much.

Ed

Ed,

The specifics that illustrate your abuse of power and control are important. That may mean any part of the argument or the history but definitely be more specific. How do you think your prior actions have affected Ellen's relationship with the children and their outlook about relationships? Also, how do you think your taking accountability affects them?

Larry

Hi Everyone,

I think my actions and events have made Ellen more guarded and suspicious. I think she will be looking to see if something like what happened to us starts happening to one of the children later on. I also think that my taking accountability will serve them well. As I learn to take responsibility for my actions, such lessons certainly will go to them, particularly when they are hurtful. I already see myself asking them to take accountability when they hurt each other's feelings—every day.
Thanks for the feedback!

Ed

How Are Social Justice Sponsors Different from 12-Step Sponsors?

Much of the wisdom of 12-step recovery programs is compatible with the philosophy of a social justice approach. Healing within a community context is a profound aspect of the recovery model, as is the concept of sponsorship.

While there are similarities, important differences exist between social justice sponsors and 12-step sponsors. Many of these differences are steeped in competing ideologies and forms of intervention. It is important to clarify some of the differences, because the term *sponsor* brings to mind the Alcoholics Anonymous (AA) sponsor.

The concept of power is fundamental to the efforts of 12-step sponsors and social justice sponsors, but in very different ways. Twelve-step programs emphasize the power of addictive illnesses and posit that recovery cannot begin until the addict acknowledges powerlessness over his or her compulsion to use substances and/or engage in specific destructive behaviors. Twelve-step sponsors help program participants acknowledge their powerlessness over their addictions and relinquish their relationship with the substance or behavior with which they have been struggling, and so begin life anew. Within the 12-step frame of reference, discussions about power focus on the relationship between the addict and the source of the addiction.

Social justice sponsors, on the other hand, identify all the ways power affects personal, social, and work relationships at every level as the fundamental interpersonal/intergroup dynamic. Sponsors emphasize how human differences such as race, gender, class, and sexual orientation have been manipulated to create hierarchies of privilege and oppression. Discussions on power within a social justice frame of reference emphasize the benefits in leveling these hierarchies and encourage action aimed at spreading equality within human relationships. A social justice sponsor supports the recovery process but requires accountability at multiple levels. For example, the addiction is *not* prioritized over domestic violence or child abuse. A social justice sponsor would bring both issues into a single healing circle.

A lesbian mother in recovery was sent to therapy for committing domestic violence against her partner. When given the power and control wheels to assess domestic violence, she became enraged over our "misuse of the language of power and control." Dramatically, she fell to the floor at the feet of one of the circle members and screamed, "I have *no* power. Do you see this arrangement? My partner has all the power. I'm the addict!" Accustomed to the 12-step language, she viewed herself as the victim; she was unable to see that as the offender of domestic violence, she held much of the power against her partner, who was the victim.

Rules of confidentiality and privacy are also handled differently in the social justice model and the 12-step model. Except in the case of victims of domestic violence, in the social justice model, sponsors encourage an open system of communication. In group interactions, sponsors encourage and participate in challenging dialogue and inquiry. On the other hand, 12-step sponsors uphold the notion of no "cross-talk" in their AA group meetings.

Male and female social justice sponsors have developed a critical consciousness and always work to balance the relational context of gender, race, class, and sexual orientation, issues that are not in the domain of an AA sponsor. Unlike some 12-step programs, there is no rigid hierarchy between sponsors and newer clients in the social justice model. Sponsors continue to work on their own issues in the same circles as the newer clients. This approach creates an open and flexible identity for the sponsors. Also, in the cultural context model, newer members of the client community are offered multiple sponsors, rather than just one, with whom to connect, which increases the potential for creative solutions.

These approaches are different, but they are not incompatible. Clients involved in a social justice approach may also be involved in a 12-step program and have the support of sponsors from each. A more focused approach to the addiction may be necessary in addition to dealing with therapeutic issues in a social justice approach.

CULTURAL CONSULTANTS

Cultural consultants are sponsors with expertise in a particular aspect of a client's life that is causing anguish or harm. They are people invited to participate in a session because of a unique perspective or skill they can offer (e.g., a policeman, a clergy member, a person of a particular race, ethnicity, or religion). In one case, a 28-year-old, single African American male was excommunicated from the Jehovah's

Witnesses because he engaged in sexual thoughts. A cultural consultant from the same faith, but holding a less patriarchal and punitive religious ideology, was invited in to meet with him and his father. The consultant was able to offer compassionate coaching to this distraught man who had lost his community. He helped him connect with other men of the same faith who shared how they dealt with their sexual desires in a manner acceptable to the church elders. The coaching helped him to reconcile his faith—which was very important to him—with his very human sexual needs and to find a way to reenter his faith community without shame.

Cultural consultants are invited to represent progressive values on behalf of religious organizations, ethnic and cultural communities, and other identity groups. For example, we have found that when a husband asserts that he will not permit his wife to work outside of the home because his fundamentalist minister preaches against this practice, the most effective voice to challenge this assertion is a minister from the same community of faith who holds more egalitarian views. The minister joins the therapy session as a cultural consultant and describes his own interpretations of scripture and his endorsement of a broader range of family patterns. During and after such a conversation, male sponsors from the same or a related faith can reinforce the minister's egalitarian views on gender. The client receives a powerful reference point, rooted in his own cultural and spiritual framework, that competes with the oppressive perspective he originally held.

Similarly, when a female client asserts that the tradition of forced marriage or forced childbearing of sons is part of her culture, we bring in women and men from similar cultural backgrounds to offer different, more expanded perspectives. Corporate executives who promote a reasonable balance between work and life can provide invaluable assistance as cultural consultants when working with clients whose work ethic leaves no room for family, home, and community. Relatives, community members, and clergy who are accepting of GLBT persons can be included in sessions with parents who are struggling to accept the sexual orientation of their gay or lesbian child. Ideally, we try to find someone of the same ethnic and religious background who is accepting of gays and lesbians, perhaps the parent of a gay or lesbian child who went through a process of acceptance and then became an advocate for queer issues. For parents struggling with the process of acceptance, this supportive environment allows them to examine oppressive religious doctrine and cultural taboos.

Liberation theologians—clergy persons who see their religious mission as ending oppressions of all kinds—can offer alternative views and interpretations of religious doctrine to people struggling to find their place. A white, Christian, battered woman considers leaving her marriage to protect herself and her son but is deterred when her church instructs her that it is an article of faith to stay with her batterer. Only through benevolent reinterpretations of scripture is she able to discover a faith that is kind to women, men, and children.

On another occasion, we invited a liberation theologist to reinterpret the suicide of a mother with seven children. The priest who had presided at the funeral services described suicide as a sin and prayed for the mother's soul. This pronouncement by the priest was devastating to her children, including her then 15-year-old daughter, who was now our 30-year-old client. The liberation theologist who was invited to participate in the session countered the original priest's punitive interpretation by reading numerous passages from the Bible recounting Christ's kindness toward people who are suffering.

While challenging oppressive traditions, cultural consultants affirm all the positive aspects of the group they represent. Cultural consultants differ from sponsors because their role within the therapeutic process is narrower in focus. Their input provides specific expertise regarding religion, ethnicity, regional background, professions, organizations, and other entities. Cultural consultants come into the therapeutic process as special guests who may or may not establish an ongoing connection to the client family. Sponsors, on the other hand, offer an ongoing mentoring relationship designed to broaden the client family's definitions of men, women, and fairness across all life spheres.

REFERENCE

Einstein, A. (1954). Albert Einstein quotes on humanity/society. http://www.spaceandmotion.com/Albert-Einstein-Quotes.

CHAPTER SEVEN

CHILDREN: SEEDS OF CHANGE

The strongest lesson I can teach my son is the same lesson I teach my daughter: how to be who he wishes to be for himself. And this means how to move to that voice from within himself, rather than to those raucous, persuasive, or threatening voices from outside, pressuring him to be what the world wants him to be.

—Audre Lorde (1995)

In this chapter, we look at children. We examine how diversity shapes their experiences and perspectives and how therapists respond to them.

We explore

- The literature on child development.
- Interdependent self-in-context as an organizing concept.
- Theory and intervention strategies that advance social justice as a primary aspect of healing.

A LOOK AT THE LITERATURE

Many classic theories of personality development promote the idea that successful maturation means adopting patterns that are prized by white, male, middle-class, heterosexual Americans. Maturity is defined in terms of independence, autonomy, striving for status within social hierarchy, and the primacy of thought over emotion (as though the two can really be disentangled). In this context, it is useful to critically evaluate all theories of personality development by asking some hard questions.

1. How do these theories address differences in gender, race, ethnicity, and sexual orientation? Do these theories deal with the power dynamics that usually accompany these differences?

2. Do these theories affirm or challenge mainstream values that identify societal norms with white people, males, heterosexuals, people of middle- or upper-class backgrounds, and Christians? Do they disempower—even pathologize—people of color, females, queers, people with disabilities, poor and working-class people, and non-Christians?
3. What aspects of these theories must be changed to accurately reflect the situation of people of all backgrounds?

Sigmund Freud's work has been criticized for devaluing women and misrepresenting children. Freud's critics offer insight into the political basis for his perspectives. Masson (1993), for example, asserts that Freud chose to report stories of childhood seduction as fantasies rather than actual transgressions, which demonstrated a lack of courage and an accommodation to male authority and power at the expense of women and children.

In his analysis of Freud's representation of race and gender, Gilman (1993) argues that as a Jew in a violently anti-Semitic world, Freud may have dealt with anxiety about his own social standing and thereby projected it onto other cultural "inferiors," including women. Therapists should keep these points in mind when considering psychodynamic hypotheses about women and children, and they should be wary of Freud's tendency to blame victims in general, females and mothers in particular.

Erik Erikson echoed Freud's insistence that maturation involves leaving our mothers and fathers behind. He claimed that healthy coming of age is defined by achieving autonomy and independence from our families of origin. His theories of human development, which are still widely used in training and clinical practice, promote competitive, hierarchical behavior over collaboration in children. Erikson's theory specifically devalues the development of communication and relational skills in favor of autonomy and self-assertion. His developmental stages do not account for variations across cultures (Rogoff, 2003).

While Erikson recognized that the self-concept and self-esteem of minority children is significantly affected by the stigma of membership in a devalued ethnic group, he did not incorporate this recognition into his developmental theory. A social justice ethic would incorporate these major differences into a theoretical framework.

Erikson's (1963; 1969) writings on Gandhi and the origins of militant nonviolence reflects his understanding of the evolution of human development and colonial oppression within other cultures. This work also displays a detailed understanding of the Indian life cycle (dharma), including differences for men and women, and reflects his own efforts to embrace an Indian spirituality. Erikson did not, however, incorporate his culturally expanded perspectives on gender into his developmental theory, an omission that raises many questions about the disconnection between his personal evolution and his expectation for others.

We encourage therapists to think of ways that Erikson's contributions can be augmented by recognizing differences linked to gender and race socialization, cultural differences, wealth, and the challenges associated with oppression. We also encourage therapists to ponder the circularity of human development because, for better or worse, most of us revisit developmental stages repeatedly across our life cycles.

Piaget and Inhelder (1969) proposed stages of physical and cognitive development. Piaget acknowledged the reciprocal contributions of environment and biological endowment. His theory posited four factors that he believed to strongly influence development:

1. Biology.
2. Interaction between the environment and cognitive structures.
3. Interactions between individuals and their social context that are universal for all societies.
4. Social, cultural, and educational factors that vary across societies.

Cross-cultural examinations of Piaget's theory have shown that there are limitations to its universal applicability (Cross, 1991; Nyiti, 1976). For example, differences in cultural and environmental factors for children in Africa and the United States significantly alter concept formation across the two populations (Hale-Benson, 1988; Ochs, 1996). The cultural and environmental differences are evident in play and relationship activities, language acquisition (fluency in several languages for African children versus monolinguism for American children), patterns of illness and nutrition, and rituals and religious beliefs.

Rogoff (1996; 2003) showed that different cultural communities expect children to engage in the same activities at vastly different times in childhood and may regard other "timetables of development" as surprising or even dangerous. For example, some cultures expect 9- and 10-year-old boys to assist their families in gathering food and repairing their homes and yards. The idea that boys of this age should focus on their schoolwork, and not participate in shared adult caretaking, raises the concern that these boys are not being socialized into eventually caring for their families.

Similarly, girls are expected at very young ages to care for other siblings and assist their mothers in domestic duties. The early socialization around caretaking of family and community certainly has great benefit for boys. In contrast, socialization that promotes self-actualization would greatly benefit girls and balance the relational field.

Cross-cultural studies on formal operational thinking reveal differences among Asian, Eskimo, and non-European cultures (Dasen, 1977). Studies also point to the strong influence of child-rearing practices on preschool philosophy and curriculum development. In technologically advanced societies, cultural tasks require a fairly high degree of formal operational thinking, making this type of thinking valuable.

In contrast, cultural tasks in other societies may not require much formal operational thinking, making it less highly valued or promoted. Studies that compare childrearing and socialization patterns in Japan, China, Uganda, and the United States challenge U.S. cultural biases and raise many questions about American child-rearing practices (Tobin, Wu, & Davidson, 1989). In Japan, the intertwining and intermixing of Shinto, Buddhism, and Christianity for over a century has created a rich tapestry of spiritual and philosophical thought that has had a profound impact on the nature of preschools.

These studies also describe the prevalence in many Asian cultures of what, by American standards, would be considered excessive indulgence and overprotection of children, the relinquishing of independent thinking in deference to authority, and the extreme priority given to communal success over personal achievement.

The New Zealand early years curriculum *Te Whariki* has created a positive *framework* for children. The ministry of education in New Zealand implemented this, and it was published by Drummond in 1996. *Whariki* in the Maori language means traditional woven mats with an infinite variety of patterns. The *guidelines* imagine the early childhood curriculum as such a mat, woven from the principles, aims, and goals defined in early education curriculum. The Whariki *framework* defines the objectives for early childhood education in New Zealand as follows:

- Well-being: The health and well-being of children are protected and nurtured.
- Belonging: Children and their families feel a sense of belonging.
- Contribution: Opportunities for learning are equitable, and each child's contribution is valued.
- Communication: The languages and symbols of children's own and other cultures are promoted and protected.
- Exploration: Children learn through active exploration of the environment.

In the United States, it would be difficult for educators to apply this conceptual framework of early childhood education because of deeply opposing values. The emphasis on learning and achievement in early education revolves around mathematics, English, and science rather than belonging, knowing, and contributing. The curricular approach in the United States focuses on acquiring textual knowledge rather than on principles and value of life.

This approach fails to examine the nature of multiple identities among racially diverse children and youth. It also fails to incorporate all of the positive ways children and youth bridge competing and conflicting messages about racial and cultural ways of being.

A social justice framework in childhood development and education attends to the interaction of school environments, community and family contexts, and identity development. Students and practitioners can assist children and youth from diverse backgrounds in developing positive, multifaceted self-concepts that contribute to their social and emotional development and self-esteem in school. Promoting positive interethnic relations requires that schools invest in comprehensive multicultural education curriculum that fosters understanding and appreciation of ethnic diversity and promotes interethnic relations. This school-based literacy creates spaces for children to develop along multiple paths. Schools can become important bridges for the development of belonging, connection, caretaking, and embracing multiple identities.

Cultural prescriptions, particularly when taken to extremes, can sometimes lead to problems. As noted in other chapters, all cultures contain some traditions that are hurtful, abusive, and even violent. The emphasis on extreme thinness as a sign of feminine beauty is one example from mainstream U.S. culture. The practice of genital mutilation in many West African societies provides another.

Similarly, some cultural practices taken to the extreme—particularly the equal and just development of girls and boys—can seriously impede child development. The rigid socialization of Japanese children, especially boys, toward success and productivity has produced increasing numbers of young Japanese men diagnosed with an agoraphobic type disorder. Many of these young men stop socializing or studying entirely. They remain isolated in their rooms, some coming out only to eat with the family, while others won't even do that. They often present with no motivation to launch and become self-sufficient. Japanese society's rigid demand that men perform and succeed is considered to be largely responsible for this tragedy.

This phenomenon among young men in Japan exemplifies their lack of differentiation of self. Healthy differentiation of self involves working to achieve one's own desires while also respecting the rights of others to do the same. It means not focusing exclusively on one's self nor entirely accepting the cultural practices put forth by the larger community.

While Freud, Erikson, Piaget, and other "classic" theorists continue to contribute to our understanding of child and adult development, a social justice perspective calls on us to evaluate and transform the ways that any theory, classic or new, supports white male dominance, mainstream male values, and power as "power over" rather than "power with." Therapists practicing from a social justice framework challenge themselves to take what's useful in each theory and expand it so that it affirms the experiences and values of people across the spectrum of gender, race, sexual orientation, class, and other human differences. Creating systems of empowerment and accountability that include diverse families and schools is critical to the well-being of our next generation.

Multicultural theorists recognize human differences as the primary foundation for inquiry rather than an "add-on" consideration. In her discussion of gender schema theory, Sandra Bem (1993) describes a generalized readiness on the part of children to encode and organize information according to their culture's definitions of maleness and femaleness. She emphasizes that gender identities vary across cultures.

While Gilligan has been criticized for working largely with upper-middle-class clients emphasizing biology (sex) over gender socialization, and more recently for lack of rigorous research standards, she and her colleagues demonstrated the major gaps between formulations designed for male children and those developmental life-cycle issues relevant to female children. Gilligan considers justice and caring as critical components for mature moral development. Caring for "other" while also safeguarding fairness to "self," in her view, are central to the development of a moral presence and the experience of justice (Gilligan, Lyons, & Hammer, 1990; Gilligan, Rogers, & Tolman 1991; Gilligan, Ward, Taylor, & Bardige, 1988). Gilligan and her colleagues did not articulate gender as a social construct.

Ou & McAdoo (1993); Powell, Yamamoto, Romero, and Morales (1983); Ramirez and Castaneda (1974); and De Anda (1984) elaborate on many of the gaps in Gilligan's work and describe the adaptation patterns of children who straddle two cultures. The key contributions of this research point to the social adaptability of identity formation across diverse cultures. In fact, the scholarship of multiple identity formation considers not only two but multiple cultures and contexts that many children navigate. In a study of children ages 4 to 7, Ou & McAdoo (1993) found that upper-class children in African American and Chinese communities preferred to identify with their own race more frequently than did lower-class children from the same communities. Information regarding race preference was obtained from questions regarding whom respondents felt closest to, whom they would prefer to be like, and with whom they would like to play.

Cole, Cole, and Lightfoot (2005) identified poverty as the most pernicious factor affecting a child's intellectual, social, and emotional development. In the United States, one in four children lives in poverty, which is associated with disproportionate risks for major illnesses, mental health problems, and school difficulties (Kaul, 2002). Others have suggested that the economic privilege and education of parents are critical elements in buffering children struggling to succeed. (Ogbu, 1981; 1988)

Havighurst (1976) focuses on how a black child's acquiescence to upper-middle-class norms might be more reflective of a process of submission than healthy development. Because of the impact of racism, assimilating to the norms of a white society means having to give up much of one's own connections to race and culture, which becomes evident in style of speech, dress, music, communication, and social distance from one's community. African American youth who succeed in suburban schools often feel isolated from their peers.

We also see this pattern in work settings where a person of color, holding a position of authority, internalizes white norms of power and control and becomes unsupportive of other people of color when they face oppression related to race, gender, or sexual orientation.

> *In a consideration of social class as an ecological factor or set of forces in human development and behavior, ethnicity always stands at the side of the stage, ready to explain some of the phenomena, which cannot be understood by social class considerations alone. (Havighurst, 1976, p. 57)*

Havighurst's model suggests that in the United States ethnicity outweighs social class for upper-middle-class Jewish, Japanese, and Chinese Americans. By comparison, he suggests that for blacks, Southern and Eastern Europeans, and Latinos/Latinas, social class overrides ethnicity.

Hale-Benson (1986) argues against these findings for African Americans. She suggests that class, defined mostly by income and occupation in mainstream America, does not reflect the larger context of socialization which, for African Americans, flows through belief systems and values across several generations. For example, African American children from an upper-middle-class nuclear family frequently receive much of their socialization from extended family members who would be considered working or lower class.

Hale-Benson (1986) describes the following patterns as typical of many African American families and their children in all social classes:

- Sociocentric view of the world. Considering the whole instead of the parts.
- Language with a wide use of coined interjections and use of Black language.
- Expression of self through affective use of body language. Systematic use of nuances and intonation such as eye movement and positioning. A preference for spontaneity.
- Reliance on words that depend upon context for meaning, resulting in a preference for inferential reasoning rather than deductive or inductive reasoning.
- Preference for oral-aural modalities for learning rather than "word" dependency in communication.
- Tendency toward altruism, a sense of justice, and a preferred focus on people and their activities rather than on things. (p. 43)

In contrast, Asian cultures emphasize the following values in their child rearing

- Cultural belonging that values connections to others.
- Emphasis on tolerance and nonviolence.
- Reliance on symbols that define context and communicate hierarchy.
- Willingness to cooperate prioritized above pursuing self-defined goals.
- Loyalty towards family and culture.

It is important to emphasize Hale-Benson's contributions to the child development literature on the range of learning styles. She challenges the convention of single dimension teaching methodology (i.e., curriculum that favor universal learning styles towards the goals standard educational literacy. This launches the necessary critique of current educational systems and their role in educating a diverse population. It also challenges child development theorists about the diverse pathways of learning, accessibility to learning, and achievement, measured. Though Hale-Benson conducted her research in the mid-1980s, it is still widely referenced in the 21st century (Rogoff, 2003).

The kaleidoscope of human diversity, with its broad and nuanced differences reflected in the research, and the power differentials embedded within these contexts require us to focus on the ethic of fairness and to challenge the assumptions that guide our assessments and practice. For example, we must remember that the concept of achievement as a discrete end point largely reflects a Eurocentric worldview (Momsen & Kinnaird, 1993). The highly structured and competitive system used to measure individual achievement in classrooms may contradict a student's cultural and community values, creating an enormous identity conflict. Development can be measured by more than intellectual performance, analytical reasoning ability, and demonstration of autonomy and self-determination.

The intellectual tasks that North American and European theorists, such as Piaget, delineated as indicators of maturity are narrow and often do not adequately

■ ■ ■ ■ ■

CASE 7.1

CHIN FINDS HIS PLACE IN LANGUAGE ARTS CLASS

Chin, a 10-year-old African American–Korean boy, is referred to treatment because, for several weeks, he has seemed depressed and highly distractible in the classroom. He speaks Korean fluently but has a strong identification with African American culture. The school wants to have him tested. Chin's parents disagree.

In assessing Chin's school-related behavior, his family reports that he is fine at home and in community life (church, recreation, extended family), as well as in most of his classes, except for language arts. Currently, his language arts class is learning to analyze classical music, but he seems distracted and has great difficulty participating with a group of mostly white children.

Because he is one of only three minority kids in a class of 24, the treatment team thinks that Chin might not be familiar with classical music and suggests that his teachers experiment by introducing music that will be more familiar to him. When hip-hop music is introduced, he becomes an animated and enthusiastic participant. The other children are also more enthusiastic, preferring this music to classical music.

The children who are less familiar with hip-hop perform less well. However, they develop a greater interest in music they apparently aren't permitted to listen to at home. The school develops a respectful, balanced curriculum featuring a mixture of music genres.

capture the rich possibilities of a child's development. For example, collaboration as a value and skill receives little attention within mainstream American schools, and European American students tend to get easily frustrated in complex social situations where they are unable to reach individual goals. Korean American children, by contrast, are encouraged to engage in more cooperative play (Best & Williams, 1997; Bloch, 1989; Farver, Kim, & Lee, 1995).

Case 7.1 illustrates that intelligence certainly goes beyond what can be measured by IQ tests. Intelligence also includes proficiency with language and communication, music and dance, bodily kinesthetic movement, logic, and social skills.

Children's development proves to be more multidimensional than many theories have indicated. Children's competencies are not milestones that are reached individually but rather accomplishments that evolve within a complex web. The constraints of a particular social context necessarily circumscribe a child's acquisition of cognitive, communicative, motivational, social, emotional, and affective skills. Our evaluation of these abilities becomes most meaningful when these constraints are considered.

Moreover, mainstream standards for successful achievement often disempower children from communities of color by narrowly defining standards of achievement. These narrowly defined conventions rarely consider the multiple cultural and social contexts of a child's life or the child's access to or lack of supportive resources. (Almeida, Woods, & Messineo, 1998).

According to Rouse, Brooks-Gunn, and McLanahan (2005), we can ultimately close the racial and ethnic gaps in educational outcomes by attending to essential aspects of children's lives before they enter school. Such aspects include health, socioeconomic status, environmental hazards, parenting and familial stress, and genetics. When 3- and 4-year-olds have access to high-quality early-childhood education, it has a marked effect on later learning. Providing children with healthy nutrition, a safe environment, and nurturing and caring adults is an investment in their academic future and emotional well-being.

Clunis and Green (1988) describe the strategy of "armoring"—building up a protective shield—as a critical adaptation to racial intolerance for minority children and their parents. For African American parents, this adaptive process, which could be described as racial socialization, is an integral part of child rearing and supports healthy maturity. Many children from upper-class backgrounds who live with two high-achieving parents do not always get the racial and cultural armoring necessary to exist and thrive in racist school systems. Dominant developmental theories do not acknowledge the critical contribution of racial socialization (Taylor-Gibbs, & Huang, 1989).

Latisha, an African American woman recalls her mother's advice:

> *My mother would always remind me to be on my best behavior when I was out with my friends. She would say, "You're not like your white friend Mary. You will not get away with anything, but a white girl will get off easy. Your punishment will be much harsher. Black people are treated differently because of the color of their skin."*

For children of color, dealing with and combating racism involves a lifelong struggle, one that is aided by parental, familial, and community support. But gay, lesbian, transgendered, and bisexual (GLTB) children, as a group, typically cannot count on anything like the collective backing available to young members of other minority groups. Queer children and adolescents, whatever their color, often live in families that openly promote homophobia and contain no GLTB role models. In such an environment, coming out may lead to the loss of all supportive connections. Queer children are rarely "armored" by their parents and communities to defend themselves against psychological assaults. Families often use the same kinds of coercive and controlling measures as those employed by society at large to maintain the invisibility of their gay or lesbian members.

> *A Latina mother reacted to her daughter's coming out by saying, "My whole life has been a struggle to try to protect you from bad men. Maybe it is a punishment from God that I shall have no grandchildren."*

When GLBT children are buttressed by family and community and have to rely entirely on internal resources, they may be able to draw strength and support from successful queer role models and gay icons from popular culture like Elton John, Billie Jean King, Ru Paul, Boy George, and many others. Like children from racially and culturally mixed communities, GLBT children must navigate a complex web of challenges which are rarely mentioned in classic developmental theories.

Studies indicate that early aspirations are equally high among most children regardless of their race, social class, culture, gender, sexual orientation, or religion. But the aspirations of children of color decline as they discover the negative messages the broader culture associates with their racial, personal, familial, and cultural selves (Majors & Billson, 1992). For many individuals, this collision of personal aspirations and societal prejudices occurs as they enter preschool at age 4 or 5. Even a strong and healthy family context cannot entirely offset these external pressures from the dominant, outside world. This is a powerful example of why we always need to situate children within their multiple contexts.

RECOGNIZING MULTIPLE IDENTITIES

A social justice perspective recognizes that negotiating multiple, often contradictory, identities is a complex process for culturally diverse school-aged children. Social, cultural, and political factors unique to their backgrounds influence the process of identity development and the extent to which children and youth balance the values of the dominant culture and their family culture (Cross, 1991). Since the competing values are often more complex than simply home versus school or single-parent home versus remarried parent home, students may choose to embrace multiple ethnicities and identities or may find safety in forming a cohesive self. Therefore, social justice practitioners should work with educators to avoid pressuring children to adapt to a norm and adopt a single identity. Instead, they should acknowledge and accept multiple identities in students without prioritizing one over the other and encourage students to appreciate their own variegated cultural heritage and norms.

Social justice students and practitioners can promote empowerment in their work with children and families by creating and supporting school and community programs that buttress racial and cultural pride. They may, for example, organize or sponsor

- Motivational speaking events and presentations by accomplished young men and women from racial, cultural, and sexual minority groups.
- Cultural events that emphasize and affirm movies, music, and traditions of marginalized groups.
- Educational programs for parents that build critical consciousness regarding the media's acceptance of white, male, heterosexual privilege. These programs can also teach parents how to help their children build such critical consciousness.
- Programs that offer parents strategies to help their children integrate all of their identities.

Programs like these can help participants recognize the many, sometimes subtle, forms of institutionalized racism and can make people of color more aware of how they may unconsciously accept and internalize self-deprecation. It is also very important to ensure that such programs acknowledge and embrace the differing identities of boys and girls and the multiple identities of both sexes embedded in complex and varying cultural contexts.

TOWARD AN INTERDEPENDENT SELF-IN-CONTEXT

Through socialization related to race, gender, class, culture, and sexual orientation, every society creates an environment within which individuals learn behaviors, beliefs, values, and ways of relating to others. Individuals are expected to demonstrate these behaviors, beliefs, and values throughout their lives. The result is a continuously evolving experience of self that we call the *interdependent self-in-context*. Most of daily life is embedded in and dependent on connections with others. Community life is crucial to the wholeness of self.

Loss—manifested through illness, death, being uprooted across oceans or continents, and societal discrimination—also shapes identities. The ordeals experienced and the stories crafted to make sense of these losses shape the lives of children, families, and societies and profoundly influence how we navigate the world, share time and resources, negotiate, and communicate. Sometimes the tales highlight strength and resilience. Often, they emphasize the extent of suffering.

At the core of an interdependent self-in-context is maturity, characterized by an identity that expands beyond restrictive and oppressive gender and cultural prescriptions. Kivel (1992; 1996), and others have shown how, for white males, classic standards for healthy maturity, centering on autonomy and independence, contribute to emotional emptiness, isolation, and a multitude of dilemmas in intimate relationships. Kivel describes the yearning of many men to leave a different legacy to their sons, one that links autonomy to collaboration within a network of mutually nurturing interpersonal connections.

We agree with Kivel that maturity extends beyond autonomy and self-determination and includes embracing interdependence with one another and with nature. Starting from our social justice perspective, we also believe that tolerance lies at the center of maturity.

In our view, maturity in its broadest sense includes

■ Affirmation of one's self while simultaneously accepting differences in others.
■ Maintaining one's values and beliefs while relating generously to others.
■ Nondefensive mindfulness regarding one's place in history and within the current global community. Remembering, for example, that Native American tribes lived in communities across most of North America and that African Americans were brought here as slaves. Remembering that one nation's interests should not override the rights of another nations' people—a refutation of "might makes right."

Tolerance embraces difference. Within the context of childhood development, tolerance acknowledges the disparity that exists among children from different racial, gender, class, and cultural backgrounds. We believe it's important to address this disparity through a conscious sharing of resources and linking of individuals across boundaries of difference.

It is common that parents who bring their children to therapy do not want them to be grouped with children who seem more problematic or too different. Parents in the middle of a divorce, for example, might want their children to be seen only with other children from divorced or divorcing homes. A white family might bring adolescent daughters who are engaged in violence and substance abuse to therapy but are shocked when their daughters join a therapeutic circle that includes young African American and Latino boys dealing with similar issues.

A social justice approach challenges this segregation as an impediment to the healing process. Allowing children to build connections to one another across different races, genders, and ethnicities builds tolerance and also accentuates their helpfulness to one another. The sharing of resources, including the sharing of the bonds they develop, builds accountability for everyone involved. The benefits of connecting "different" children to one another deserves more attention than it has received in therapeutic literature.

Trust, the experience of safety and support within one's home and community, and a welcoming rather than dominating approach to difference, is also essential to developing a healthy interdependent self-in-context. Infants and toddlers begin to develop trust in their immediate environment, which, ideally, supports their safety and development. Developing trust involves orienting to one's cultural group and its position in the world.

Developing trust is more difficult for those who come from stigmatized groups. When a child of color or one who is disabled develops a sense of basic trust, that child has accomplished something more remarkable than a white, able-bodied child who arrives at the same degree of trust. Collaboration and respect are also essential to creating a healthy interdependent self-in-context. Sharing efforts, resources, and power with others demonstrates collaboration. Respect is demonstrated through actions that nurture self, home, and community, as well as relationships with those who are different from us.

Respect for different styles is a hallmark of mature interdependence (Chisolm, 1996). Children benefit from exposure to different sounds, smells, toys, dolls, games, books, food, and people. They also benefit from exposure to a variety of learning styles. Recognizing and valuing many styles enhances the valuing of self and others and promotes communication across differences. One view of the continuum of learning styles locates analytical/rational types (mostly boys) at one end and relational/emotional types (mostly girls) at the other. We assign importance to helping children (and adults) develop flexibility in understanding and relating to others across gender and cultural styles.

For example, we encourage a girl who prides herself on helping others to also focus on identifying, sharing, and receiving assistance with her difficulties. We encourage a white boy to listen to others, provide thoughtful feedback, and describe his own difficulties in a respectful and nonblaming manner. We encourage a minority child to describe how respect is a necessary and valuable part of communication within family life, thereby elevating the notion of respect over self-centeredness.

Baumrind (1980) identifies three primary parenting styles: authoritarian, authoritative, and permissive. Authoritarian parents tend to produce children who are withdrawn, are other-directed, and lack social competence and curiosity. Children of authoritative parents are likely to be self-reliant, self-controlled, curious about the world around them, and basically content with life. The children of permissive parents demonstrate poor impulse control, relative immaturity, and inordinate dependence on others.

From a social justice perspective, we are interested in using these styles less as a vehicle for assessing the relative health or pathology of individual parents and more as a framework for helping parents understand the needs of children and how best to meet those needs. The complex demands of parenting exact an especially heavy toll on single parents. They benefit from being included in therapeutic circles that connect them to other single parents and two-parent families who can share and exchange expertise and resources.

Behavioral styles shape our interaction with the world. These styles shape how we use language and writing. They affect our choices in music, dance, religion, art, work, leisure activities, problem-solving approaches, sports, and other avenues of self-expression. Our behavioral styles link us to our own cultural groups and distinguish us from those who are different, making every style relevant and important to the functioning of a diverse society.

White children are born into a world that, in general, reflects their own image, affirming their styles across all dimensions of expression. For example, most of the children featured in books, movies, and television shows are white. Silvern and colleagues (1984) describe the vulnerability of young children because of their limited ability to distinguish reality from distortions promoted by trusted adults. In one study, children of mixed races and genders were asked about the race of the "real" Santa Claus. After viewing images of a black Santa, they reported that he was black.

In order to promote the development of an interdependent self-in-context, we find it helpful to ask children, regardless of their presenting problems, to bring in pictures and stories of children who are different from them. We ask them to discuss the similarities and differences. This bridging of narratives provides a context within which presenting concerns can be addressed through connection rather than compartmentalization.

BRINGING A SOCIAL JUSTICE PERSPECTIVE ON CHILD DEVELOPMENT INTO THE THERAPY ROOM

We suggest that therapeutic work with children, as with adults, include raising critical consciousness and creating systems of empowerment and accountability. The developmental chart (Table 7.1) provides a summary of classic developmental expectations compared with transformational expectations. This chart will assist

TABLE 7.1   Classic and Transformational Developmental Expectations

AGE IN YEARS	TRADITIONAL THEORY* DEVELOPMENTAL TASKS (No Gender or Race Differentiation)	DEVELOPMENTAL TASKS DIFFERENTIATED BY GENDER AND RACE		
		Boys	Girls	Children of Color
0–1	Develop trust Overcome fear of new situations	Learn that men are also nurturing and trustworthy as caretakers Learn that caretaking by men does not mean abandonment by women	Learn to expect fathers to be equally as nurturing as mothers Learn that caretaking by men does not mean abandonment by women	Appreciate and value your own cultural group Begin to identify with cultural group through exposure to toys, dolls, games, music, foods, and books that represent own cultural background
1–3	Increase motor skills Learn that behavior is self-determined Develop autonomy Decrease self-doubt Assert self Learn gender roles	Express sadness Learn that it is okay to cry Learn cooperative play Delay gratification	Engage in both traditional male and female play Express anger Learn nonverbal symbols of power Develop trust of own intuition	Recognize your difference Begin to negotiate between two worlds (white world and the world of one's own culture or race)
3–5	Develop initiative Separate self from others Identify with heroes Recognize own power Learn to compete Learn respect for authority	Begin to define self through connection rather than achievements Begin to feel rather than act on feelings Allow others, especially girls, to take leadership roles in play Learn respect for females Recognize heroines	Express pride in accomplishments Begin to be clear about needs and wants Increase leadership in group play Determine and assert degree of physical and emotional closeness in relationships Identify with heroines and heroes	Develop pride in cultural identity and race Identify with powerful heroes and heroines of color Learn to protect self in racist society

*Traditional Theory from Kohlberg and Erikson   *(continued)*

TABLE 7.1 (continued)

| 5–12 | Recognize accomplishments
Master new skills
Seek approval from adults
Develop peer attachments
Increase interests outside of family
Maintain social order for its own sake
Concretely follow rules and regulations | Recognize power given to males and whites in society
Learn that this power can be destructive or constructive
Become more nurturing
Increase self-disclosure
Recognize and welcome difference in race, culture, and gender roles
Develop curiosity differences in race, culture, and gender roles
Begin to challenge norms that increase power of white males and decrease power of others | Recognize that females are granted less power in this society
Learn to take self seriously
Reassert power
Prioritize self
Contradict self-deprecation
Express and defend thoughts, ideas, and feelings
Expect to be listened to; speak out
Challenge traditional gender roles
Increase awareness of subordination
Counter experiences of subordination | Recognize power and privilege differentials between white people and people of color
Learn about history and heritage of your racial/cultural group
Verbalize feelings of difference and demand to be heard
Participate in activities that celebrate cultures marginalized by mainstream society
Counter experiences to increase awareness of subordination and rejection by society
Seek out safe places and opportunities for personal achievement |
| 12–18 | Develop identity
Begin to resolve conflicts about role in the world
Begin to consider occupational choices
Develop conscience
Learn to appeal to logic and consistency | Become more relational and less self-focused
Make choices that are more collaborative rather than self-serving
Build relationships based on caring and nurturance
Challenge sexism and racism in peers and self
Develop friendships with females, people of color, and GLTB people
Cultivate nonsexual relationships with females
Tolerate inconsistencies
Develop healthy curiosity and acquire knowledge about women and other cultures and races | Make choices that are more independent and self-serving
Learn to balance role overload
Begin to plan for economic independence (school, career)
Exercise leadership roles
Become clear and decisive regarding own values
Learn to love your body and to be in charge of your own sexuality
Develop curiosity and knowledge about other cultures and races | Acculturate (develop ways to fit into larger culture without losing one's own culture)
Make choices that strengthen your cultural identification
Take on leadership roles
Plan for economic independence (school, career) |

you in formulating interventions for children that challenge unfairness and create equity linked to gender, race, and culture.

Children's sense of security evolves through connection to and identification with those who care for them: mothers, fathers, siblings, nannies, baby-sitters, grandparents, aunts, uncles, and all the others who participate in their lives. Many theories of child development have ignored this rich context and instead have focused almost exclusively on the mother–child relationship. In many cultures throughout history, mothers have not always been the primary caretakers because they have been busy with other work. Grandparents and other elders, as well as older siblings, have filled that role.

When we overemphasize mothers, we ignore and invalidate the richness of the total environments in which children generally grow up. We also fall into sexist stereotyping. By expanding our lens, we can more realistically examine the characteristics that help children attain their full potential—and recognize the people who provide such help. We find it helpful to view all the connections within a child's life as part of the child's nurturing circle. Therapeutic work with children within culture circles takes full advantage of the learning adults can offer children as well as what children can offer one another. Therapy should include helping parents who are less connected (often fathers) to develop relational skills. For example, fathers are coached on how to talk more engagingly with children by using a softer voice and manner, sitting on the floor, or kneeling down to talk eye to eye.

Building Friendships across Difference

Case 7.2 is an example of how a children's culture circle might approach a discussion about friendships.

Experiences within such a culture circle teach children to reach across differences of age, gender, race, culture, and class. Together, they experience support from people of other ages, challenges to gender-role expectations, and truth telling. For example, boys in the group might be taught to prepare the group snacks, set the table attractively, and clean up. Girls may plan a group activity or establish rules for a game or discussion. While seemingly simple, these tasks, performed in a collective, powerfully impact traditional gender-role socialization. If Sally's difficulties continued at school, her parents would be coached to intervene with that system. If the school was unresponsive, therapists or sponsors would help to advocate on the family's behalf.

The ethical decision about when to intervene on a family's behalf depends on their ability to navigate systems and advocate in the face of adversity. Case 7.3 example involves a family that is unable to navigate systems on its own on behalf of its children. Using a social justice lens, you will see multilayered interventions designed to empower the family, hold the children's school accountable, and deliver results that further the academic progress and emotional well-being of the children. Investing in the academic entitlements of children is key to social justice.

This case highlights the importance of critical consciousness, empowerment, and accountability within the helping process. Sometimes people assume that just

■ ■ ■ ■ ■

CASE 7.2

FINDING NEMO AND FRIENDSHIP

Children of mixed ages, cultures, and genders gather together to watch movie clips designed to address the broad social justice implications of their presenting problems. The circle is composed of seven children—four girls and three boys—ranging in age from 4 to 12. The group is racially and economically diverse. Boys and girls are asked to describe in detail their daily activities and the skills required to perform those activities. Therapists then validate the skills and direct the children to borrow from one another in order to broaden their levels of adaptation and maturity.

The group then watches clips from the movie *Finding Nemo*, (Stanton & Unkrich, 2003) which tells the story of a father, Marlin, and his son, Nemo, both fish. Marlin loses Nemo, who has been scooped up by a diver. Although Marlin is overly cautious, he must search land and sea to find Nemo. He befriends another

fish, Dory. In order to be successful in his quest, Marlin must accept Dory's help and shore up his own courage. With her help, Marlin develops the courage and strength to find and recover Nemo. After watching the clips, the children discuss the qualities of friendship, the importance of friends, and the skills needed to make and keep friends.

Sally, a six-year-old only child of Italian American parents, achieves academically but has difficulty making friends. She describes her sadness at never finding friends to play with during recess. Shari, a 12-year-old African American boy, suggests that she ask one of the children in her class to play with her before recess begins. He likens it to making a play date. Her face beams. She thanks him and tells him she will try his suggestion. The children end the session by making friendship bracelets.

■ ■ ■ ■ ■

CASE 7.3

WHEN SCHOOLS COLLUDE IN MAKING MINORITY CHILDREN INVISIBLE

Salim is an African American man in his 50s. He is employed by the state as a sanitation worker. His second partner in life, Celia, who is Puerto Rican, doesn't work outside the home and has a restraining order against Salim. They have three daughters: Cara, 6; Lateesha, 9; and Sameera, 12. Salim has supervised visitation at the therapy center. Celia has two daughters—Kim, 21; and Lateesha, 19; from another partnership.

The children have had excessive absences during the two preceding school years, and the two older girls are failing most of their classes. Celia isn't in therapy and is preoccupied with another man and a new grandchild, Kim's daughter. She seriously neglects her three younger daughters.

The school intends to retain the girls, but there are no parent conferences, reports from the truant officer, or any larger system interventions regarding their neglect.

When Salim presented the situation, his men's group encouraged him to see that as their father, he needed to be consistently involved with the girls' education even though he doesn't have joint custody of the girls.

Social justice interventions require that the therapeutic team first gather information from all systems with which families have contact. In the specific case of urban schools, it is important to consider institutional bias, cultural misunderstandings, and potential teacher incompetence. The treatment team was concerned that the school seemed unaware of the multiple risk factors these children faced, such as the daily stresses of urban life, stress related to race, possible learning style differences, and a lack of cultural enrichment activities. The school had limited expectations for academic success of girls and children of color. This is not unlike many urban schools that are confronted with the challenges of complex social problems that children bring with them, when learning and educational goals are not always a priority.

The treatment team collected information about the school's protocols for children with excessive absences and failing grades. In addition, there were members of Salim's culture circle who were teachers and parents from high-performing school districts and knew about the rights of parents and children in the public schools.

Together, the culture circle, parents, and team planned an intervention. Salim and the therapist requested a conference with the principal, the guidance department, and the teachers. Their plan was to hold the school accountable for not having had a plan at the end of the last school year to address the failing path of Salim's children and to work with the school personnel to develop a course of action for the coming year.

In the first meeting, Salim and his white sponsors met with school personnel, who were defensive. They blamed the children for not completing work and for being tardy. They also blamed Salim and Celia for their noninvolvement and their inability to get the girls to school regularly and on time. Neither parent was informed that the children had not been turning in their homework. The father, Salim, had not been informed about the children's chronic tardiness by the school's truancy officer.

Family members must accept their own portion of responsibility for school problems, but in this case, the school failed Celia, Salim, and the girls through its lack of follow-through. The school is obligated to ensure that the girls get to school. It is obligated by law to report neglect and chronic absence. The school has leverage that could make a difference in the lives of these girls. It is also obligated to address the shortfalls of academic performance and propose options for academic achievement. During the meeting, the principal, who is also African American, tried to placate Salim without getting to the root of the problems. Finally, the school personnel agreed to a second meeting to create a plan to move forward, although they still wouldn't commit to providing remedial help or ability testing for the children.

After the second meeting, Salim, the therapist, and the sponsors sent a letter to all the school personnel who were present at the meetings and sent a copy to the superintendent. As a result of this letter and a third meeting, a plan of intervention was worked out to improve the girls' academic performance.

The school agreed to test the girls to determine their learning needs and provide the necessary academic support they needed. Moreover, the school agreed to begin remedial tutoring. The truancy office was directed to work with Celia on getting the girls to school regularly and on time. The results of the testing revealed that two of the three girls had learning disabilities and needed enriched learning opportunities. The school, knowing that it was being challenged by a cohort of this family's community, provided the rightful educational plan.

These improvements were achieved without legal intervention. While children might face this same dilemma in tax-rich school districts, families are able to use the legal system to get justice. In this case, justice was granted by a community of concerned citizens.

In the meantime, Salim is working to get joint custody so that he can be more consistently involved in the girls' lives. And the girls were brought into therapy and began participating in the children's culture circle. Efforts to enroll their mother into this program and AA continue.

---

*Social problems that children bring with them, and learning and educational goods are not always a priority.

because those in authority are of the same race as those seeking justice, fairness will prevail. Often this proves untrue. People of color who reach positions of authority may assume mainstream (racist) values in order to gain and keep positions of power. Others, as in Case 7.3, are fighting an uphill battle with institutional racism and tend to take the path of least resistance when advocating for children.

Moreover, the quality of education that children of color receive is often so inferior that even when children perform at the top of their classes in their own (segregated) schools, they find they need remedial classes in college just to bring them up to the level the rest of the students (Gay, 2000).

In the case of Salim, the social justice therapy consisted of education regarding the institutional bias and incompetence of the school system his children attended and he was coached to challenge the system and the specific people in power to get the school to be more proactive in helping his two daughters. This process also taught Salim to be a more effective parent. Sadly, Salim, as a working-class African American man, was never able to generate the same results on his own as his therapist and white sponsor, people with more power and privilege, could when they confronted the school.

Nonetheless, Salim's participation in this collaborative effort was empowering to him. Through it, with the help and guidance of the treatment team, he gained the confidence to demand meetings with school officials. In these meetings, he held the school accountable for its failure to educate his children and got the school to hold Celia, their mother, accountable for the attendance of their daughters. Salim also enrolled his daughters in therapy, where they received support and coaching in their culture circle, and he learned skills for effective parenting.

Because the circle members helped Salim in an area in which he felt deficient, he was less defensive when moving toward being accountable himself regarding his previous domestic abuse charges.

Affinity Counseling Group in New Brunswick, New Jersey provides a good example of the use of justice–based models of intervention with high-risk youth and their families.

The group works primarily with youth of color—many of whom are involved with the criminal justice system. Using a social justice approach to treatment, Affinity Counseling Group incorporates the following goals:

1. Building the youths' critical consciousness through dialogue, inquiry, and reflection of current music lyrics, art, and movie clips.
2. Using adult sponsors to model healthy adult relationships in family and community life. Sponsors become the bridge for youth between violence and nonviolence in urban community life. They partner with parents whose children are dead or incarcerated and help reconnect parents and siblings who are, or have been, incarcerated.
3. Engaging youth and their communities in civic participation and community re-integration through numerous social action projects such as, letter writing to local newspapers regarding police profiling of youth of color, meeting with school boards to challenge institutional bias, participating in white privilege conferences, and joining voter notification and registrations drives.

4. Creating partnerships with local social action groups aimed at academic opportunity and economic viability.
5. Creating safe, nonviolent, **physical borders** for youth through partnerships with sponsors, community members, religious leaders, and business leaders.
6. Offering information on health, nutrition, and medical access.
7. Helping youth generate safe income-earning opportunities and learning how to be responsible with their finances.

Children of Divorce

Researchers who study divorce typically define "good" and "bad" divorces. In a good divorce, parents sort through their differences and collaborate to promote the best interest of the children. Bad divorces, on the other hand, involve acrimonious negotiations (sometimes made extraordinarily difficult by a history of domestic violence or extreme gender inequity), custody battles, and questions about supervised or unsupervised visitation. Research substantiates that over time, children of divorce fare well as long as their parents do not engage in ongoing conflicts after the divorce, their lifestyle is not radically altered, and they do not lose connection with parents. In fact, many children report that their relationships with fathers actually improves after divorce (Ahrons, 2004; Furstenberg & Cherlin, 1991).

We have found it helpful for children going through the divorce of their parents to build connections with other children who are going through similar as well as different life experiences. In these groups, we work to validate and normalize the experiences of all the children and their adaptations to the many challenges they face.

As Weingarten (2003) eloquently writes, "Listening well, listening to allow the heart of another person's meaning to emerge even if that person does not fully or clearly appreciate what she knows is . . . the heart of empowerment" (p. 74). Weingarten emphasizes that instead of exposing the "sick context" that produces problems for adolescent girls, bestselling books end up pathologizing the girls who are the product of that context. She encourages therapists to "undermine these interpretations of young people as destructive or self-destructive" and instead to emphasize young people's creative "resistance to destructive conditions" (p. 74). The culture circle format provides an ideal forum for doing so. Children learn they are not alone in their concerns and are eager to empower one another and their family members as they grow in critical consciousness.

Case 7.4 recounts how a therapeutic team and a culture circle helped a brother and sister cope with confusion about their racial identity, difficulty with peer relationships, and abandonment issues.

When parents are separating, children benefit from therapists who help them gain comfort with the concrete changes that lie ahead, such as changes in living arrangements and visitation schedules. Children respond well to stories, films, and activities that depict these changes. When the circle watches a movie in which a divorce occurs and then discusses what happens, the children are able to detoxify the experience of divorce and all the changes and loss that go with it. Most children also find it helpful to identify and discuss advantages as well as disadvantages of the divorce.

■ ■ ■ ■ ■

CASE 7.4

KAHLID AND MINLEE ESTABLISH A PLACE AMONG THEIR PEERS

Jane, 35, is an African American single mother, divorced from her Chinese American husband. She has a 12-year-old son, Khalid; a 10-year-old daughter, Minlee; and 5-year-old son, Lamar. Jane and her children are practicing Jehovah's Witnesses. The father abandoned the family several years ago, and has not been heard from since.

Khalid and Minlee both had difficulty with peer relationships in school, being unable to break into either the black or Asian peer groups. Their religious affiliation did not allow them to participate in many celebrations, which ordinarily would provide points of social entry. Khalid was performing poorly in most of his classes. To deal with his bruised male pride, he would go on and on about his elevated status in the church, which did not endear him to his peers.

The therapeutic team approached the school on each child's behalf, suggesting that each be connected with mentors and peers who were a year older and could help them get more connected with their classmates. The team and sponsors also helped the school organize a celebration of biracial and bicultural students.

In therapy sessions, they discussed the loss of their father and their confusion about their racial identity. With the other children in their circle, they read books on cultural leaders and critiqued films together. They discussed the pain that Khalid, Minlee, and other members experienced when they did not fit neatly into one ethnic group. Most importantly, they celebrated the richness of their complex cultural identities.

Children of GLBT parents

Homophobia prevents many queer parents from coming out, which limits the accuracy of information available regarding the incidence of gay and lesbian parenting. But many kids are being raised in gay and lesbian households today. The National Adoption Information Clearinghouse, a service of the U.S. Administration for Children and Families, estimated that as of 1990, about 6 to 14 million children in the United States were being raised in gay and lesbian households. The American Psychological Association, the American Academy of Pediatrics, the National Association of Social Workers, and many other agencies agree that children of GLTB parents are as healthy, happy, and well adjusted as those raised by their heterosexual counterparts.

Children of GLBT parents also have similar responses on measures of gender identity, sexual orientation, intelligence, moral reasoning, behavioral problems, and a sense of connectedness with the world (Ariel & McPherson, 2000). There is no evidence that children are psychologically or physically harmed in any way by having GLBT parents. And, there is a lot of evidence that shows they are not. Gays and lesbians possess the same abilities as heterosexuals to nurture and provide stable homes (Stacey & Biblarz, 2001).

It is important that social justice workers arm themselves with information and statistics to counter mistaken notions about GLBT people as partners and as

■ ■ ■ ■ ■ ▬▬▬▬▬▬▬▬▬▬▬▬▬▬▬▬▬▬▬▬▬▬▬▬▬▬▬▬▬▬

CASE 7.5

A BIRACIAL GIRL FACES HER MOTHER'S DIVORCE AND COMING OUT

Susie, a 10-year-old biracial child with a Jewish mother and an African American father, had to deal with the divorce of her parents and her mother's coming out as a lesbian. Her father expressed his homophobia by buying Susie sexualized clothing, letting her watch adult-rated films, and generally adding to her fear of becoming gay.

When the mother and daughter came to the treatment center, Susie was invited to join a culture circle that included adolescents who were raised in racially mixed lesbian- and gay-parented families. She was also invited to read Rebecca Walker's *Black, White, and Jewish* (1995) and discuss her own complex identity. Walker's biography addresses the layered aspects of cel-

ebrating and questioning her biracial identity as the daughter of a Jewish–African American partnership.

Susie's participation in treatment was limited because her father denied consent. Susie learned, however, that being gay is not something one catches from breathing the air that GLBT people breathe or from embracing the love of a parent. She also learned from the other children of GLBT people in her circle that she has much to be proud of and to celebrate. She is part of a growing group of children from healthy and loving GLBT families who are expanding the understanding of what constitutes family and compassionate civic behavior.

parents. Rhetoric that equates GLBT persons with pedophiles or vilifies them as people and parents damages all of us. Social justice workers must work to correct false stereotypes and to rectify discrimination in all forms. Consider case 7.5.

"Gay bashing" is a frequent and cruel way for children and adolescents to dismiss each other, and it must be confronted. In this regard, therapists must be mindful of their own heterosexism when they ask a young male whether he has a girlfriend or a girl if she has a boyfriend. These unconscious and heterosexist questions by the therapist make queer youth feel invisible.

EXPANDING THEORIES TO PROMOTE THE DEVELOPMENT OF CHILDREN

While the most prominent child development theories offer important insights, they typically place too much emphasis on patterns typical of white, heterosexual, middle- and upper-class males, such as independence, autonomy, and striving for status within the social hierarchy. We advocate expanding these theories to affirm and promote the development of children across the spectrum of diversity, recognizing that there exists a multitude of adaptive styles. We suggest the term *interdependent self-in-context* as the description for these adaptive styles.

When children get affirmation of the values of their own family and cultural group along with exposure to a wide range of different genders, cultures, races, and sexual orientations—each of which has value and interest—they begin to develop an interdependent self-in-context. Boys of all races start to focus more on relationships and less on self, and they place nurturing rather than domination at the top of their relationship agenda. When they start to accept differences, boys become free to adopt learning styles less oriented toward logic and problem solving and more oriented toward understanding context and its relation to the development of problems. Boys can then experience success as the result of shared power rather than as the result of holding power over others.

On the other hand, girls of all races make choices that are more independent and self-related rather than striving just to please others. Girls gain clarity and decisiveness regarding their own values. They more fully celebrate their own achievements.

White children also benefit from learning about their interdependence with racially and culturally different children. Making friendships across these divides enhances individual as well as community development.

When social justice–based therapists, sponsors, and clients interact with schools, they can expand programs and curriculums, helping youth discover the works of diverse authors, such as James Baldwin, Carlos Fuentes, Paula Gunn Allen, V. S. Naipal, Meena Alexander, Jamaica Kinkaid, Alice Walker, Maxine Hong Kingston, Fatima Mernissi, Bharti Mukerjee, Cherrie Moraga, Amy Tan, Howard Zinn, Cornel West, and Isabelle Allende, who reflect the experiences of people of color, gays, immigrants, and people of other cultures. They also can establish learning modules that acknowledge America's genocide against native people, (Gunn Allen, 1992; Gunn Allen, 2003) the holocaust of slavery, and the current war on immigrants.

Social justice–based therapists provide a therapeutic environment that helps children and their families affirm that there are many ways to live a healthy life.

REFERENCES

Ahrons, C. (2004). *We're still family: What grown up children have to say about their parents' divorce.* New York: Harper Collins

Almeida, R. Woods, R., & Messineo, T. (1998). Child development: Intersectionality of race, gender, class and culture. In Almeida, R. (Ed.) *Transformations of gender and race: Family and developmental perspectives.* New York: Haworth Press.

Ariel, J., & McPherson, D. (2000). Therapy with lesbian and gay families and their children. *Journal of Marital and Family Therapy. 26,* 421–432.

Baumrind, D. (1980). New directions in socialization research. *American Psychologist. 35,* 639–652.

Best, D. L., & Williams, J. E. (1997). Sex, gender, and culture. In J. W. Berry, M. H. Segall, & C. Kagitcibasi, (Eds.), *Handbook of cross-cultural psychology: Social behavior and applications.* (2nd ed., Vol. 3; pp, 163–212.) Needham Heights, MA: Allyn & Bacon.

Bem, S. L. (1993). Gender schema theory and it's implications for child development. *Signs 8*(4), 598–616.

Bloch, M. N. (1989). Young boys' and girls' play at home and in the community: A cultural-ecological framework. In M. N. Bloch, & A. D. Pellegrini, (Eds.), *The ecological context of children's play.* Norwood, NJ: Ablex.

Chisolm, J. S. (1996). Learning "respect for everything": Navajo images of development. In C. P. Hwang, M. E. Lamb, & I. E. Sigel (Eds.), *Images of childhood* (pp. 167–183). Mahwah, NJ: Erlbaum.

Clunis, D. M., & Green, G. D. (1988). *Lesbian couples: Creating healthy relationships for the 90's.* Seattle, WA: Seal Press.

Cole, M., Cole, S. R., & Lightfoot, C. (2005). *The development of children* (5th ed.). New York: W. H. Freeman.

Cross, W. (1991). *Shades of black: Diversity in African American identity.* Philadelphia Temple University Press.

Dasen, P. R. (1977). *Piagetian psychology: Cross-cultural contributions.* New York: Gardner Press.

De Anda, D. (1984 March–April). Bicultural socialization: Factors affecting the minority experience. *Social Work, 29*(2), 101–107.

Drummond, M. J. (1996). Play learning and the national curriculums some possibilities. In T. Cox (Ed.) *The national curriculum and the early years,* London: The Falmer Press.

Erikson, E. H. (1963). *Childhood and society*(2nd *ed.).* New York: W. W. Norton.

Erikson, E. H. (1969). *Ghandi's truth: On the origins of militant nonviolence.* New York: W. W. Norton.

Farver, J. M., Kim, Y., & Lee, Y. (1995). Cultural differences in Korean- and Anglo-American preschoolers' social interaction and play behavior. *Child Development 66,* 1088–1099.

Furstenberg, F. F., Jr., & Cherlin, A. J. (1991). *Divided families: What happens to children when parents part.* Cambridge, MA: Harvard University Press.

Gay, G. (2000) *Culturally responsive teaching : Theory, research, and practice.* New York: Teachers College Press.

Gilligan, C., Lyons, N. P., & Hanmer, T. J. (Eds.). (1990). *Making connections: The relational worlds of adolescent girls at Emma Willard School.* Cambridge, MA: Harvard University Press.

Gilligan, C., Rogers, A., & Tolman, D. L. (Eds.). (1991). *Women, girls and psychotherapy: Reframing resistance.* Binghamton, NY: Harrington Park Press.

Gilligan, C., Ward, J. V., Taylor, J. M., & Bardige, B. (1988). *Mapping the moral domain.* Cambridge, MA: Harvard University Press.

Gilman, S. L. (1993). *Freud, race and gender.* Princeton: Princeton University Press.

Gunn Allen, P. (1992). The sacred hoop: Recovering the feminine in American Indian traditions. Boston: Beacon Press

Gunn Allen, P. (2003). *Pocahontas: Medicine woman, spy, entrepreneur, diplomat.* San Francisco: Harper San Francisco.

Hale-Benson, J. E. (1986). *Black children: Their roots, culture, and learning styles.* (Rev. ed.) Baltimore: John Hopkins University Press.

Hale-Benson, J. (1988, January). African heritage theory and Afro-American cognitive styles. *Educational Considerations, 15,* 6–9.

Havighurst, R. (1976) Education through the adult life span. *Educational Gerontology, 1,* 41–51.

Human Rights Campaign foundation (2007) Professional Opinion. Retrieved on April 2, 2007 from http://www.hrc.org/Template.cmf

Kaul, C. (2002). *Statistical handbook on the world's children.* Westport, CT: Oryx.

Kivel, P. (1992). *Men's work: How to stop the violence that tears our lives apart.* New York: Random House.

Kivel, P. (1996). *Uprooting racism: How white people can work for racial justice.* Gabriola Island, BC: New Society Publishers.

Lorde, A. (1995). In Marita Golden, (Ed.), *Saving our sons: Raising black children in a turbulent world (p.3).* New York: Anchor Books Doubleday.

Majors, R & Billson, J. M. (1992). *Cool pose: The dilemmas of black manhood in America.* New York: Lexington.

Masson, J., M. (1993). *My father's guru: A journey through spirituality and disillusionment.* Reading, MA: Addison-Wesley.

Momsen, J., & Kinnaird, V. (1993). *Different places, different voices: Gender and development in Africa, Asia and Latin America (International studies of women and place).* New York: Routledge Press.

Nyiti, R. M. (1976). The development of conservation in the Meru children of Tanzania. *Child Development. 47,* 1122–1129.

Ochs, E. (1996). Linguistic resources for socializing humanity. In J. Gumperz & S. Levinson (Eds.), *Rethinking linguistic relativity* (pp. 407–438). Cambridge, UK: Cambridge University Press.

Ogbu, J. U. (1981). Origins of human competence: A cultural-ecological perspective. *Child Development, 52*(1), 413–429.

Ogbu, J. U. (1988). Black children and poverty: A developmental perspective cultural diversity and human development. *New Directions for Child Development. 42,* 11–28. San Francisco: Jossey-Bass.

Ou, Y., & McAdoo, H. (1993). Socialization of Chinese American children. In H. Pipes McAdoo *Family ethnicity: Strength in diversity.* Newbury Park, CA: Sage Publications.

Piaget, J., & Inhelder, R. (1969). *The psychology of the child.* New York: Basic Books.

Powell, G., Yamamoto, J., Romero, A., & Morales, A. (Eds.) (1983). *The psychosocial development of minority group children.* New York: Brunner/Mazel.

Ramirez III, M., & Castaneda, A. (1974). *Cultural democracy, bicognitive development, and education.* NY: Academic Press.

Rogoff, B. (1996). Developmental transitions in children's participation in socio-cultural activities. In A. I. Sameroff & M. M. Haith (Eds.). *The five to seven year shift: The age of reason and responsibility.* Chicago: Chicago University Press.

Rogoff, B. (2003). *The cultural nature of human development.* New York: Oxford University Press.

Rouse, C., Brooks-Gunn, J., & McLanahan, S. (2005). Introducing the issue. *The Future of children (School readiness: Closing racial and ethnic gaps), 15*(1), 5–14.

Schacher, S. J., Auerbach, C. F., & Silverstein, L. S. (2005). Gay fathers extending the possibilities for us all. *Journal of GLBT Family Studies.* New York: Haworth Press.

Silvern, S., Surbeck, E., Kelley, M. F., Williamson, P. A., Silvern, L. R., & Taylor, J. (1984). The role of racial identity constancy of children's perceptions. *Journal of Social Psychology. 15,* 223–226.

Stacey, J., & Biblarz T. (2001). How does the sexual orientation of parents matter? *American Sociological Review, 66,* 159–184.

Stanton, A. (Director), & Unkrich, L. (Codirector). (2003). *Finding Nemo* [Motion Picture]. United States: Walt Disney Pictures, Pixar Animation Studios, and Disney Enterprises.

Taylor-Gibbs, J., & Huang, L. N. (1989). Children of color: Psychological interventions with minority youth. San Francisco: Jossey-Bass.

Tobin, J. J., Wu, D. Y. H., & Davidson, D. H. (1989). *Preschool in three cultures: Japan, China and the United States.* New Haven, CT: Yale University Press.

Walker, R. (1995). *Black, White, and Jewish.* New York: Anchor Books

Weingarten, K. (2003). Repairing the world: An adolescent and her parents. In L. Silverstein & T. J. Goodrich (Eds.) *Feminist family therapy: Empowerment in social context.* (pp. 65–78) Washington, D.C: American Psychological Association.

RECOMMENDED READINGS

Carter, R. T. (1991, September–October). Cultural values: A review of empirical research and implications for counseling. *Journal of Counseling and Development, 70*(1), 164–173.

Golden, M. (1995). *Saving our sons. Raising black children in a turbulent world.* New York: Anchor Books.

Helms, J. E. (Ed.). (1990). Black and white racial identity: *Theory, research, and practice.* New York: Greenwood.

Flisher, A. J., Brown, A. L., & Mukoma W. (2002). Intervening through school systems. In W. R. Miller & C. Weisner (Eds.). *Changing substance abuse through health and social systems* (pp. 171–182). New York: Kluwer Academic/Plenum Press.

LaFromboise, T., Coleman, H. L. K., & Gerton, J. (1993, November). Psychological impact of biculturalism: Evidence and theory. *Psychological Bulletin, 114*(3), 395–412.

Lutz, C. (1985). Depression and the translation of emotional worlds. In A. Kleinman & B. Good (Eds.), *Culture and depression: Studies in the anthropology and cross-cultural psychiatry of affect and disorder* (pp. 63–100). Berkeley: University of California Press.

Markus, H. R., & Kitayama, S. (1991, April). Culture and the self: Implications for cognition, emotion, and motivation. *Psychological Review, 98*(2), 224–253.

Markus, H. R., Mullally, P. R., & Kitayama, S. (1997). Selfways: Diversity in modes of cultural participation. In U. Neisser & D. A. Jopling (Eds.), *The conceptual self in context: Culture, experience, and self-understanding* (pp. 13–61). New York: Cambridge University Press.

Payne, Y., & Brown, A. L. (in press). Sites of resiliency: A reconceptualization of resiliency for young black men living in the inner city. In M. Pierre, (Ed.), *A new psychology for African-American men: A critical analysis toward understanding black male behaviors.* Westport, CT: Greenwood Publishing Press.

Yeh, C. J., & Hwang, M. Y. (2000, Fall). Interdependence in ethnic identity and self: Implications for theory and practice. *Journal of Counseling and Development, 78*(4), 420–429.

CHAPTER EIGHT

SPECIAL ISSUES: DOMESTIC VIOLENCE AND SUBSTANCE ABUSE

Black women are being murdered in Boston, Massachusetts White women are being murdered in California. Native American women are being murdered in New Mexico. Hispanic women are being murdered in New York. Chicana women are being murdered in Texas. All of us are being attacked because we are women, and no one really cares about us but us.

—Alice Walker (1997)

Domestic violence exists at every level of society. Women of all colors are at a greater risk of being battered than men, raising the question: What are the forces in our society that invite domestic male violence against women?

In this chapter, we examine the prevalence of violence, the lack of justice in cases involving violence, and violence's fundamental link to gender socialization. Domestic violence is not an aberration, the result of a few individuals whose pathology places them in need of anger management.

Instead, a social justice perspective finds the roots of domestic violence in socialization that teaches men—and, more broadly, those who hold more power—to dominate. In contrast, women and those who hold less power are socialized to accept and even promote domination.* Extreme valuing of privacy and autonomy for men, the hallmark of patriarchal values, are contributing factors.

In GLBT relationships, violence is equally prevalent, but because of lack of police reporting, accurate statistics are difficult to compile. When domestic violence and substance abuse coexist, the system for intervention is more complex and involves competing ideologies.

---

*In heterosexual relationships, domestic violence is perpetrated by the man against the woman in more than 90% of cases. We therefore refer to *he* when discussing perpetration in heterosexual relationships.

VIOLENCE IN CONTEXT

Imagine how clients who are queer and/or people of color respond when thera-pists challenge them to take responsibility for their perpetration of abuse without a word of acknowledgment regarding the abuse they endure in public. Imagine what it's like to be a poverty-stricken, battered woman facing not only her batterer but a series of well-meaning but grossly mistrained therapists who expect positive change to result simply from conversations in the woman's home. The battered woman knows that these conversations will not transform her batterer because they include no consequences or incentive for him to change. Instead of elevating her power and diminishing his control, the conversations result in exactly the opposite. If she acknowledges further abuse, the therapists can take her children away.

This chapter provides

- An overview of domestic violence: definition, prevalence, link to gender socialization.
- A discussion about the importance of race, sexual orientation, and class to assessment and treatment.
- An overview of social justice–based intervention.
- Considerations when addiction coincides with domestic violence.
- A developmental perspective about the challenges facing child survivors of domestic violence.

Definition of Domestic Violence

The National Coalition Against Domestic Violence defines domestic violence as the "willful intimidation, assault, battery, sexual assault, or other abusive behavior perpetrated by an intimate partner against another." We extend this definition to include "the patterned and repeated use of coercive and controlling behavior to limit, direct, and shape a partner's thoughts, feelings, and actions" (Almeida & Durkin, 1999, p. 313).

Tactics of domestic violence include

- Physical abuse.
- Emotional abuse.
- Economic abuse.
- Threats and intimidation.
- Isolation and entrapment (including job relocation and language barriers).
- Sexual abuse and exploitation.
- Control and abuse of children.

Undocumented immigrant women are at greater risk than others for domes-tic violence because of the threat of deportation. Women of color and GLBT individuals are also at greater risk because of bias and discrimination within the criminal justice system. These realities, discussed later in this chapter, show how violence at broader systems levels shapes violence at home.

While domestic violence continues to be a crushing problem for families, there have been positive developments over the past decade. According to the Bureau of Justice Statistics (U.S. Department of Justice, 2005), the rate of family violence in this country has dropped by more than half since 1993. A lot of the credit belongs to people quietly working in the field: social workers, women's crisis centers, police forces, and prosecutors. The Violence Against Women Act, passed in 1994, and amended in 1998 and 2006, expands women's legal rights to safety at home and within intimate relationships. These statutes also apply to GLBT couples. But all of these efforts are part of a larger story. The decline in family violence results from a web of positive, mutually reinforcing social trends.

Work and Domestic Violence

In a study of 2,400 U.S. workers, Ellen Wulfhorst (Reuters, Friday, 18 August, 2006) reports the staggering loss of work hours for domestic violence victims. Victims of domestic violence suffer at work as well as at home, losing costly work hours to distraction and absenteeism. Wulfhorst states that in 2005, women who were victims lost an average of 249 work hours—40% more than nonvictims.

Overall, about 40% of women and 29% of men reported violence from intimate partners at some point in their lives. According to the Centers for Disease Control and Prevention and the National Center for Injury Prevention and Control, intimate partner violence costs nearly $1.8 billion in lost productivity every year, with nearly 8 million paid workdays lost (Wulfhorst, 2006).

To determine how many U.S. companies have programs dealing with the issue, in 2005 the Corporate Alliance to End Partner Violence (Wulfhorst, 2006) conducted a survey and found that nearly a third of workers believe their companies have such a program. Companies support a number of intervention strategies to keep victims safe and minimize lost profits. Strategies range from changing employees' telephone numbers to helping them relocate. Still, companies often face challenging situations, including how to protect a victim when the abuser works in the same firm. Companies often struggle to keep the abuse private, sending the abused and abuser to couple's or mediation therapy instead of applying a policy of zero tolerance for violence. More egregious forms of corporate denial include situations in which upper management is protected at all costs, with threats to both victims and abusers that their benefits and income will be withdrawn if there is a protective order in place. While legal intervention is always possible, it is costly and remains a barrier to enforcing justice in the workplace for victims of domestic violence. The lack of a systematic program to hold abusers accountable further weakens strategies to keep victims safe.

Despite progress, violence toward partners in our society and others remains widespread. Family violence still accounts for approximately 1 in 10 violent crimes, or 11% of all reported and unreported violence. Forty-nine percent of such crimes were perpetrated against intimate partners, 11% against children by a parent, and 41% against other family members. The majority (73%) of family violence victims were female. Females comprised 84% of spouse abuse victims and 86% of victims of boyfriend or girlfriend abuse. Most family violence victims were white (74%), and the majority of those were between ages 25 and 54 (65.7%). Most family violence offenders were white (79%) and most were age 30 or older (62%) (U.S. Department of Justice, 2005). Nearly a quarter of the murders committed from 1998 to 2002 were against a family member (p. 8).

GENDER LAYS THE FOUNDATION FOR DOMESTIC VIOLENCE

Domestic violence can be evaluated as gender norms taken to the extreme expression. Patriarchy's definition of family as a private domain governed by men (Avis, 1992a, 1992b; Bograd, 1984; Bograd, 1986; Bograd, 1988; Dobash & Dobash, 1979; Duneier, 1992) has long perpetuated unequal power between the genders and separation between community and home life. Accordingly, most societies have tolerated husbands' oppression of their wives as a normal pattern. After all, "what goes on behind closed doors is private" and "a man's home is his castle." Less than 100 years ago, men were criminally prosecuted for beating strangers but could legally beat their wives (Coontz, 2005).

Even today, although we have seen important increases in community support for enforcement of restraining orders against batterers and regulations mandating police reporting of domestic violence, many people still see physical assaults against partners as less objectionable than crimes against strangers. There remains significant hesitancy toward public involvement in the "private" matter of domestic violence. From 1992 to 2000, less than half (44%) of intimate violence was reported to police; and only 24% of rape or sexual abuse was reported (National Coalition Against Domestic Violence, 2005). The most common reason victims cite for not reporting family violence is that the "incident was a private/personal matter" (U.S. Department of Justice, 2005, p. 2); 12% of nonreporting family violence victims seek to "protect the offender" (p. 2).

In addition to patriarchal gender norms that assert men's right to dominance within the home, there are other reasons survivors of domestic violence refrain from reporting to police. Advocates within immigrant communities, communities of color, and the queer community seek alternative options because of the dangers inherent in exposing their families to police and the courts, both of which have treated them less than fairly. The intersection of gender, race, and class conspire to silence victims so that many crimes committed within the home continue to evade public scrutiny. Men of all colors still hold power over women and children when there is no community oversight.

Men in most cultures historically have promoted group solidarity through the devaluation of women. "Being men together" requires verbally objectifying or degrading women (e.g., pornography), bragging about sexual exploits, and defining "feminine" characteristics as antithetical to being male (Farley, 1992; Kivel, 1992). Devaluation of women sometimes escalates to activities such as gang rape ("wilding" and men on the "down low") or men/boys going to brothels together. These acts join sexuality and violence with the domination of women. Men on the "down low" or DL are men who have secret relationships with other men, but choose to be in relationships with women as well.

Americans of all ages, educational levels, and income levels agreed on what traits are masculine. As described in Chapter 3, men are expected to aggressively strive for dominance, avoid emotional vulnerability, practice self-reliance and independence, support their families economically, treat sexual partners as objects, avoid "feminine" behavior, and be competitive, rough, unaware of others' feelings, and homophobic.

Women are expected to be more or less the opposite: to claim fault for interpersonal conflict and take responsibility for making things better and to prioritize relationships above all else, including the self. Although anger in men is seen as masculine and a hallmark of strength, in women it is viewed as unfeminine and aggressive. While most women may learn that education and paid jobs are important, they are also made to feel that nothing proves more essential than having a man and children. They are often raised to pursue relationships with dogged perseverance and seek to please men. In addition, they are raised to gain and keep men's love and approval.

Chapter 3 describes women's role as "culture bearer." Fulfilling this role, women often conspire with their male partners to distort evidence of domestic abuse and deny the long and harsh effects of violence on their children. With this in mind, it is important to not label survivors of domestic violence entirely as hapless victims but to assist women in evaluating the ways in which they accommodate misuse of power and personally misuse and abuse power. Women who physically discipline their children when perpetrators have left the home, and in some cultures, mothers-in-law who abuse authority, all need to be challenged when their behavior demonstrates abuse (Almeida, 2004).

Women uphold patriarchal practices and structures in many ways. A white mother from a fundamentalist church might justify the violence toward her children, saying it is done calmly and serves to teach respect. An Asian Indian woman might argue that in her culture it is important to support the dowry system, subjugate her daughter-in-law, ignore the sexual harassment of her daughter-in-law by the father-in-law, and support her son's violence toward his wife to keep the daughter-in-law in place.

Regardless of the violence and humiliation directed toward them, mothers from all cultural backgrounds often feel compelled to model respect toward husbands and for traditional male patterns of behavior. Case 8.1 is about a mother who resists acting as a culture bearer. She instead helps her sons to counter culture- and gender-based patterns that support violence.

■ ■ ■ ■ ■

CASE 8.1

HOW SHEILA STOPPED THE CYCLE OF DOMESTIC VIOLENCE AND RECLAIMED HER SONS

After living for years in a violent marriage and with several dropped protective orders, Sheila obtained a protective order and filed for divorce from her husband, Matt. After Matt's removal from the home, their boys—Brian, 8, and Charles, 10—became angry with Sheila because Matt had told them that their mother was mean and did not want him to live with them. They are Irish American.

Because most of the physical violence toward Sheila—rape and battering on intimate parts of her body—occurred behind closed doors, the boys were not aware of it. The boys, however, had witnessed verbal abuse—derogatory name-calling and put downs—and were anesthetized to it. In language their father taught them, the boys engaged in numerous power struggles with their mother because she had "thrown their father out of the home."

A social justice intervention requires that men be brought into the circle of conversation around the ethics of respect and care for women and mothers, so Sheila used the community culture circle that included men. The women in her culture circle helped her understand the limited power of mothers within the larger social context and the paradox of still being able to raise good sons. One African American woman talked about raising three sons in the face of numerous sources of adversity. She set a standard and stuck to it, getting a lot of support for herself and the boys from places where she knew they would get the right messages. This testimony from another mother greatly reassured Sheila, who began to internalize the notion that she did not have to give up work to be a competent mother, a message her husband continually barraged her with. It also permitted her to seek parenting support from the members of her culture circle and support for accountability from her sons within the men's culture circle. The men assisted her in writing a letter to her sons describing all of the reasons for which she made the difficult decision to end the marriage.

Sheila's brother, Mark, who was very connected to the boys, was also invited to witness the reading of her letter. Mark shared with the boys his own feelings of loss and explained all of the ways in which his friendship with their father had been damaged because of the violence toward his sister.

The opportunity for the boys to speak to their uncle about the violence they did not understand removed them from the loyalty-binding position of having to be loyal to one parent or another. They could speak with their uncle Mark—another man—who supported their connection with their father. And, they learned that Mark would stay connected to their father providing their father completed his participation in a batterer's intervention program and engaged in supervised visitation.

Mark's firm break with the masculine code of violence provided a powerful loop of accountability and empowered Sheila as a mother. She was able to accept coaching that helped her redefine some of the parenting boundaries that were inconsistent during the years of violence.

DIASPORA/IMMIGRATION AND DOMESTIC VIOLENCE

The following story of Chitra and Anant (Case 8.2) reflects the tragedy that confronts many immigrant women (Almeida & Dolan-Del Vecchio, 1999). Full of hope and eager to create a new life, they are confronted with the daily struggles of succeeding

CASE 8.2
AN IMMIGRANT COUPLE BREAKS THE CYCLE OF DOMESTIC VIOLENCE

In this case, a South Asian couple, Chitra and Anant, had recently immigrated to the United States. Theirs was a love marriage. They had met in Bombay on a work assignment. Anant was from North Asia, and Chitra was from Kerala in the South. After 4 years of marriage and a history of domestic violence that began on their honeymoon, Chitra escaped from her home on a treacherously cold winter night to meet with us.

Contacting the police was out of the question because Chitra and Anant were awaiting their green card documentation. Chitra requested that we contact Anant, which we did, and they began attending their separate circles, while living separately. Anant began his accountability work acknowledging his abuse toward Chitra, which included a pervasive attack on her body by criticizing her looks, her hair, her breasts. While in India, he had forced her to get skin bleachings because she was not, in his opinion, sufficiently light skinned. He slapped and punched her, ripping her lip on one occasion. He blocked her from working outside of the home even though she was as educated as he was and had planned to move forward with her career. He told her repeatedly that if she truly loved him, she would do whatever he requested.

After beginning his accountability work, and after numerous conversations with the sponsors and other men in his circle, Anant was able to prepare an accountability letter, which included the promise of reparations. During this time, he stepped into sponsoring the male adolescent circle, helping single mothers with their sons' homework, teaching the boys to play chess, and challenging new men about the abuse and exploitation of their partners. His reparations included a number of financial paybacks to Chitra: the transfer of about $36,000 of their money that he was holding in his savings account; an offer to financially support Chitra and pay her tuition for 2 years while she realized her goal of going back to school to get an advanced degree; and setting her up in her own place if she chose not to return to their marital home. After he read his accountability letter to Chitra and offered reparations, she accepted and told him that she had not yet made a decision about returning to the marriage. She also confronted Anant about the ways in which his mother colluded with him. She was convinced that on many nights when he was battering her, her mother-in-law was aware of it.

During the separation, her mother-in-law traveled to the United States to coax Chitra to return to the marriage. Chitra boldly suggested to Anant that working on his relationship with his mother would be key to partnership in his marriage to her, or with any woman.

Several weeks after the accountability and reparations, Chitra decided she no longer wanted to be married to Anant. Although he accepted her choice, Anant was deeply disappointed and regretted what he had done during the marriage. We assisted them in splitting their assets and waited until they obtained their legal documents before assisting them in filing for divorce. They both remained in the community, giving back to others for several years. Anant eventually returned to India, and Chitra continues to live in the United States.

in a new world while simultaneously living with their enemy. Without close friends or family and no legal protection, they are forced to survive with few options.

In keeping with the mainstream definition of power as "power over" rather than "power with," many men experience the empowerment of women as the loss of their own power in family and community life. They react to it as a threat. One manifestation of this can be seen within the judicial system, where this past decade has witnessed an increasing level of misogyny toward battered women and their children. For example, parent alienation syndrome (Gardner, 1998), considered by many professionals to be a bogus diagnosis and therefore unethical, can weigh heavily in the courts in favor of father's rights and against the rights of battered women who are mothers.

CONTEXT OF INTIMACY FOR PEOPLE OF COLOR

Many social factors assail the experience of intimacy for people of color. Mainstream images of ideal love relationships often reflect white stereotypes. Standards of beauty, intelligence, and economic security are very often "whitewashed." The partnerships of people of color are portrayed as unstable, with black men caricatured sexually as satyrs and rapists and black women as insatiable nymphomaniacs.

Both images serve to nullify whites' responsibility for their own history of sexual violence. Across the board, women of color face stereotypes as exotic temptresses. Stereotypes of men of color within couple relationships are more varied: Asian men are portrayed as cold, asexual, or effeminate; Latinos as controlling "machos"; Arabs as chauvinistic, seductive brutes.

Unions between whites and people of color have been both sensationalized and discouraged. Overall, people of color are sensationalized by images and films that negatively depict them and their partnerships—even when the movie producers are themselves black. Television dads may be portrayed as benevolent despots who disempower their children in the name of discipline and family values—for example, Bill Cosby's bumbling efforts at providing dinner for his children by serving chocolate cake. Even Spike Lee, who has defied Hollywood's marginalization of black directors, leaves much to be desired in the way he represents black women in his films. While he dramatically depicts the victimization of black men and is sympathetic to the plight of black women, he does not hold black man accountable for their exploitative and entitled behaviors toward black women.

In our society, racism weaves race and class together, relegating people of color disproportionately to the lower socioeconomic strata. When masculinity is defined substantially by a man's earning power, men of color and men of lower socioeconomic classes disproportionately suffer in their self-definitions as adequate males (Lui, Robles, Leondar-Wright, Brewer, & Adamson, 2006).

When men cannot meet social standards for manhood, they often balance this deficit by exaggerating their performance in meeting other masculine criteria. This compensation is evident in the social evolution of gangs within inner cities—a violent response to a violent context. Research in gang violence identifies factors such as loss of middle-class role models within communities of color compounded by female-headed households and a societal aspiration to succeed economically as a man. Young men in urban settings lack role models of successful adult men and legitimate pathways to economic success.

Part of the backlash against women's empowerment comes from men of diverse racial, cultural, and socioeconomic backgrounds who mistake women's changing roles as the "disintegration of culture." In a world that teaches all men to expect women's subservience at home, men who face disrespect and limited opportunities within the public sphere often feel a heightened pressure to enforce this prescription at home. Kevin, a Trinidadian black male referred for physically assaulting his wife Margaret, insisted: "I must have complete respect in my house. My home is the only thing I own in this country."

Holding such men accountable for their use of violence at home while also acknowledging the violence they face within the public world become concurrent tasks in the process of intervention.

COLONIZATION, RACISM, AND THE SHACKLES OF GENDER

Women of color who confront domestic violence often experience triple jeopardy. Many of their own communities conspire with the perpetrator by trumping race or culture over gender. The following narrative in Case 8.3 reflects a dismantling of these forces.

■ ■ ■ ■ ■

CASE 8.3

KEVIN CONFRONTS A LEGACY OF OPPRESSION AND HIS OWN VIOLENCE

Born and raised in Jamaica, a former British colony, Kevin is the son of an indentured servant from India. Beginning in the 19th century, the British were largely responsible for the indentured-servant market between India and the Caribbean, cutting off men from their families until they realized that bringing the wives would assure even greater servitude.

Kevin was a legacy of the "kinder" policy of bringing indentured families. As an adult immigrant to the United States in search of a better life, he shared a history with many others from nonindustrialized nations. Confronting generations of colonization, he became challenged by a new face of racism.

In therapy, Kevin addressed his violence toward his wife, Margaret, within his cultural and racial legacy. Therapeutic treatment focused on raising Kevin's critical consciousness regarding his use of power through money, sex,

emotional stonewalling, isolation, and physical violence within his intimate life.

Among many films, Kevin was shown clips from *Crash* and *Straight Out of Brooklyn*. *Crash* highlights the complexities of race, ethnicity, power, and family life, demonstrating the fluidity and intersectionality of oppressors and oppressed. It also portrays black and white men with power. *Straight Out of Brooklyn* depicts an African American couple in which the husband repeatedly strikes the wife. It also displays the degradation that the husband experiences daily at his job as a gas station attendant. Some of the experiences include name-calling, people spitting at him, and ultimately job loss. With a family to feed and a 14-year-old son who looks up to him, the husband finds himself without money to pay the rent or buy his son a winter coat. The film examines the multiple levels of abuse that occur in the

(continued)

■ ■ ■ ■ ■

CASE 8.3 CONTINUED

outside world, exacerbating tension within the home and heightening the husband's desire to be a man or his desire to reach for the masculine grade.

After he viewed the films, Kevin's culture circle challenged him to differentiate his experiences in the public world from the experiences of white men. He was also asked to describe the public experiences his wife Margaret faced. He was then challenged to recognize the private experience of oppression that he daily forced on his wife.

Kevin confronted his violence toward Margaret while simultaneously identifying the

multiple levels of public assault that he and his family, as people of color, experience daily. His culture circle generated discussion about why Margaret, who also faced the same public assaults, was not violent in the relationship. He was asked to examine the following questions: How is it that some people respond with violence and others do not? What are the gendered variables operating in the behavioral options?

With a newly developed critical consciousness regarding these multiple layers of oppression, Kevin could then begin his accountability work.

A white, middle-class man in the same circle faces different challenges. Therefore, treatment would proceed differently. His sense of privilege and entitlement both within and outside of the home should be challenged in the first stage of treatment. His family of origin or community experiences of victimization are addressed after his consciousness is raised with respect to racial privilege and male entitlement. This approach to men who come from dominant standpoints balances the larger culture's privileging of their wounds and victimization over the ways in which they as a collective victimize others. For men of color, we simultaneously hold the polarities of both experiences: gender entitlement and racial oppression.

We encourage therapists to pay special attention to the following factors when assessing dimensions of violence for people of color:

1. *Economic:* Because men and women of color are often relegated to low-paying positions offering no benefits and limited upward mobility, they are frequently the last to be hired and the first to be fired. Once hired, job stability is precarious. As a result, men and women of color are less likely to speak out in support of fair labor practices for fear of losing their jobs or jeopardizing their chances for promotion. Immigrants are especially vulnerable.

Immigrant workers in low-paying jobs are subject to racism from white people and cross-racial hostility from people of color, both of whom are also threatened by wage and labor conditions. Because of fear of or actual job loss, displacement, and economic disenfranchisement, racism intersects with ethnocentrism and nationalism to create cross-racial hostilities against immigrants of color who occupy the lowest paying positions that offer few or no benefits and limited upward mobility.

2. *Sexual:* Historically, both women and men of color have been objectified sexually: men were represented as animals with mythical and "inhuman" sexual

prowess, and similarly, women were portrayed as "exotic" and sexually insatiable. Because of these stereotypes, men and women of color are exploited and objectified in pornography.

3. *Perceptions of Family:* Children of color are often perceived as delinquent and are devalued on the basis of their appearance or speech patterns. Children of color are overrepresented in detention and other disciplinary actions as well as in child abuse investigations.

4. *Physical and Psychological:* Instances of police brutality and harassment are far more likely when the suspect is a man of color. Men of color are more often singled out for investigation at police road checks. Latino men are stopped as often as African American men. And, post–September 11, men perceived as Arab and South Asian men have been racially targeted.

5. *Emotional Isolation:* The homes and family lives of women and men of color are frequently exposed to intrusions by police, welfare workers, school personnel, and other public institutions. The dearth of positive role models and negative representations of persons of color in the media reinforce the notion that white culture is the ideal to which other cultures may only aspire. As Case 8.4 illustrates, differentiating these aspects of public abuse from private displays of power and privilege for men of color proves essential.

■ ■ ■ ■ ■ ■

CASE 8.4
FROM OPPRESSED TO EMPOWERED: NATE CLAIMS HIS HERITAGE

Nate, a mixed Cherokee and African American man with copper-colored skin and semi-curly hair, was referred for brutally beating his Puerto Rican wife, Rosa. With two prior restraining orders and another in effect, Nate had previously been referred to therapy. However, he did not follow through with treatment.

In describing his work as a janitor, Nate related the racial slurs that were hurled at him in the cafeteria, mostly by children but sometimes by staff. He spoke of the humiliation that his children faced because of his job and his concern regarding possible lay-offs. In response to questions about his family of origin and connections to Cherokee lands, he cried and spoke of hearing stories about land his great-grandparents had owned. His parents, now deceased, were moved off his grandparents' land. Two of his siblings were in jail and

two others died from substance abuse–related accidents.

Unaware of entitlements due him as a First Nation son, he lamented that he would never be able to afford to buy land on a janitor's salary. In therapy, he was referred to a legal clinic to begin proceedings that would guarantee him some form of financial reparations for this loss of his family's land. He also began to transform his violent behavior and create a more positive relationship with his children.

As part of this effort, he offered tangible reparations to his partner, Rosa, who accepted them. When he received reparations through the legal system, he divided the newly accrued assets equally, bought life insurance naming his wife as the primary beneficiary, and set up trust funds for their children. Rosa was encouraged by his changes and his growing participation in co-parenting their children.

For men of color, demands of accountability for intimate violence must be paired with an acknowledgment of their experience of public abuse.

CONTEXT OF INTIMACY FOR GLBT PEOPLE

> Homophobia is the irrational fear and hatred of those who love and sexually desire those of the same sex . . . Like racism and anti-Semitism, it is a word that calls up images of loss of freedom, verbal and physical violence, death.
> —Pharr (1988)

By defining what is publicly acceptable and intolerable, the dominant culture creates rules for intimacy. Nate's presenting case, (Case 8.4) described how those rules add pressure to the lives of people of color—pressure that must be addressed in cases of domestic violence. In this section, we examine how the rules create similar pressures for GLBT people.

Heterosexism legitimizes intimate bonds of male and female partnerships. Within a heterosexist context, intimacy among women is acceptable as long as it does not have a sexual component. Intimacy between men, while acceptable in rituals of sports, work, and recreational activities, is seldom supported and often suspect when it also has emotional overtones.

Like the intimate lives of heterosexuals of color, the intimate lives of GLBT people of all races are not publicly acknowledged. Instead, GLBT people are devalued, even pathologized. (Island, & Letellier, 1991; Kanuha, 1990; Morales, 1990). Rules of privacy used to maintain the oppression of women are similarly used to maintain homophobia in the public sphere. Tactics of power and control used to maintain social invisibility for queers, include

1. Economic exploitation.
2. Sexual abuse.
3. Triangulation of children.
4. Physical abuse and threats.
5. Emotional abuse and isolation.
6. Loss of spiritual and religious freedom.
7. Loss of heterosexual privilege.

Intimacy for GLBT people is often rendered pornographic as it is for heterosexuals of color. Moreover, the public violence to which gays and lesbians are subjected is often compounded by the rejection GLBT people face from their own families.

Homophobia sanctions the invisibility of partnerships, placing enormous pressure on the person to maintain a semblance of "normal" intimate life. Everyday issues become stressful elements of a GLBT couple's life because they, like people of color, experience all the interlocking barriers of racism, homophobia, misogyny, and classism simultaneously. For example:

1. Who will pay rent?
2. How will medical benefits be supported?
3. Should we have children?
4. How will we pass our wealth/assets to our children or to each other?
5. How will we acknowledge normal life-cycle transitions such as weddings, engagements, and pregnancies?

These pressures serve to maintain secrecy around dimensions of power and control within GLBT relationships. If one or both partners recognize that they are exploiting the other for money or sex, but are reluctant to identify overtly with what resembles heterosexual practice, they may tend to deny the problem until it manifests in the form of verbal and physical violence. When the couple decides to acknowledge the problem, finding a safe place to gain help also presents challenges. If the couple is gay, they are rendered vulnerable to being criminalized in many states. Consequently, because the couple may be breaking sodomy laws, the violence they face is either ignored or thought to be deserved.

GLBT couples know the extent to which society will blame the problem on their sexual orientation or lifestyle rather than on the imbalance of power that promotes oppressive practices among intimates. As with couples of color, it is important to situate the private violence that some couples experience in their intimate lives within the broader context of public oppression.

The following are key factors for the therapist to consider when assessing violence within the interior of a GLBT couple's life:

1. *Economic:* If "out," the GLBT person risks losing his or her job. Legal protection of civil rights for gays and lesbians is still not formally secured in all states, and where it is, GLBT people may face informal discrimination. Like heterosexuals, GLBT people of color have far less economic privilege and power than white GLBT people have.

2. *Sexual:* Most of society still views GLBT people as abhorrent and abnormal. Therapists and religious leaders may pathologize sexual orientation. In particular, heterosexuals have historically subjected lesbians to sexual abuse. Abuse ranges from the eroticization of lesbians in pornographic magazines and movies aimed at heterosexual male audiences to the more physically violent rapes enacted to "make them straight."

3. *Triangulation of Children:* The privacy of GLBT parents can be infringed upon by social agencies. Many GLBT parents have difficulty in obtaining custody of their own children and/or have been accused of being poor parents or pedophiles. Accusations attacking the credibility of GLBT parenting persist despite research showing that gay parenting does not have ill effects on children (Ariel & McPherson, 2000; Green, 1978; Hitchins, 1980; Kirkpatrick, Smith, & Roy, 1981; Megan 2004; Schacher, Auerbach, & Silverstein, 2005).

4. *Physical Abuse and Threats:* Gay bashing and other forms of physical violence, as well as threats of being disowned by families and threat of arrest, present ongoing

challenges for GLBT people. In addition, they face the prospect of being "outed"—having their sexual orientation disclosed to the public without their consent—by other GLBT people as well as by heterosexuals.

Like people of color, GLBT people are not always legally protected from violence. In fact, findings from the Comstock Survey (Comstock, 1991) indicate that 73% of victims of all forms of anti-GLBT violence did not report incidents to the police. Of the victims of color, 82% did not report the crimes, compared to 72% of white victims who did not report. In response to very serious violence, 58% of all victims did not report. Again, victims of color showed a higher percentage of nonreporting than did white victims.

5. *Emotional Abuse and Isolation:* GLBT people are subjected to name-calling, pejorative language, exclusions, and rejections by heterosexuals. Lesbians are accused of being "manhaters," and gays are accused of hating women.

6. *Spiritual/Religious Alienation:* Organized religions generally view GLBT people as sinners. Many are ousted from their religious traditions and are alienated from their spiritual heritages. Spirituality, as a larger form of human interconnectedness, is compromised for gays and lesbians. Religion has historically helped people define and punctuate major life stages through rituals and celebrations. Exclusion from religion can mean exclusion from spiritual resources that mark important milestones in the life cycle.

7. *Denial of Heterosexual Privilege:* GLBT couples are offered little in the way of legal protection (marriage, tax deductions, and joint insurance coverage). Though some states now allow gay lesbian marriage, and some companies offer partner insurance coverage, equity is still a long way off.

Because most of the world assumes heterosexuality to be the norm, many gays and lesbians remain invisible. This invisibility allows gays and lesbians access to the same level of privacy and privilege afforded to heterosexuals, provided they remain "closeted." However, the price for privacy includes great psychological and emotional costs (Berger, 1990; Clark, 1987).

Being "out" can bring psychological, emotional, and financial cost, and, may entail the loss of numerous heterosexual privileges, such as participation in the military, housing, maternity/paternity leaves, funeral leaves, medical decision making for partners, inheritance, family insurance coverage, and legal protection from violence in both public and private life. Gays committing violence through militarism is not a privilege; however, the benefits of being in the military for underprivileged men and women is an economic reality. These losses, combined with other direct forms of public violence, are sufficient to coerce many GLBT people into a position of invisibility by "passing" as heterosexual lest they become the next victim (Berk, 1990).

Invisibility as an expression of homophobia is a form of public abuse in that it intrudes on the private lives of GLBT people by requiring them to be "secret." As we witness in this next case (Case 8.5) the intricacy of couples' lives add another layer of oppression to the complexity.

CASE 8.5

CREATING AN INTIMATE PARTNERSHIP: SARA AND JULIE CONFRONT HOMOPHOBIA

Sara, 37, and Julie, 40, an interracial lesbian couple, experienced many violent fights during their 6-year committed relationship. Sara was of African-Cuban descent and Julie of English-Irish descent. Sara worked for a well-known publishing house with an annual income of $175,000. Julie was a nurse in a pediatric office, earning about $80,000. Both had good benefits: medical and pension. They owned a modest home in a highly desirable neighborhood.

While they were open about their sexual identity with friends, families, and coworkers (Julie had been "out" to her family since adolescence), Sara's family was unforgiving about her sexual orientation.

The violence in their relationship was usually initiated by Sara toward Julie. Julie usually used *retaliatory violence*, a term for physically defending oneself.

Treatment consisted of having each woman join different culture circles where they received social education separately. Like other GLBT couples, they had internalized norms of dominance that they used to resolve conflict.

Julie's whiteness had more power in the outside world. Her family's acceptance of her sexual orientation early in life gave her the foundation many GLBT children do not receive. She learned early to tap into the cultural safety nets of the GLBT communities. While not classically feminine, she certainly passed as feminine.

Sara, on the other hand, was dark skinned. The outside world reminded her of her skin color on a daily basis. Since she presented as butch, she didn't have the illusion of protection that femme lesbians garner from the heterosexist mainstream. As a black Cuban lesbian, her economic situation, in terms of earned income, was in direct contradiction to mainstream stereotypes.

While Julie's economic status afforded her a more-than-decent income, she also received family support, the down payment on her and Sara's mortgage, and money from a trust left to her from grandparents. No such generational assets were passed on to Sara.

These are critical dimensions to consider in assessing power within the interior of a couple's life. Much of Sara's frustration was driven by the fact that while she made more than twice Julie's income, she had none of the wealth accumulation that Julie inherited. Should there be a medical crisis, Sara would have to tap into their equity line, while Julie was assured that someone in her family would take care of her.

Since the couple commingled their funds, most of Sara and Julie's fights, many of which escalated into violence, occurred around money and how it should be spent. Sara wanted a budget and the comfort of being able to accumulate wealth. Julie wanted a budget but was less concerned about wealth accumulation or saving for emergencies. Both had internalized heterosexual norms by automatically commingling funds without conscious dialogue or an investigation regarding how money and expenses are equitably handled.

Both viewed dominance (e.g., aggressiveness) as a strength, feeling they could take on the world if they had to. For example, Julie defined her response to her partner's physical abuse as "fighting back" as opposed to internalized dominance behaviors. She was encouraged to do her work by looking at different threads of empowerment. She and Sara participated in the same process of social education in their separate culture circles, learning about dimensions of power and control that thread into violence and family legacies around sexual orientation. They had conversations and witnessed numerous letters of accountability and reparations from other perpetrators to their victims.

(continued)

■ ■ ■ ■ ■

CASE 8.5   CONTINUED

Empowerment for both involved developing a critical consciousness about the painful effects of homophobia that were threaded into their relationship, balancing Sara's sense of security with Julie's by creating a joint financial plan, and by putting both of their names on the deed for their home, which was only in Sara's name. Sara's income had qualified her for the mortgage.

Finally, Julie wrote a letter of accountability to Sara about her white privilege and the assaults that she brought into the partnership. She offered to participate in a young women of color empowerment project through photography. A year later, they decided to adopt a child and a had an announcement celebration with their families.

For GLBT couples, dimensions of abuse exist first in public arenas and often get mirrored in their private lives (Comstock, 1991; Herek, 1990). For example, in some Asian–Middle Eastern communities, if they are found to be in a lesbian relationship, women may be forced to marry or face death through "honor killings." The statistics reported in the Comstock study indicate similarity among experiences of GLBT people, people of color, and battered women. That is, without society's structural supports to maintain familial survival, these populations' private lives are publicly vulnerable. With few safe public places to go, the GLBT people must solve their problems within the privacy of home. When "out," they sometimes can rely on the support of family and friends, but they remain vulnerable in the public world.

Queer People of Color Face Multilayered Oppression

GLBT people of color face racism, classism, and immigrant marginalization, compounded by homophobic abuse. In addition to overlapping effects of homophobia and racism in the mainstream, GLBT people of color are vulnerable to attacks of racism that exist within the GLBT community. The difference in relation to identity of self between white GLBT people and those of color lies in the prominence attributed to race. Thus, for GLBT people of color raised in the United States, self-definition may occur first by race and second by sexual orientation (Morales, 1990). The coming out process is different for GLBT people of color than it is for their white counterparts, particularly with respect to racial socialization.

BRINGING A SOCIAL JUSTICE MODEL TO DOMESTIC VIOLENCE INTERVENTION

A social justice model evaluates all problems that interfere with the safety and health of families and communities (including domestic violence) from a perspective that takes power, privilege, and oppression into account. A social justice perspective transforms assessment questions that guide intervention by taking a question such as. *What kind of individual pathologies cause abuse to occur?* and reframing it into an inquiry that asks, *Under what conditions do those who hold more power and privilege over others abuse their power and privilege?*

The cultural context model originated as a means to treat domestic violence. Over time, it became clear that the distinction between families who experience domestic violence and families who avoid this tragedy is a difference in degree, and not kind. In other words, gender socialization results in most men abusing their power over women to some degree, though not always to the extreme of domestic violence.

In same-sex couples, abuse occurs with a frequency similar to that found in heterosexual couples. For this reason, we strongly advise that all clients, whatever their presenting concern, be screened for the presence of abuse. For example, in Case 8.6, the couple's previous five therapists had entirely missed the domestic violence.

■ ■ ■ ■ ■

CASE 8.6

THE CHALLENGE OF EXPOSING THERAPEUTIC PRACTICES: HIDDEN DOMESTIC VIOLENCE

Gary and Gail, a professional, upper-middle-class couple in their 40s, experienced roughly 12 years of diverse forms of couple's therapy. They were referred to us by one of Gary's friends who had been in therapy with us a few years earlier. Gary and Gail had three children, one of whom had Tourette syndrome. Gail was increasingly unhappy with the state of their marriage.

On the surface, Gary appeared to have total disregard for domestic justice, for fairness and equity regarding child care and household responsibilities, and for managing two high-powered careers. Gail carried the management of social, medical, school, and recreational activities for all three children. What also existed, but was not immediately apparent, was a story of serious domestic violence—violence that was never addressed in prior therapies. Gail's rib cage had been broken and her eardrum punctured in the first few years of their marriage.

While Gail appeared to be strong, astute, and competent, it became clear that the lines of power and authority were drawn early on in the relationship, marked by the violence. The string of therapists this couple saw (five in all) failed to inquire about power and control issues, missing not only the gender disparity but also the violence within this relationship. Such an oversight is not an unusual scenario. The more couples present with a smooth outer veneer, the less likely the therapist is to believe there is domestic violence or to investigate it.

Gary, emboldened by his past therapies that had leveled the playing field, was insistent that Gail had a part in orchestrating the violence. Gail alternated between outrage and acquiescence that her competence might be a factor. Gary fired us five times but kept coming back. Significant to his process of staying and doing his work was the fact that Gail developed strong connections with the women in her circle and with men as allies.

We invited Gary's friend who referred him to also join us for a few sessions. It took the power of this collective of men and women to help redefine the parameters of Gail and Gary's relationship, demanding that Gary become accountable to Gail and their children. There was a brief separation of 6 months before the accountability work began and continued successfully.

The issues that bring couples and individuals to treatment may include child-focused concerns, loss, chronic illness, extended family conflicts, depression, anxiety, or addiction. While couples nearly always frame their difficulty as a "communication problem," rarely are their issues mutual or gender-neutral. If gender is never investigated as an essential part of the landscape, violence in the relationship will become even more difficult to assess unless there are bruises to document.

We recommend the following sequence for assessing couples: Upon intake, we suggest that partners be seen conjointly, very briefly, to gather a description of their presenting concerns and information on their families of origin. Always have a sponsor or invited guest present to begin the linking of private and public contexts. During the conjoint session, we recommend that the therapist not raise the subject of abuse. The remainder of the initial assessment (or, perhaps, the second session) can be devoted to individual time with each partner. At that time, the therapist can obtain specific information regarding power and control dimensions. Gathering this information within private meetings provides safety. Victimization revealed in the presence of a perpetrator usually wounds the perpetrator's pride and can fuel additional violence. If the therapist is not sensitive to the needs of both the batterer and the battered, too often violent attacks can follow couples sessions.

To assist in your inquiry, refer to the power and control wheels introduced in Figure 1.2 and Figure 2.1, which define spheres of organization for couples and families. For example, when we use the control wheel, we say to the individual, "Misuse of power within relationships takes many different forms. I'm going to ask you to take a look, one at a time, at the description in each section of the pie in this power and control wheel. Let me know if you (or your partner) have done any of the things mentioned or anything similar to what's mentioned."

Violence occurs at all stages of the life cycle. Teens in particular struggle with dating violence. We recommend using similar wheels for assessing and educating teens about violence in relationships (see Figure 8.1). Teenage girls often mistake controlling behaviors on the part of their boyfriends for love. It is not until the control leads to coercive demands that they become aware of the problem.

> Both Susan and Shakira spoke of the warmth and love they felt when their boyfriends kept calling them, sending them candy and flowers. It took them a while to realize that all of their fights and challenges occurred after they failed to return phone calls—phone calls tracking their whereabouts.

Teen violence does not receive the same level of attention and legitimacy as adult violence. Using the wheels of teenage dating along with films that depict gendered norms is enormously helpful to teens in general.

Violence is grossly underreported by both batterers and victims. Interviewing partners together, and then individually, allows therapists the opportunity to safely assess for danger and to begin an education process about patterns of domestic violence. It also provides the therapist the ethical opportunity to inform

FIGURE 8.1   Teenage Power and Control in Dating

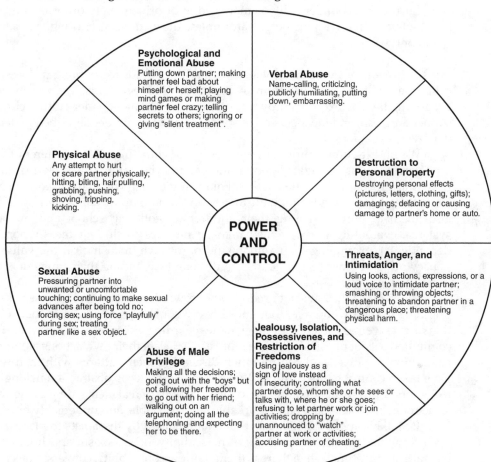

the victim about legal rights and ways to obtain an order of protection. The therapist might want to suggest to the batterer that he or she continue working in a group context (Adorando & Mederos 2003). And if necessary, suggest protective measures for the batterer's partner, such as a temporary separation.

When violence is described, we thoroughly assess for danger and lethality using the following checklist (Bograd & Mederos, 1999):

GOALS OF ASSESSMENT
- Determine the nature, frequency, severity, and consequences of aggression.
- Obtain a detailed behavioral description of the sequence of events in context.
- Understand the intended function of the violence and its impact.
- Evaluate the degree of fear and intimidation.

- Expand your inquiry to explore broader patterns of control and domination.
- Ensure that confidentiality is managed to prioritize safety (information will not be shared with the perpetrator unless the victim consents while in a safe context).

Treatment of domestic violence within a social justice paradigm does not differ markedly in structure from treatment of other problems. We recommend expanding the context of therapy through the use of same-gender culture circles, social education, and the inclusion of sponsors, all of which are described in detail in previous chapters.

We find it counterproductive to segregate court-mandated batterers from other clients. Court-mandated people and people who voluntarily seek treatment have much to learn from one another. For example, men who have used violence learn to embrace friendships with men who do not support abusiveness. They also get help with parenting their children, negotiating school and medical systems, evaluating the way they manage finances (including the support of dependents), examining their understanding of love, focusing on the value of housework and other second-shift activities, and expanding their range of emotional expressiveness.

When men who have not used violence toward intimates find themselves sitting next to men who have, they more easily confront similarities in their own thinking, as well as choices they have made regarding violence. Men who have not committed acts of physical violence more easily locate their own actions along the continuum of power and control when discussing their patterns with men who have taken control to the extreme. Violence no longer is an abstraction belonging to "others" but a reality demonstrated by the actions of real men, sitting in the very same room, men who seem unremarkable, approachable, and undeniably human.

By talking together, both sets of men are helped by therapists to place their actions within broader frameworks of masculinity, heterosexism and homophobia, race, and culture. When there is therapeutic accountability, conversations provide a perspective that loosens defensiveness, makes personal accountability less onerous, and clears the way for new choices.

Accountability in the field of domestic violence has frequently included linking the criminal justice and shelter systems with the system offering intervention to the batterer. All too often, however, accountability focuses exclusively on prosecution and punishment rather than reparation. We believe there is an important difference between prosecution-oriented domestic violence programs and programs that incorporate redistributive justice. Prosecution-oriented programs offer only punitive and institutionalized constructs of accountability, outgrowths of oppressive control mechanisms of patriarchal culture. These programs tend to exacerbate oppression against racially or culturally marginalized batterers and their victims. They also do not offer a way for people to repair or heal from the harm they have created.

Domestic violence victims from marginalized groups often do not opt for safety within dominant systems because these systems tend to make matters worse rather than better. We have heard more than one black woman say, "I didn't call the police because I was afraid they'd kill him." GLBT people fear a similar fate should they request police intervention. Moreover, calling the police outs both partners, making it a dangerous choice. It exposes them to state censure and, in some instances, violation of civil rights by state agents. Immigrant women, among whom violence is very prevalent, and/or their violent partners are often deported if they involve the authorities. Though an immigrant woman needs freedom from abuse, she also is often dependent on her abuser for financial support. If he is deported or denied legal work status, she and her children may become destitute.

By creating forums that privilege the victim's voice and allow her to speak about her experiences, the distribution of power between victim and offender can be rebalanced (Curtis, 2005). This was Chitra's experience in Case 8.2. We also witnessed a rebalancing of power with Chitra's husband, Anant. Because we emphasize taking responsibility and making reparations, he learned to accept accountability through restorative justice instead of through punitive consequences.

The batterer's therapeutic work focuses on gaining an empathic understanding of the victim's experience of his violence and coming to see his partner as a human being equal in value to himself. Once he claims responsibility for the violence he has perpetrated, he can be assisted by the members of his culture circle and therapists in offering meaningful reparations for harm done.

A batterer's accountability often involves reading a letter to his victim in which he describes his violence, what it may have been like to be on the receiving end, and the reparative actions he proposes. He does this in the presence of a community that includes both his and his victim's culture circles. This ritual assists both parties toward healing, creating a powerful new memory, and reinforcing new norms of nonviolence and justice. The accountability letter is often the first step—the truth-telling step, which is followed by reparations, reparative behaviors, or actions that are meaningful to those who were offended. They can be monetary reparations, for instance, or assuming household and/or people care tasks, but they must take the form of extraordinary good deeds that begin to repair the harm done in ways that are meaningful and healing to the partner and others who were harmed.

While an ethic of caring is the holding context for this work, accountability must come first. Therapists often elevate caring over accountability because it allows them a way to feel more comfortable with a batterer who may also make them feel fearful. Because the batterer does not yet understand gendered power differentials in male and female patterns of socialization, he often does not understand the roots of his own violence. Developing critical consciousness is key to a therapeutic/accountability platform.

Therapists encourage women's empowerment by acknowledging their roles within and outside of family life while at the same time encouraging them to expand self-nurturing patterns. Therapists can also encourage strategizing for economic independence, acknowledging and respecting one's body, striving for leadership, and coming to rely on a collective of conscious women for support. We encourage women to stop overfocusing on their guilt and to begin to experience anger as an appropriate response to control and abuse.

Empowerment has an added dimension for victims who are parents. When a batterer leaves the home, the mother emerges from a recent history that found her huddled and protective of her children—a position that can level the generational hierarchy. Children often assault and make demands on her, much as her abuser did. Because she has been undermined as a parent by the batterer, her children may have negative impressions of her skills and abilities to parent. She may face confusion about her role as parent and must work to regain her status as an adult.

In addition, she must find ways to get healthy and get respite from all that she had to negotiate in the relationship. With some batterers, the legacy they leave to their children is disdain for their mother and tools to undermine her. Parenting in this new family configuration requires both a healing context and new rules and boundaries.

A social justice–based system of intervention offers a range of new options for the battered partner: the possibility of rebuilding a relationship with the abusive partner, of having a civil and safe divorce, and when the criminal justice system is not an option, of maintaining safety by way of the therapeutic community.

Women survivors of abuse face pressure from their male partners to accept conjoint couple's therapy. "How can our issues be resolved if we don't talk with one another?" is a typical male complaint. Men may exert pressure by "making deals" or promising to change if a woman insists on couple's therapy. Women are also influenced by well-intentioned religious leaders, extended family members, or adult children to seek more traditional (conjoint) marriage counseling. Layers of rigid gendered construction need dismantling prior to couple's therapy.

Even when couples insist they want to be together, the safety of the battered woman and her children must come first. It is therapists' ethical responsibility to postpone seeing the couple together until the abuser claims full and sole responsibility for the violence he committed. That said, since partners are being seen by the same treatment team, working with them in separate same-gender circles does not prevent negotiating the numerous issues they face, such as managing support and child care expenses, visitation, contacts with extended family, and the children's recreational activities. Because therapists and sponsors can act as go-betweens, the activities of one partner are immediately known by the treatment team for both partners and can be handled appropriately. This approach is different from most domestic violence treatment programs, which deal with only one half of the couple (perpetrators or victims).

Intermittent couples or family work for nonviolent men begins earlier than for those who physically battered their partners, depending on nonviolent men's awareness of how they may have used other means of gaining power and control in their families and on the willingness they show to change those patterns. Learning from these couples benefits those waiting to engage in couple's work. For those who are single or do not have partners, participation in our circles provides numerous insights into negotiating the complex dimensions of couple and family life.

We use power and control wheels and the list of rigid male and female norms regularly to evaluate the degree to which men (or perpetrators of violence) are working to change patterns of dominance and adopt more relational ways of being. We determine their effort not only by the attitudes, behaviors, and participatory responses that batterers offer in their culture circles but also by what the women (including victims) report in their culture circles.

Changes by men (or batterers) are reflected in all aspects of the couple's relationship, including nonthreatening behavior, respectful and affirming ways of relating, gaining trust and giving support, accountability that includes reparations, admitting to being wrong, accepting responsibility for self and behavior, communicating openly and truthfully, responsible parenting and caregiving, and economic partnership. Finally, changes are reflected through negotiation and fairness, by seeking mutually satisfying solutions to conflicts, by demonstrating relational compassion, and by developing ability to compromise.

All of these behavioral changes are necessary before initiating couple's work. Since power over others is maintained by forgetting specific acts of abuse, a community of concerned others, such as culture circles, claims the power of remembering that provides the balance necessary to create change.

Change and accountability are also measured through interactions and projects with women and children, such as helping single mothers manage their children's homework, organizing home and auto repairs, accompanying battered women in courts, and advocating for children in schools. Within the accountability framework for therapy, the boundaries of the couple system are open and flexible for both heterosexual and GLBT couples. Therefore, couple's work progresses in conjunction with each partner's ongoing participation in his or her respective culture circles. Very often, partners come together encircled by a larger collective (the men's, women's, or community circles) to discuss their issues. The culture circles provide safety for the victim and accountability for promises made by the perpetrator of violence.

Change for batterers is a lifelong process. It goes beyond anything a single program can offer. When violence stops, this change can only be sustained if the batterers continue to be connected with community and social systems that support nonviolence in multiple ways.

In the cultural context model, after completing their therapeutic program, men who stay connected to their sponsors are more likely to be effective in maintaining nonviolence in all intimate relationships, with positive reverberations in other family and community connections.

Current research that measures only the effectiveness of programs fails to measure the enormous power of communities and institutions that refuse to sanction violence in both private and public spheres. The solution to ending violence does not rest solely within the walls of mental health communities but rather within society at large. Evolving systems that support nonviolence, such as the National Organization for Men Against Sexism (NOMAS), Physicians for Social Responsibility (PSR), faith-based organizations that particularly support the end of violence against women, and many other activist community organizations, are crucial to expanding options for nonviolence.

COUPLE'S THERAPY IN THE AFTERMATH OF DOMESTIC VIOLENCE

Couple's therapy that follows a history of domestic violence proceeds only after all forms of violence (verbal, physical, sexual, economic) have stopped and only if the victim initiates the request for such assistance (Almeida & Durkin 1999). Ethical standards for treatment of domestic violence require that conjoint counseling (with both partners present) be considered only when the following criteria are met (Bograd, 1999, pg. 295):

- Both partners voluntarily agree to couple's counseling, meaning that therapy is not mandated. In court-mandated cases, the violence tends to be more severe and the perpetrator's motivation for treatment is questionable. He is often manipulative and coercive of his partner with economic threats or threats to have child protection workers remove children.
- The violence that has occurred is relatively minor in nature, such as "slaps, shoves, grabbing and restraining without bruising or injury" (p. 304).
- "Use of psychological abuse does not create a climate of constant anger or intimidation, and is neither terrifying nor debilitating" (p. 29).
- There is no sexual abuse or relationship rape.
- There is no access to and use of weapons, substance abuse, history of physical violence or violent crimes, threats, obsessive or controlling behavior toward partner, presence of unusual or sadistic forms of violence—burning, animal abuse, sleep deprivation.
- The partner displays no fear of retaliation.
- The abusive partner takes full responsibility for his or her abusive behavior, demonstrates commitment to control angry and blaming emotions, and can tolerate a detailed description of the abuse without defensiveness. If the abusive partner "shows no remorse, denies his actions, blames the woman, and has little commitment to change" (p. 304), couple's work is contraindicated.

DOMESTIC VIOLENCE INTERVENTION AND 12-STEP PROGRAMS

Chapter 6 describes the differences in sponsorship between social justice sponsors and addiction sponsors. Much of the wisdom of 12-step recovery programs is very compatible with the philosophy of the cultural context model. We strongly advise that every client with a substance abuse problem attend Alcoholics Anonymous (AA) or Narcotics Anonymous (NA) meetings regularly and consistently and adhere to the fundamental principles outlined in the 12 steps and *The Big Book of Alcoholics Anonymous*.

However, we monitor the advice handed down by individuals in the AA and NA fellowships and recommend that clients who are both addicts and batterers stay in close touch with their sponsors in the cultural context model who are veterans of negotiating both programs.

Despite the overwhelming evidence of a correlation between the misuse of alcohol and other substances and domestic violence, these two issues are frequently treated separately and with little or no coordination between treatment centers. The compartmentalizing of treatment for these two lethal problems creates grave dilemmas.

In the addiction treatment community, as well as in the general population, there is a longstanding belief that the ingestion of alcohol or drugs causes violence. This belief fosters the myth that violence will end once abstinence is achieved. It also fosters its corollary, that in the process of treating addiction violence is also being addressed. In that context, victims may let down their guard, fail to notice key signals that the violence is escalating, and/or remove safeguards (that is, restraining orders, physical separations, safety plans).

Furthermore, the conventional wisdom of the addiction recovery community is that addiction is primary, and thus every issue in an addict's life can only be addressed after sobriety is stabilized. It may be true that a second-order shift in family relationships cannot be achieved while clients are under the influence. However, when there is domestic violence, consideration for the safety of the victims must be the driving force and overarching blueprint for treatment. The social and structural interventions compromising the early stages of domestic violence must be activated as soon as domestic violence is assessed. At the same time, a plan to facilitate recovery must be put in place for the perpetrator and for victims who are drug or alcohol dependent. Victims who use drugs or alcohol are also often vilified and blamed for the violence perpetrated against them.

Treatment for the addiction, with an aim toward recovery, cannot be in lieu of treatment for domestic violence. It is not uncommon for the recovery community to advise its members to postpone any activities that would threaten recovery. Any activity that makes the addict uncomfortable can be labeled as threatening. Clearly, writing an accountability letter, being challenged by a group of men about his violence, being confronted with the discrepancy between his version of the history and his partner's narrative, are all examples of activities that would raise the addict's level of anxiety.

Yet, these activities are central to batterer's intervention work. If the addict refuses to do these things—which often happens with the support of the recovery community—the family must understand that no change in the level of risk for violence has occurred. Finally, the 12-step position on privacy and confidentiality creates competing and dangerous notions regarding issues of safety.

In recovery circles, the convention of prescribing Al-Anon for partners of addicts often creates additional difficulty. For battered women, the Al-Anon principle of focusing on one's self obscures the need for the victim to hold her partner 100% responsible for his violence. Since women are universally socialized to take responsibility for every aspect of a relationship, this principle adds more weight to the tendency for women to blame themselves for the violence.

In addition, addiction counselors and rehabilitation programs emphasize the need for spouses of addicts to stop "enabling the addict." This advice obscures the existence and impact of the violence and places the responsibility for both the violence and the change process on the victim (see Figure 8.2).

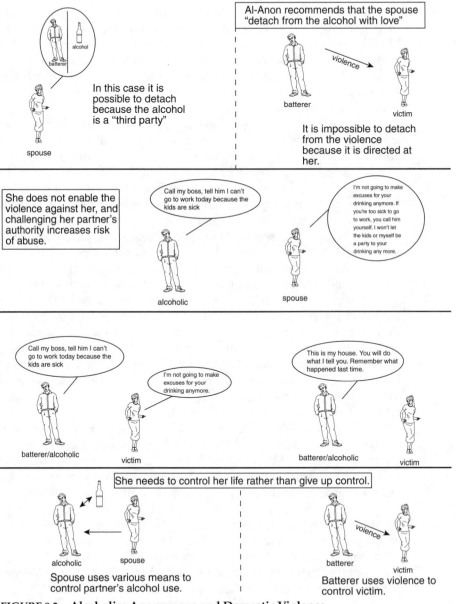

WHY 12 STEP PROGRAMS ARE NOT ALWAYS HELPFUL FOR BATTERED WOMEN

FIGURE 8.2 **Alcoholics Anonymous and Domestic Violence**

In the cultural context model, a fundamental part of treatment for families experiencing domestic violence who have been socialized in the 12-step model is to help them understand the dangers of that model. The AA and Domestic Violence Power and Control Wheel was devised (Figure 8.3) to help deconstruct the differences. This wheel exemplifies the graphic in Figure 8.2. It is a powerful tool in delineating the ways in which violence gets minimized, confidentiality is misused, and the victims are blamed and pathologized. It also exposes how 12-step programs privilege the addiction over competing life-threatening problems such as domestic violence. The competing language of power with 12-step and domestic violence programs is also re-interpreted on the wheel.

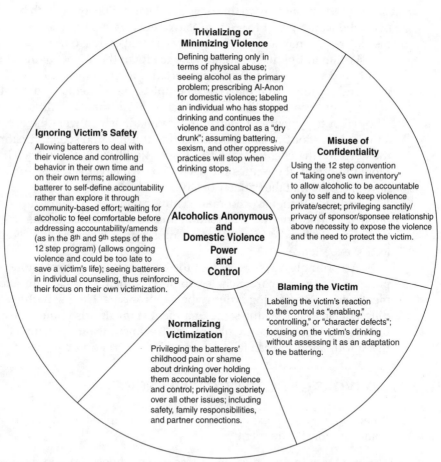

FIGURE 8.3   The Dangers of the 12-Step Addictions Model in Working with Domestic Violence

Source: This instrument was created by Juditn Lockard, Institute for Family Services.

THE DANGERS OF INDIVIDUAL THERAPY

Because individual therapy reinforces rules of privacy that are at the core of patriarchy, it is contraindicated for people who use violence against their partners (Kaufmann, 1992). The structure and process of individual therapy privileges batterers' tendency to focus on their own victimization and ultimately supports their entitlement.

Victimization is a more comfortable focus than accountability-focused conversations for both therapists and clients. These conversations about the batterer's victimization often persist for months, even years, while the batterer continues to offend. How could it be otherwise? He now can rest assured that his offenses are the unfortunate but predictable result of early wounding rather than crimes for which he alone bears responsibility. His entitlement to violence and abuse grows stronger with this newfound validation, often with help from a therapist, who would prefer to see him as wounded rather than help him recognize that his violence is an unacceptable response to that early wounding.

Within individual treatment, the reality of the impact of the violence on others often becomes secondary in importance to explorations of the batterer's feelings and history. Well-meaning therapists help clients address their abusive behavior by reconstructing early psychological traumas. Although many people who resort to violence in their intimate relationships were themselves targets of abusive behavior by others, investigating this link too soon in treatment obscures the need for the client to take full responsibility for the violence he perpetrates. More important, it obscures the need to do whatever is necessary in the here and now to ensure that the batterer behaves safely and respectfully.

Individual therapy, no matter how radical in content, runs counter to the public nature of group conversation and accountability. It fails to build a collective of support and critical consciousness, and it lacks the answerability of a collective experience.

Accordingly, we suggest that the best practice for men, women, or same-sex partners is to join separate circles, to unpack their issues, create rules for engagement, and get restraining orders when appropriate. Having partners participate in different circles led by the same treatment team affords immediate accountability. If there is a recurrence of violence, the treatment team immediately has access to that information and can take action with the perpetrator.

CHILD SURVIVORS OF DOMESTIC VIOLENCE

Whether or not they experience physical abuse personally, children who survive domestic violence frequently

- Feel torn in their loyalties. Pressured to choose sides in the conflict between parents, they become weapons in the marital battle.
- Blame or feel alienated from their mothers, often physically attacking them.

- Feel a need to protect their mother.
- Identify with the power of the abuser.
- Experience deprivation of the protection to which they are entitled.
- Have their developmental tasks derailed or sidetracked by the secondary trauma of witnessing and/or experiencing abuse.
- Embrace exaggerated traditional norms and/or violent behavior.

A social justice approach in domestic violence situations requires going beyond coaching parents how to ensure that they and their children stay connected and out of their acrimony. This approach may be fine for parents in divorcing situations, when there is domestic violence. However, therapists ethically must investigate the harm by the abusing parent toward the children.

While these issues can be contentious in any divorce, predictably they will be even more so when an angry batterer seeks revenge for the ending of his control over his victim. Often, a victim may spend years in court fighting to protect her children from contact with a dangerous parent or to enforce court orders for financial support (Hoult, 2006).

Victims who have been able to use the legal system to gain physical safety through a protective order now discover that they are mired in a divorce court that seems to have discarded its concern and awareness of her plight as a victim of domestic violence. A social justice therapist is aware of the psychological and economic damage done to victims and their children by these protracted legal proceedings.

Harm by the abuser toward children goes beyond physical abuse. It constitutes withholding funds for medical treatment, not paying child support that often serves as the security for housing and other essentials for daily living, parentifying children under duress, humiliating them, threatening them in subtle and covert ways about their relationship with the nonoffending parent, and threatening to abandon them.

The nonabusing parent needs guidance in learning how to speak to her children about the violence, how to teach them the value of nonviolence, and how to resist succumbing to the larger culture's demands that she keep the other parent involved at all costs. It is a huge abuse of power for the helping professional to collude with the abuser and not help him understand that children are not possessions but precious human beings who deserve care, protection, and nonviolent nurturing.

Table 8.1 describes developmental challenges faced by boys and girls who experience domestic violence.

REFRAMING DOMESTIC VIOLENCE

Domestic violence should be considered not as an individual pathology but as the escalation to its most extreme limit of domination within an intimate relationship. By reframing the issue of domestic violence, therapists can begin a more contextual

TABLE 8.1   Developmental Tasks Designed to Mitigate Impact of Domestic Violence on Children

AGE	BOYS	GIRLS
0–1	Experience nonviolent caretaking and nurturing from adults. Expect needs to be met.	Experience nonviolent caretaking and nurturing from adults. Expect needs to be met.
1–3	Exposure to nurturing males. Express sadness, fear, and disappointment rather than anger. Learn to protect self. Learn that children are not responsible for violence. Seek other adults for nurturance. Exposure to protective and assertive females.	Exposure to nurturing males. Express anger and fear. Exposure to protective and assertive females. Learn to protect self and assert own concerns and needs. Learn that children are not responsible for violence. Seek other adults for nurturance.
3–5	Learn collaborative problem solving rather than aggression. Begin to speak publicly about violence. Differentiate feelings about abusive behavior from feelings about abuser as a person. Identify anger and disappointment toward nonabusing parent for lack of protection.	Learn to assert self and speak about violence. Recognize and express both loyalty and hatred toward abuser and victim. Differentiate feelings about abusive behavior from feelings about abuser as a person. Identify anger and disappointment toward nonabusing parent for lack of protection.
5–12	Break privacy rule around domestic violence. Learn to depend on external control of violence (police, state youth and family services, teachers, counselors). Learn to express range of emotions and gather multiple ways to solve problems. Associate with different groups of kids, not just those from abusive families. Differentiate between violent and nonviolent worlds. Connect with nonviolent males. Learn to expect and receive help from other adults.	Break privacy rule around domestic violence. Learn to depend on external control of violence (police, state youth and family services, counselors). Externalize anger and rage rather than internalize it as depression and suicidal feelings. Associate with different groups of kids, not just those from violent homes. Differentiate between violent and nonviolent worlds and between adult and child worlds. Focus on caring for self rather than caring for family. Seek support from other adults. Learn to respect self as a female.

12–18	Assess peer relationships for equity and nonviolence.	Assess peer relationships for equity and nonviolence.
	Seek entry into adult world through means other than violence and devaluation of women and children or crime or drug use.	Seek entry into adult world in ways other than through seduction and victimization by men.
	Find entry through academics, sports, employment.	Find entry through academics, sports, employment.
	Verbalize fear of homicidal thoughts toward abuser or aggression toward siblings.	Verbalize fear of own suicidal thoughts.
	Plan for healthy "escape' from violent world.	Plan for healthy "escape" from violent world.

inquiry, asking the following questions:

- Under what conditions do those with power over others abuse their power?
- How is this power misused and abused?
- What is the trajectory of harm and violence?

Understanding institutional oppression toward racial, ethnic, and GLBT minorities does not mean that members of these same groups cannot be held wholly accountable for their own social and political transgressions. We encourage you to use these questions as a standard part of your assessment (with guided tools) even when abuse or violence is not the presenting complaint.

We ask you to think beyond programmatic structures and question the very definition of domestic violence. We also encourage you to question remedies that include a pro-prosecution philosophical stance and to also question the largely institutionalized systems of batterers' intervention programs predicated on the Duluth model—a largely cognitive literacy–based approach that defines victims as hapless souls who cannot be held accountable when they direct their abuse of power toward children, women, and some men (Pence & Paymar, 1993). While Pence the originator of the Duluth model, has revised the model on numerous counts, attending to some of the intersectionalities laid out in this chapter, the mainstream domestic violence movement continues to endorse the simplicity of the original model. The problem, nonetheless, with the Duluth model's practice approach is that it is cognitive, embedded in individual psychology and literacy. A cognitive approach in general does not create larger systems of empowerment and accountability.

Throughout this book, we challenge the effectiveness of separating people by their presenting problem. Change requires a social context that promotes nonviolence and resilience on all levels and forms. Viewing the problem of domestic violence as located solely in the interior of family life, disconnected from other forms of power and oppression, limits solutions. Seeing batterers and victims as homogenous populations without connections to their gendered counterparts limits creative responses.

This conceptual shift opens up intervention to a variety of possibilities as well as systematic change. Indeed, all institutions in a community must rise to an ethic of caring that holds nonviolence as its core. Couple's treatment should occur only with people who have received social education about, and made substantive changes in, their destructive uses of power and control over partners and children.

Even when subtle patterns of domination resurface, therapists should take them seriously and not go with "business as usual." When men (or women) resort to old patterns, they should be challenged within a larger community context and not within private couple's therapy sessions. Instead, therapists should take information gained in marital and family sessions back into a larger collective context (e.g., culture circle) to maintain a process of accountability that will ensure safety for the family. In our 20-year experience using this process, no battered partner has been physically harmed or endangered.

Although the battered women's movement began as a grassroots activist group, through the years it has become largely institutionalized, perhaps dangerously so. It operates within a "mythology of activism," though it often does not provide an understanding of the multilayered analysis of gender, race, culture, and class. Most important, it doesn't address how those dimensions of our lives are linked to access structures that promote and ensure safety. White, middle-class feminism as a mainstay advocacy forum for battered women is flawed and unsafe for women on the margins of society (Almeida & Lockard, 2005; Crenshaw, 1994).

While it is true that many women of color and immigrant women are served by this system, many more are not. Further, although the criminal justice system is necessary as a backdrop to ensure protection for victims, given its inherent racism, classism, sexism, and homophobia, a heavy reliance on this structure to end family violence is hazardous. We must create alternatives both within and outside of this subculture of patriarchy and white privilege.

We still live under patriarchy, which reveres, rather than challenges, traditional male roles that reinforce misuse of power and privilege. A therapeutic context that requires perpetrators of violence, as well as those who misuse power and privilege, to change is revolutionary. For example, if we consider that batterer programs are virtually the only institutions in our culture in which men are required to change, we can begin to expand on the potential. Working to change the behavior of individual men is not enough. We must challenge patriarchal values by creating expanded norms of masculinity and fostering a cultural morality based upon nonviolence. Parallel to this process, we must empower and structure accountability for women as victims while simultaneously holding women accountable for the role they play in maintaining violence against women. Efforts toward changing rigid gendered norms in all of our institutions, from schools to work sites to recreational and political spaces, is key to creating nonviolence in our families and communities.

Compliance with nonviolence standards, in the broader context of a social justice approach, is part of critical consciousness. It includes dismantling the links between patriarchy and family abuse in addition to ceasing battering within families.

While the public illumination of private lives has proven to be a powerful experience of empowerment for white women trapped by intimate violence, it is less useful in sanctioning the lives of heterosexuals of color and GLBT persons of all races. The largely heterosexual public offers "legitimized" safety for white heterosexual women in domestic violence situations (Rahman, 1989). For her, the public world is less ambiguous. For heterosexuals of color and queers, however, transforming the private lie, making the invisible visible, means confronting various public oppressions and privileges while simultaneously relocating the dimensions of power and control. For many GLBT people of color, their own racial communities deny and attack their sexual orientation. Religious damnation of queers is a legitimized form of antigay violence.

The therapeutic constructs offered in this chapter embrace a collaborative context within which the dilemmas of the gender, race, and sexual orientation are untangled. By bringing together the struggles of both the privileged and the oppressed, we dislodge the compartmentalization of experiences through hierarchical separation. Because many of these families remain on the fringes of society, social and family agencies must stretch for relational initiatives that insert a level of safety within the center of public life. They must not only expand existing conceptions of therapy but also step outside of the therapist's office to forge alliances with community support structures friendly to women, families of color, and GLBT families.

As we end this chapter, consider the different nuances of power, privilege, and oppression experienced by Margaret (Jamaican), Chitra (Asian Indian), Sheila (Irish), Rosa (Puerto Rican), and Gail (Jewish). Consider their partners as well: Kevin (Jamaican), Anant (Asian Indian), Matt (Irish), Nate (Native American), and Gary (Jewish). How did their narratives of violence, of abuse of power and privilege with their intimates, situate them within the power and control wheels? What about their diverse social locations?

Finally, consider Sara and Julie? Were you drawn to any of their truths? How does this narrative fit with your practice or what you've been taught about domestic violence in relationships of same-sex, interracial couples?

A social justice approach locates empowerment, compliance, accountability, and reparations within a larger social context. Accountability and reparations are also linked to social activism: going to high schools to socialize boys and girls to a life of nonviolence, shifting norms within corporations, and testifying in the legislature on behalf of victims' rights, or making sure that all have access to necessary resources, including adequate medical care or school advocacy to ensure safety and learning choices for all children. To succeed in altering patterns of violence among intimates, we must recognize the degree to which oppression of women, oppression of men and women of color, and oppression of GBLT people normalizes acts of public violence.

REFERENCES

Adorando, E., & Mederos, F. (2003). *Batterers intervenion in a diverse society.* Kingston, NJ: Civic Press.

Almaguer, T., Busto, R., Dixon, K., & Lu, M. (1992). Sleeping with the enemy? Talking about men, race and relationships. *Outlook, 15,* 30–38.

Almeida, R. (1996). Hindu, Christian and Muslim familes. In M. McGoldrick, J. Giordano, & J. K. Pearce (Eds.), *Ethnicity and family therapy* (2nd ed. pp. 395–423). New York: Guilford.

Almeida, R., & Bograd, M. (1990). Sponsorship: Men holding men accountable for domestic violence. *Journal of Feminist Family Therapy, 2*(3/4), 243–256.

Almeida, R., & Dolan-Del Vecchio, K. (1999). Addressing culture in batterers intervention: South Asian communities as an illustrative example. *Violence Against Women, 5*(6), 654–683.

Almeida, R., & Durkin, R. (1999). Couples therapy when there is domestic violence. *Journal of Marital and Family Therapy, 25.*

Almeida, R., & Lockard, J. (2005). The cultural context model. In N. Sokolov (Ed.), *Domestic violence at the margins: Readings on race, class gender and culture* (pp. 301–319). New Brunswick, NJ: Rutgers University Press.

Ariel, J., & McPherson, D. (2000). Therapy with lesbian and gay families and their children. *Journal of Marital and Family Therapy, 26,* 421–432.

Avis, J. M. (1992a). Where are all the family therapists? Abuse and violence within families and family therapy's response. *Journal of Marital and Family Therapy, 18*(3), 225–233.

Avis, J. M. (1992b). Current trends in feminist thought and therapy: Perspectives on sexual abuse and violence within families in North America. *Journal of Marital and Family Therapy, 4*(3/4), 87400.

Berger, R. M. (1990). Passing: Impact on the quality of same-sex couple relationships. *Social Work, 35*(4), 328–332.

Berk, R. (1990). Thinking about hate motivated crimes. *Journal of Interpersonal Violence, 5*(3), 334–339.

Bograd, M. (1984). Family systems approaches to wife battering: A feminist critique. *American Journal of Orthopsychiatry, 54,* 558–568.

Bograd, M. (1986). Family therapy and violence against women. In M. Riche (Ed.), *Women and family therapy* (pp. 34–50). Rockville, MD: Aspen Systems.

Bograd, M. (1988). How battered women and abusive men account for domestic violence: Excuses, justifications or explanations? In T. Hotaling, D. Finkelhor, J. Kirkpatrick, & M. Straus (Eds.), *Coping with family violence.* Newbury Park, CA: Sage.

Bograd, M. (1999). Strengthening domestic violence theories: Intersections of race, class, sexual orientation, and gender. *Journal of Marital and Family Therapy, 25,* 275–289.

Bograd, M., & Mederos, F. (1999). Assessing the presence of domestic violence and lethality. Battering and couples therapy: Universal screening and selection of treatment modality. *Journal of Marital and Family Therapy, 25,* 291–312

Clark, D. (1987). *The new loving someone gay.* Berkeley, CA: Celestial Arts.

Comstock, G. D. (1991). *Violence against lesbians and gay men.* New York: Columbia University Press.

Coontz, S. (2005) *Marriage, a history: From obedience to intimacy, or how love conquered marriage.* New York: Viking.

Crenshaw, K. (1994). Mapping the margins: Intersectionality, identity politics and violence against women of color (pp. 93–118). In M. Finemen, & R. Mykitiuk (Eds.), *The public nature of private violence.* New York: Routledge.

Curtis, S. (2005). Gendered violence and restorative justice: The views of victim advocates. *Violence against women, 11*(5), 603–638.

Dobash, R. E., & Dobash, R.P. (1979). *Violence against wives: A case against the patriarchy.* New York: The Free Press.

Duneier, M. (1992). *Slims Table: Race, Respectability, and Masculinity.* Chicago: University of Chicago Press.

Farley, N. (1992). Same–sex domestic violence. In S. Dworkin, & Gutierrez (Eds.), *Counseling gay men and lesbians: Journey to the end of the rainbow.* Virginia: American Association of Counseling and Development.

Gardner, R. (1998). *The parental alienation syndrome* (2nd ed). Cresskill, NJ: Creative Therapeutics.

Green, R. (1978). Sexual identity of 37 children raised by transsexual parents. *American Journal of Psychiatry, 135,* 892–697.

Herek, C. M. (1990). The context of anti-gay violence: Notes on cultural and psychological heterosexism. *Journal of Interpersonal Violence, 5*(3), 316–333.

Hitchins, D. (1980). Social attitudes, legal standards, and personal trauma in child custody cases. *Journal of Homosexuality, 5,* 89–95.

Hoult, J. (2006, Spring). The evidentiary admissibility of parental alienation syndrome: *Children's Legal Rights Journal,* Science, law and Policy American Bar Association, Vol 26, 1.

Island, D., & Letellier, P. (1991). *Men who beat the men who love them: Battered gay men and domestic violence.* New York: Harrington Park Press.

Kaufman, G. (1992). The mysterious disappearance of battered women in family therapists' offices: Male privilege colluding with male violence. *Journal of Marital and Family Therapy, 18*(3), 233–245.

Kanuha, V. (1990). Compounding the triple jeopardy: Battering in lesbian relationships. In Brown and Root (Eds.), *Diversity and complexity in feminist therapy.* New York: Harrington Park Press.

Kirkpatrick, M., Smith, L., & Roy, R. (1981). Lesbian mothers and their children. *American Journal of Orthopsychiatry, 51,* 545–551.

Kivel, P. (1992). *Men's work: How to stop the violence that tears our lives apart.* New York: Ballantine Books.

Lui, M., Robles, B., Leondar-Wright, B., Brewer, R., & Adamson, R. with United for a Fair Economy. (2006). *The color of wealth: The story behind the U.S. racial wealth divide.* New York: The New Press.

Megan, K. (2004). *Children of gay parents say they do just fine, and studies support them.* Hartford, CT: Courant

Morales, E. (1990). Ethnic minority families and minority gays and lesbians. In F. W. Bozett, & M. B. Sussman (Eds.), *Homosexuality and family relations.* New York: Harrington Park Press.

Narayan, U. (1995) "Male-order" brides: Immigrant women, domestic violence and immigration law, *Hypatia, 10*(1), 104–120.

Pence, E., & Paymar, M. (1993). *Education groups for men who batter: The Duluth model.* New York: Springer.

Pharr, S. (1988). *Homophobia: A weapon of sexism.* Little Rock, AR: Chardon Press.

Rahman, Q. A. (1989). *Getting our house in order: Racism in the battered women's movement NCADV Voice.* Washington DC: National Coalition Against Domestic Violence, 6, 1–2.

Schacher, S.J., Auerbach, C.F., & Silverstein, L.S. (2005). Gay fathers extending the possibilities for us all. *Journal of Family Studies.* NY: Haworth Press.

Walker, A. (1997). *Anything we love can be saved.* New York: Balantine Books.

Wulfhorst, E. (2006). Domestic violence takes toll in the workplace. Reuters, August 18th, 2006.

U.S. Department of Justice. (2005). Bureau of Justice Statistics. National Coalition Against Domestic Violence (2005). Retrieved on March 8, 2007, from http://www.ncadv.org/files/DV_Facts.pdf

RECOMMENDED READINGS

Berrill, K. (1990). Anti-gay violence and victimization in the United States. *Journal of Interpersonal Violence, 5* (3), 274–294.

Clunis, D. M., & Green, C. D. (1988). *Lesbian couples.* Seattle, WA: Seal Press.

Ganley, A. (1981). *Court mandated treatment for men who batter.* Washington, DC: Center for Women Policy Studies.

Gondolf, E. (1985). *Men who batter: An integrated approach for stopping wife abuse.* Homes Beach, FL: Learning Publications.

Gondolf, E. (1985). Anger and oppression in men who batter: Empiricist and feminist perspectives and their implications for research. *Victimology, 10,* 1–4, 311–324.

Gondolf, E. (1988). How some men stop their abuse: An exploratory program evaluation. In T. Hotaling, D. Finkelhor, J. Kirkpatrick, & M. Straus, *Coping with family violence.* Newbury Park, CA: Sage Publications.

Greene, B. (1992). *An African-American perspective on racism and anti-Semitism within feminist organizations.* Seventh Black International Cinema, Berlin. Kino Arsenal, Welserstrade 25, 1000 Berlin 30.

Hammond, N. (1986). Lesbian victims and the reluctance to identify abuse. In K. Lobel (Ed.), *Naming the violence: Speaking out about lesbian battering.* Seattle, WA: Seal Press.

Hart, B. (1986). Lesbian battering: An examination. In K. Lobel (Ed.), *Naming the violence: Speaking out about lesbian battering.* Seattle, WA: Seal Press.

King, D. (1988). Multiple jeopardy, multiple consciousness: The context of black feminist ideology. *Signs, 14*(1).

Lorde, A. (1984). *Sister outsider: Essays and speeches by Audre Lorde*. New York: Crossing.

Lorde, A. (1987). Turning the beat around: Lesbian parenting. In S. Pollack & J. Vaughn (Eds.), *Politics of the heart: A lesbian parenting anthology*. Ithaca, NY: Firebrand Books.

Pharr, S. (1986). Two workshops on homophobia. In K. Love (Ed.), *Naming the violence: Speaking out about lesbian battering*. Seattle, WA: Seal Press.

Renzetti, C. (1988). Violence in lesbian relationships: A preliminary analysis of causal factors. *Journal of Interpersonal Violence, 3*(4), 381–399.

Vera-Sanso, P. (1999). Dominant daughters-in-law and submissive mothers-in-law? Cooperation and conflict in South India. *Journal of the Royal Arthropdogical Institute, 5*(4), pp. 577–593.

CHAPTER NINE

CASE STUDIES: POWER, PRIVILEGE, AND OPPRESSION IN FAMILY LIFE

The story told in Case 9.1 by Frank, a 51-year-old Irish Catholic insurance broker, conveys some of his experiences in a social justice–based treatment program dedicated to addressing issues of power and privilege in family life and society. In Frank's case, domestic violence brought him and his wife to therapy. After 5 years in the treatment program, Frank is now an advocate for domestic violence prevention, speaking to churches and civic groups about his personal experience and process of healing.

Two family-centered practices in New Jersey follow the cultural context model. One center, the Institute for Family Services (IFS) in Somerset, supported Frank. It serves diverse families, with about 4% of its cases involving domestic violence. The other center, in New Brunswick, also serves diverse populations, with about 60% of its caseload made up of adolescents and their families involved at various levels of the juvenile justice system.

The Cultural Context Model: Two Studies

BY LYNN PARKER

My relationship to the programs began with an independent research project in which I interviewed prominent national feminist social workers and family therapists about how they address issues of power and privilege in therapeutic sessions with couples (see Parker, 1997, 1998a, 1998b). One of the therapists I interviewed was Rhea Almeida, director of the IFS (see Box 9.1) in Somerset, New Jersey, and founder of the cultural context model.

In a subsequent study (Parker, 2003), I concentrated on Almeida's unique model, which I selected because of its unambiguous political approach and because it places issues of social justice at the center of its therapeutic program

CASE 9.1

FRANK SPEAKS OF HIS VIOLENCE AND AWAKENING

Almost 5 years ago, when I joined the men's group, they began asking me some pretty tough questions. I was very resistant, very angry, yet I showed up every Thursday. Typically, I didn't want to hear what they had to say, but on the way home I would think about the things I heard, and those things would sink in.

I also remember on more than one occasion some of the guys telling me that during our group meeting they were really frightened, because they thought I was going to jump across the room and grab somebody. There's an interesting aspect to that because I had no idea I might have appeared that way to my wife, Rita.

I used a lot of verbal abuse and intimidation with her for a long, long time. That's the way you control someone. On the few occasions when Rita didn't follow her usual pattern of backing off, but challenged me, that was when I physically abused her. Her challenges would enrage me, and it became important to do whatever was required to be absolutely in control of that situation. This included physically abusing her, grabbing her, pushing her down, and on a few occasions even kicking her.

In the group, I slowly realized that I had a lot in common with these other men. I realized that these sponsors are there for a purpose, that they are much farther down the road than I am. I didn't relate to all of them, but there were a few, like Stan, who had a history very similar to mine. He was my sponsor. It was clear that we were very similar in the way we abused our partners. But the difference was that Stan was making changes, and I was just starting. Of course, there's a lot of accountability in this program, a lot of challenging that I think would be extremely difficult when you work one on one with a therapist.

I've had a lot of therapy. But the individual therapy Rita and I had, it's just not the same thing. I'm not sure what it takes for most of us men. Probably it takes some kind of a cri-

sis to get us here in the first place. And then we have to break down these barriers and get right down to the very essence of what is really going on inside us. How could we do these things and hurt our families? Then, finally we realize how absolutely terrible and unacceptable that kind of behavior really is.

You would think that we would know that. But it's not necessarily so. I spent some months of being very guarded and trying to be very much in control. But at some point, I started to get in touch with the terrible things that I've done. Then it just came to me very quickly that this behavior was absolutely wrong and totally unacceptable. It just could never happen again.

It might sound kind of simple, but for guys who are in this program, it's not simple because their whole life has been this course of rigidly trying to be in control. It's not an easy thing to let that go or even to see how absolutely wrong it is.

One of the group members asked me, "When you're at work and you're angry at someone at work, what do you do about it?"

The answer is, "Not much."

What they meant was, "You don't say the things to colleagues at work that you do to your wife because you would be fired!"

They were trying to convey to me that my behavior was a choice, even though I didn't think that it was. I thought that I was being provoked, that I had to react, and that my reaction was legitimate.

But they were saying, "When someone really pisses you off at work, do you walk over and get in their face? And if they come back at you, would you throw them against the wall? No. But you do that with your wife. So it's a choice."

They were making the point that abusive, controlling behavior is a choice, but I wouldn't accept that. One night, on my drive home from group to the motel where I stayed for 5 months after Rita and I separated, somebody pulled right in front of me and cut me off. I was furious! I was ready to climb out of my car at the stop light, yank the guy's door open, and pull him right out. Then I saw how big the guy was, and I didn't do a thing.

At that moment, I realized what it was like to be a bully. You have to be real careful who you pick on. You're not going to pick on a big guy. It's a very humbling, even humiliating, thing to see that in yourself. But I think we need to.

structure. More recently, I began studying the Affinity Counseling Group (see Box 9.2) in New Brunswick, New Jersey, which has also adopted the model. Along with other family services, Affinity provides clinical and family case-management services to youth and families involved with the juvenile justice system. I participated in both programs as an independent researcher to learn more about the practical applications of the cultural context model.

For both studies, I chose the single case-study method of qualitative research. Information was gathered from multiple sources: interviewing clients, staff, and sponsors; observing all aspects of the program; and reviewing program documents (Stake, 1995). The research with IFS was conducted from 1995–2000; the research with Affinity took place in 2006.

Interviews followed a "general interview guide approach" (Patton, 1990, p. 280), using a set of open-ended, very general questions. Candid perceptions from clinicians and clients were sought. The clinicians spent many hours meticulously describing the philosophy and process of the program.

BOX 9.1

INSTITUTE FOR FAMILY SERVICES

The Institute for Family Services (IFS) is a team of family therapists committed to producing change that embraces safe, respectful, nurturing, and empowering relation- ships for all communities and families. The IFS is acclaimed throughout New Jersey and the nation for its innovative programs for families and communities, raising critical consciousness, and instituting empowerment and accountability. The IFS faculty teaches its expanded model of family therapy to postgraduates and offers training in the cultural context model at the state, national, and international levels.

At IFS, clients receive the same attention, support, and care regardless of financial resources. IFS therapists work to create and sustain a broad community of helpers, clientele, friends, and professionals.

■ ■ ■ ■ ■

BOX 9.2
AFFINITY COUNSELING GROUP

Affinity Counseling Group was established by social workers and family therapists who wanted to offer high-quality, innovative systems thinking and therapy to families in crisis, particularly families from marginalized populations. Using a team approach with therapists specializing in various fields and paraprofessionals with rich community-building experience, Affinity is committed to empower all persons to contribute meaningfully to their relationships and communities; to engage and challenge families to work collaboratively toward community and social justice; and to respect, support, and forward the rights of all people including youth, women, people of color, people with disabilities, people of all religious backgrounds, and lesbian, gay, bisexual, and transgender individuals.

Among the questions posed to clients were

- What have been your experiences in the program here?
- What has been helpful or not helpful?
- For whom does (does not) this program work?

My intent was to provide a portrait of a therapeutic model, the mission of which is to promote social justice. Below are some themes uncovered in my interviews with clients that illustrate how empowerment and accountability—primary components of a social justice approach—are integrated into therapeutic work.

CLIENTS' IMPRESSIONS

What do clients say about their experience with the cultural context model? Following are five themes characteristic of the responses clients gave.

1. *Therapy was very different than I thought it would be.* Several clients said the therapy they received was different from what they expected. Some talked about their initial resistance to the same-gender culture circle format.

The following quote is from Stan, a 34-year-old German American construction worker who came with his wife, Gretchen, to the program because their arguments were becoming more intense and frequent.

Therapy was such a different experience than I had expected it to be. I thought we would be in couple's sessions. When I was put in with a bunch of men, and only had a short period of time to talk, I was always wondering what was happening with Gretchen. At first it was hard, because the things people said in the men's group went against all the roles I grew up with in my household—the role of the male, the husband, the son. The men's group challenged those fundamental ideas. But when I look back, I think it was for the best to first concentrate on what's going on with me, and not as a couple. I tell the men who come here not to get all excited and angry about things just because you're uncomfortable confiding in men.

As he mentions, Stan was initially uncomfortable with the structure of the program, where he found himself in a men's group and his wife in a women's group instead of both participating together in couple's therapy, because he did not know and could not control what his wife was saying in the women's group. He was also discomforted by a situation that required intimate sharing with other men.

Both are structurally imposed changes in the ways the partners ordinarily relate to each other. The structure is designed to encourage people (particularly males) to take responsibility for their own emotional lives by requiring that they first break down their interpersonal issues in the context of the culture circles. Rather than insulating themselves in what may be the more comfortable environment of couple's counseling, partners first go to same-gender culture circles to expand their view of themselves and their situation.

Couple's counseling is done in the men's, women's, or couple's circles. Many men I interviewed agreed with the one who told me that learning to "carry my own emotional burden instead of putting it on my partner, learning to feel my own feelings and to share significant events with other men, frees me to be more intimate with my wife and family."

In all-female culture circles, women more readily learn "I'm not crazy; my situation is," because in the larger IFS community, "crazy making" issues of power and privilege are directly and specifically tackled by both genders, although they do so separately. Most clients, especially the men, initially expressed reservations about being in gender-specific culture circles, but all the clients I interviewed came to appreciate their value.

2. *Breaking down barriers.* Many clients said that the diversity of the membership of the culture circles—encompassing people of different ages, races, problems, sexual orientation, and social class—helps to break down barriers between people who are different and who would otherwise have no contact with one another. Clients were surprised by the commonalities they found. William, a 31-year-old African American male psychology student, initially said that if he had to participate in a group, he preferred to be in a black men's group. He later came to appreciate the value of the diverse men's culture circle:

The program helped me draw connections between men of color, men of different classes, and men at different places on the power and control wheel. It also helped to bring us together and to see the ways we use power and control in our own lives. Through the media, society tells us that we're all separate, and there really aren't many similarities between us. The program here breaks down a lot of the differences that we otherwise might use to put up walls that keep us from communicating with each other. These walls prevent us from coming to terms with the way we use power and control in our lives.

I bought into that separation. Then, sitting right next to me in the group was a white male cop who physically abused his wife! And on the other side was a white man who is three times my age and who sexually abused his daughter!

I would ask myself, "What am I doing here? That's not my background. I haven't used my power in those ways." Early on, I was putting up walls and saying, "I'm not really sure this is for me because of the obvious differences."

Over time, I've realized it is all connected. The way we men use power in our workplace and family life crosses cultures, professions, races, and ages. Without my culture circle, I probably wouldn't have seen the connections.

If I tell myself I'm not a child molester, I'm not a rapist, I'm not a woman abuser, that makes the things I am doing seem kind of small, as opposed to "Wow, I'm doing almost exactly what he's doing, just to a lesser degree."

Maybe I ostracize my girlfriend. Although I don't play around or drink, she still feels just as isolated as the cop's wife. I'm able to see myself in them, and that goes hand in hand with breaking down those barriers and accepting that maybe I do need to be here. Maybe there is some work that I need to do.

When university police, using racial profiling, stopped and harassed William, IFS clients and staff members gave him the financial and emotional backing he needed to take legal action, which he did and won. In his men's circle, William also had many opportunities to give older white men advice, breaking traditional racial and social norms, which he could not have done in a more traditional therapeutic setting or in a black men's group.

William speaks for many clients when he says that hearing other men talk about the diverse problems for which they come to therapy helps individuals see their own misuses of power. This is a central focus at IFS and the reason for creating the culture circle structure. Men who do not at first recognize their own power and control issues come to see that they are not so different from members who are in the program as court-mandated perpetrators of violence.

Group members also say, like William, that they learn to locate themselves somewhere on the spectrum of power abuse as opposed to seeing a dichotomy between "us" nonviolent guys and "them" violent guys. This more inclusive frame of reference (along with the social education format) gives people a broader understanding of power and inequity.

Layla, a female college student who is black, Colombian, Palestinian, and Muslim, talked about the initial resistance she felt toward her culture circle group because the women seemed so different from her. Then, like William, she became aware of where connections were possible.

I didn't think that they had any concept of what I was going through. I was much younger than most, but I felt that they couldn't identify with me culturally. I had always attributed the problems in my family to my cultural background. I never really saw that women share a lot of common difficulties. We live in a patriarchal society across the board. It's not just something inherent to my family, like my father's culture and religion.

Growing up, I had the sense that women were being controlled, but I thought that it was only happening in my family because of the religion and the customs. I thought that it was my family that was nuts! I thought that women in white America didn't experience those types of controls in the same way I did. So, I couldn't really appreciate that, as women, we have this common thread—oppression—and that in that regard we are very similar regardless of our cultural background.

Particularly helpful to Layla was a social education component on diversity in which videotapes were shown to her women's group to help non-Muslim women understand Muslim women in the context of Islam. Layla felt that she was safe to explore these issues within a community of women committed to building a critical consciousness.

Clients talked about how they were able in the diverse culture circles to break down long-held stereotypes and realize that while there are significant differences, there are also universal threads that connect people. One 16-year-old Latino male, a former gang member, shared the insights he had gained into the influence of "patriarchy" and "male privilege" (his words) on men and women. This use of language and connection of personal issues to broader contextual issues were commonplace in the interviewees. If the post-structuralists are correct, and our words create the world we behold (Fraser, 1997; Moules, 1999), we need a new language system.

In order for the world to become a more equitable environment for those with less power and privilege, their voices need to be heard by those with more power and privilege (Weick, 2000). The clients at IFS and Affinity are learning how to articulate their needs and interests.

3. *Public forum and collective memory.* Clients often remarked about the value of the culture circles, the sponsorship program, and advocacy work as a "public forum" where all sorts of things are explicitly stated and discussed in the presence of a group of interested people. Sometimes men who initially resisted the culture circle format became its greatest proponents. Clients also appreciated the culture circles' ability to function as what they called a "collective memory." For example, clients remember each other's past misdeeds or commitments that were made but have not yet been kept regarding behavioral changes. Beth, a 42-year-old Irish accountant stated that "the public forum and the collective memory of the culture circle are so helpful" because "if I'm in la-la land over here, they say, 'Remember when he did this? And, you need to make sure that you don't forget that he is capable of x, y, and z.' That is a very powerful tool, although it never feels good."

Beth wanted to reunite with her husband, Kevin, who was out of the home because of inappropriate behavior toward their 8-year-old daughter and his involvement with sex clubs that had cost the family more than $90,000 over the past 10 years. The women's culture circle provided a "collective memory" for Beth. They pointed out that even though there were significant improvements in Kevin's behavior, he had recently violated "boundaries" with their daughter.

Feedback from the culture circles and sponsors serves a powerful accountability function. When the "heat" of the moment has slipped from the memory of clients in cases of abuse, as it often does, those memories are kept alive by culture circle members committed to empowering silenced voices and holding each other accountable.

Additional accountability is provided through "public forums" in several culture circles running simultaneously. For example, Beth and Kevin's two daughters attend the children's circle, where they revealed recent boundary violations by their father. Beth was then able to address this issue in her culture circle. In Beth's words:

> Our daughter knew that it would get back to both of us and that her dad would be held accountable; and that was important to her. She now sees there's a safety net in bringing the problem here. She didn't have to tell him directly, "Daddy, that doesn't feel good when you say that." An 8-year-old is not going to say that. But it's a tremendous benefit for the girls to know that it will be taken care of!
>
> My husband is held accountable in a public way. He's not confronted with this information in private. It's brought into the men's circle, and they say, "What the hell are you doing putting your daughter in that position?" He is on the spot and publicly has to acknowledge, "Well, I did that." And he is unlikely to do it again. We have been in therapy for 9 of our 12 years of marriage, and no real change occurred until we came here.

Having several family members participate in the various culture circles seems to be the norm rather than the exception. Rather than going private within individual, relationship, or family therapy, clients are encouraged by the structure of the therapy in the culture circles to go public. This promotes differentiation (McGoldrick & Carter, 2001) within an intimate context that is not necessarily one of family of origin. Clients learn to be responsible, maintain their sense of selves, and manage reactivity to others while being emotionally present with significant others. Personal and relational responsibility are reinforced within the context of culture circles. Clients are offered layers of support for life changes yet are simultaneously challenged to be responsible, generous, and accountable to those in their culture circles. When emotional reactivity that individuals may carry with them from their family of origin erupts, they are helped to understand their reactions and offered new perspectives. When relationship or family work is deemed appropriate, it is available—again in the context of a public forum within the men's, women's, or couples' culture circles.

Ann, a 32-year-old Irish secretary, related an IFS adage: "We are encouraged to call our culture circles before trying to resolve issues in relationships. This has changed the intensity of my husband's and my arguing and fights." Clients report that going to their culture circle first allows issues to be aired in a context where clarity can be gained outside of the turmoil of the relational moment.

This strategy is similar to conflict management strategies employed by Notarius and Markman (1993) and Gottman (1994) in that people are encouraged to take time away from situations to gain perspective on conflictual issues before confronting those issues with others. But at IFS, clients first consult their community of helpers instead of taking time outs. Doing so seems to help clients break down isolation and secrecy surrounding family life and dilemmas and allows them to muster resources and support for less reactive responses and behavior.

4. *No secrets.* Several clients related how secrecy had contributed to their problems. They said that affairs, pornography, and private psychotherapies left "real" problems unchallenged and therefore intact. If both partners and/or family members are to be treated by IFS, they must first agree that secrets will not be kept from people or culture circles under the guise of confidentiality.

As a result, the team knows immediately and can respond if threats of violence are made or boundaries are violated. This approach is different even from group-oriented domestic violence therapy in which partners tend to be seen by different treatment providers who are therefore limited in learning the full story from both partners.

According to clients and treatment providers, all aspects of the program at IFS emphasize:

1. Safety and empowerment for victims of abuse.
2. Responsibility and accountability within an ethic of care for perpetrators of abuse.

Accordingly, the therapists stressed that they are careful to discern whether revealing information would put someone at risk. Partners are seen in different centers (though by the same treatment team) to ensure both safety and accountability. Several female clients, some with current restraining orders against their partners, said they felt physically and psychologically safer because the IFS team was treating their partner. Their feelings of safety flowed from the knowledge that their partner was being held accountable for maintaining nonviolent behavior by the men's circle and treatment team. Both partners knew if violent behavior occurred, the treatment team would be informed and would take action.

5. *Giving Back.* Many clients emphasized their wish to give to others some of what they learned in the therapeutic process. They related that becoming a sponsor of new clients in the cultural context model was a way to give back as well as a way to keep their consciousness raised.

Sam, a 35-year-old Puerto Rican, stated that "after I graduated from the program, I told myself that I don't have to be here on a weekly basis anymore. My marriage is going well. I'm a better person than when I first started. But the sponsorship program is the perfect opportunity for me to stay in touch with the community and to give back to other men some of what I've learned. It's really been very helpful."

In a similar vein, Al, 51 and Scotch-Irish, recalled that, "I became a sponsor for two simple reasons: to continue with my consciousness-raising and to give back what was given to me. The way you really blossom is when you find opportunities to give to other people what was given to you. Then it just comes back to you, and that's a wonderful thing."

The sponsorship programs and the active advocacy projects work to dismantle power, privilege, and oppression on a broader societal level. In the context of their wish to give back what they learned at IFS, several male clients established the first chapter of the National Organization of Men Against Sexism (NOMAS) in New Jersey. Others formed a white privilege group. Some speak to schools and churches on such topics as the prevention and remediation of domestic violence and sexism.

Other community action projects that have come out of the model include a successful basketball tournament planned and initiated by Affinity's adolescent clients to raise money for Katrina flood victims in New Orleans and a voter registration drive. The adolescent clients were very proud that they were able to register more new voters than the American Civil Liberties Union. Action projects such as these provide a way for clients to begin to enact social education in ways that are meaningful to them.

The projects also empower clients. In this case, adolescents who previously were involved with the criminal justice system discovered they could be leaders in contributing meaningfully to others and to their community. In addition to garnering positive feedback from others, the participants developed a more positive sense of themselves as well as a feeling that there were new possibilities for who they could become.

Many clients try to give back by serving as sponsors to newer clients. The sponsors are not therapists. Sponsors are support persons who serve in a variety of roles:

- They serve as mentors to those struggling with issues of equity and nonviolence in relationships.
- They offer expanded notions of masculinity, including nurturing, gentleness, and empathy; and femininity, including financial viability and empowerment.
- They model respect for women, children, people of color, sexual minorities, and others who are different from them.
- They sometimes serve as a special resource to a client of the same cultural or religious background or provide needed and missing information to a culture circle on a particular topic.

FOR WHOM DOES THE PROGRAM WORK?

Clients say the therapeutic program offered at IFS "works when you work it." Everyone I interviewed claimed the program was a success for them. They say it is not an easy or brief therapy. In the opinion of Ann, a 27-year-old African American student, the program might not work for people "who are invested in finding some instant cure or some biomedical approach where someone throws a couple of pills at you and says 'see you in six months.'"

Ann added that "if you think you're going to go to brief counseling, or something that is totally removed from a community atmosphere, or that it is not going to address all aspects of your being, you are in for a surprise. This program is a lot of work!" She warns "you've got to be ready to confront what you've been taught since you were a fetus and to look at the world differently. And we have plenty of people who come in and know it's not for them right from the jump because they're not ready."

Similar themes ran through many clients' remarks. Others emphasized how the program challenges fundamental belief systems as well as behavioral patterns. As 34-year-old Stan said, "It's very different to challenge society's view. People don't like that."

Not every client who comes to the program stays with it. Those who do and who are successful need to be willing to challenge fundamental belief systems and to do so in the public context of the culture circles.

CONCLUSIONS

What can we learn from the case studies throughout this book about applying a social justice perspective in our therapeutic work with others? First, we must structure therapeutic work so that issues of power, privilege, and oppression are integral to each step of the therapeutic process. Second—and this aspect is still missing even from most feminist therapeutic programs—we must find ways to engage and hold those with more power and privilege accountable to change the unequal power structure.

Engaging and holding those with more power and privilege accountable is what makes the therapeutic experience different for clients who engage in the cultural context model. When clients (or therapists) step into IFS or Affinity, they have stepped into another therapeutic world—one where men, heterosexuals, and people of light skin and middle- or upper-class background are not automatically granted the loudest voice. Instead, clients are asked to systematically examine their privileges and how they impact others. Rather than placing the onus for change on the shoulders of those with the least power to affect it, the social justice approach places responsibility squarely on the shoulders of those with more power. This shift empowers women and others with less social power, the very people who in most therapeutic settings carry most of the responsibility for change.

Furthermore, the cultural context model conveys the message that problems are better solved in communities that nurture empowerment and answerability than in isolation. The culture circles and sponsors help break down traditional rules of privacy that serve to maintain positions of power and privilege (and therefore inequality) in relationships and society. As the clients say, "This is not a brief therapy."

It is far more than therapy. It is also resocialization.

REFERENCES

Fraser, N. (1997). *Justice interruptus: Critical reflections on the "poststructuralis" condition.* New York: Routledge.

Gottman, J. M. (1994). *Why marriages succeed or fail.* New York: Simon & Shuster.

McGoldrick, M., & Carter, B. (2001). Advances in coaching: Family therapy with one person. *Journal of Marital and Family Therapy, 27,* 281–300.

Moules, N. (2000). Postmodernism and the sacred: Reclaiming connection in our greater-than-human worlds. *Journal of Marital and Family Therapy, 26*(2), 229–240.

Notarius, C. I., & Markman, H. (1993). *We can work it out: making sense of marital conflict.* New York: Putnam's Sons.

Parker, L. (2003). A social justice model for clinical social work. *Affilia, 18,* 272–288.

Parker, L. (1998a). The unequal bargain: Power issues in couples therapy. *Journal of Feminist Family Therapy, 10*(3) 17–38.

Parker, L. (1998b). Keeping power on the table in couples therapy. *Journal of Feminist Family Therapy, 10*(1), 1–24.

Patton, M. Q. (1990). *Qualitative evaluation and research methods.* Newbury Park, CA: Sage.

Stake, R. E. (1995). *The art of case study research.* Thousand Oaks, CA: Sage.

Weick, A. (2000). Hidden voices. *Social Work, 45,* 395–402.

CHAPTER TEN

DIALOGUE: THE WAY FORWARD

You can't be neutral on a moving train.
—Howard Zinn (1995)

As you approach this book's end, we hope that you are energized and ready to implement changes that bring social justice into the center of your work. We know that moving in this direction can be difficult because most professional healers practice within settings governed by the profit motive and a host of related values that don't support social justice.

Therefore, in this final chapter, we conduct an imaginary dialogue with you that addresses questions that are often asked by our live audiences after the presentation of this material.

Our dialogue touches on

- Incorporating the social justice strategies we have described into your practice.
- Resolving discomfort with intervention that defies "neutrality."
- A thoughtful approach to confidentiality.
- The importance of courage and risk-taking for clients and for professional healers as well.

Reader: *I understand that ethically we cannot ignore our society's unjust power structure. But how do we construct a treatment plan that addresses injustice in the world at large while also keeping the client family's presenting issues as the focal point?*

Authors: You can focus on the points where injustice intersects with the client family's particular dilemmas. Consider the following case. Daniel, a Korean American working-class man, who works as a supervisor at a major U.S. corporation, came to therapy because of increasing exhaustion, which contributed to growing isolation from his wife, Amy, who is also Korean American and is a graduate student at an art institute.

Over the previous three years, Daniel's work team had endured repeated "downsizings" without a corresponding decrease in workload. He and all the other members of his department were routinely working 14-hour days. His team's morale was suffering, and two of his staff members were out on "stress disabilities." Before he began therapy, Daniel started picking up signs that his own job was likely to be cut in the next reorganization.

In addition to the fear that Daniel's job might disappear, the couple faced additional stress. Their home, which was their pride and joy as well as their primary asset, is located next to public land that was zoned as a wildlife refuge when they bought it 5 years earlier. Recently, the county and town signed a deal with one of the country's largest toy retailers to rezone much of this undeveloped acreage for the construction of a 24-hour regional warehouse and distribution center. This project would destroy the wildlife sanctuary, damage the environment, and devalue Daniel and Amy's property by bringing constant truck traffic into their mostly working-class neighborhood.

Daniel and Amy felt worn down, exhausted, and hopeless and were constantly irritable toward one another. They both feared they were suffering from clinical depression, and at their intake session, they raised the idea that perhaps they should begin taking antidepressants.

Reader: *In this case, a lot of what you describe is material that therapists often wouldn't cover. They would stay with the symptoms that characterize depression or focus on the details of conflict within the couple.*

Authors: You're absolutely correct. Too often, therapists shape the assessment and findings by exploring some aspects of the client's situation in great detail while paying no attention at all to other aspects. In order to make a broader contextual assessment, it is useful to begin by creating a genogram that includes ethnicity, occupation, family roles, work roles, assets, and financial status. In addition to focusing on those aspects, we advise helping the clients expand their understanding of the presenting problem through social education, and whenever possible, linking them to progressive contacts outside their family circle.

For Daniel and Amy, therapy began with the therapeutic contract to meet other employees dealing with similar issues and a number of reading assignments. They were encouraged to find out if any resistance was brewing within their community to the proposed distribution center. They were also invited to meet George, a Chinese American, middle-class man who, in his own workplace, had faced many of the same challenges as Daniel. George's partner, Magdalena, an Italian American nurse, was also brought into the circle.

The therapist directed the couples to a number of articles and books from which they could choose their reading assignments. Among the suggested readings were "The Reincarnation of Rumpelstiltskin," a chapter from Arundhati Roy's *Power Politics* (2001); "Nitassinan: The Hunter and the Peasant," from Winona LaDuke's *All Our Relations: Native Struggles for Land and Life* (1999); Naomi Klein's *No Logo* (2000); and the International Forum on Globalization's *Alternatives to Economic Globalization: A Better World Is Possible* (2002).

They were also referred to Web sites documenting activist struggles in South Korea against dam projects, and they watched some of the movie vignettes highlighted in Chapter 2: *Roger and Me*; *The Corporation*; *Wal-Mart: The High Cost of Low Price*; *In Good Company*; and *Working Girl*.

Reading, watching films, and discussing what they were learning about the dark side of corporate globalization helped Daniel and Amy put the warehouse project threatening their neighborhood in a more comprehensive frame of reference. They recognized that as a working-class family living in one of more modest neighborhoods in the county, it was entirely predictable that their community would face the current environmental challenge from the corporate elite in partnership with government authorities. The readings and discussions also put the corporate threats to Daniel's and George's livelihoods in better perspective.

Reader: *I can see that therapists need to be up on their readings and movies.*

Authors: Social education applies to therapists and students as well as clients. To effectively guide our clients, we must continuously expand our own critical consciousness by reading, watching films, and making connections to community efforts.

Amy and Daniel learned that people had indeed gotten together to oppose the planned distribution center. With encouragement from the therapist, they began participating in the group's weekly meetings, letter-writing campaigns, and other activities. George and Magdalena helped with these efforts.

Through their studies, Daniel and Amy were able to link Daniel's uncertain job status to the efforts of global capitalism to move labor to low-wage, low-benefit countries, where economic and political conditions make nonunion, sweatshop working conditions the norm. They could see that even if the jobs did not actually move, this global pattern inspired fear and desperation within the United States as well, and it pressured employees to accept increasingly stressful and untenable workplace demands.

George, who had been downsized several times in the past several years, led a weekly discussion circle for survivors of corporate downsizing at a local YMCA. Although most of the participants were recently laid off, some participants, like Daniel, were proactively assessing their current employment situation and options. Members of this circle referred Daniel, George, and their partners to some articles in *The Guardian*, a British newspaper. One predicted that at least 30,000 positions in Britain's finance and insurance industries were likely to be transferred to India over the next 5 years. Another *Guardian* article reported that the railway information call center in Britain was likely to

---

BOX 10.1

**NOW THE JOBS WE STOLE 200 YEARS AGO
ARE RETURNING TO INDIA**

There is nothing new about multinational corporations forcing workers in distant parts of the world to undercut each other. What is new is the extent to which the labor forces of the poor nations are also beginning to threaten the security of our middle classes. The most vulnerable communities in Britain are losing the jobs which were supposed to have rescued them. Almost two-thirds of call-center workers are women, so the disadvantaged sex will slip still further behind. At the same time, extending the practices of their colonial predecessors, they will oblige their Indian workers to mimic not only our working methods but also our accents, our tastes, and our enthusiasms in order to persuade customers in Britain that they are talking to someone down the road. The most marketable skill in India today is the ability to abandon your identity and slip into someone else's (Monblot, 2003).

---

move to Bangalore, India. Two days later, the same paper reported that the HSBC Bank was cutting 4,000 customer service jobs in Britain and relocating them to Asia.

The discussion circle read another article from *The Guardian* [see excerpt in Box 10.1] pointing to the rise of call centers overseas that eliminated these types of jobs at home. Even the jobs of well-educated professionals are now being threatened with outsourcing.

Reader: *It seems that much of the work of therapy took place outside the consultation room and was actually facilitated by other people, like George and the members of his discussion group.*

Authors: That's an important observation. A central aspect of the therapeutic task is to help clients join with others to examine and resist injustice. The cultural context model's culture circles function within the therapeutic practice setting. In the case of Daniel and Amy, there was no culture circle per se but rather links to progressive community elements like George's survivors' discussion circle and the taskforce fighting the distribution center. Critical consciousness, accountability, and empowerment—the primary vehicles of social justice–based therapy—can be constructed in different ways.

George became a mentor in Daniel's life. Two years earlier, George had decided to start giving more priority to connections with family and friends than to the ever-expanding demands of the corporate workplace. George's role bridged what we described earlier as the roles of the cultural consultant and the sponsor. As a cultural consultant, he helped Daniel reexamine the culture of the corporate workplace from a human-values perspective. As a sponsor, he shared his own experiences and provided ongoing support and encouragement to Daniel.

George and the other men in the survivors' discussion circle encouraged Daniel to spend less time at work and more with Amy and to begin setting limits on how many assignments he accepted for his team from the manager of his department. The therapist supported these recommendations.

Reader: *But what if George or other members of the group were giving Daniel bad advice? What would the therapist do then?*

Authors: That's an important question. There needs to be a corrective feedback loop. In essence, the therapist would try to broaden the network of contacts still further, and through direct consultations with Daniel, George, and the group, try to directly shape the pattern of support Daniel was getting.

Similar input is necessary when dealing with addictions. While 12-step programs can be lifesavers, they tend to prioritize individual recovery over relational responsibilities, even when domestic violence or child abuse is present. Therefore, we invite 12-step sponsors in for consultation with clients and connect our clients to 12-step sponsors who have developed critical consciousness about this aspect of their recovery support programs.

Reader: *What would that look like in this case? Would you invite George into your office? Would you attend one or more of his group meetings?*

Authors: Either might be an option. There would always be a connecting loop between the therapist and clients because these are not self-help groups but circles predicated on critical consciousness. The goal really is to build a growing web of contacts that will help advance a progressive agenda, one that's good for individuals, families, and communities. Empowerment and accountability are the cornerstones for change.

Any meetings with George would include Daniel and Amy. In this case, the therapist had a preexisting personal connection to George because George was a former client who had started his discussion circle as a way to continue to resist the corporate culture while empowering his family and community.

Reader: *What happened when Daniel started setting limits at work? Did he lose his job?*

Authors: At first, Daniel was sure he would lose his job, so he updated his résumé, began refreshing his network of professional contacts, and started exploring career-change options. Feeling empowered by these actions, and by his growing understanding that the expectations from his superiors were unreasonable, Daniel eventually went well beyond the suggestions offered in therapy and by his mentor. He began leaving work promptly at 5 o'clock and encouraged those reporting to him to do the same. He sliced his team's workload by saying no to a great many assignments. He spent more time and energy on family activities and expanding his network of friends.

Interestingly, Daniel's job was not eliminated. It was noted that his staff members were performing more effectively than ever before, and their morale made them the envy of the department. Daniel recently reported, "My manager now refers to me as her 'work/life guru' and is inviting me to share my strategies with all her groups."

Daniel and Amy were enjoying major changes in their lives. The isolation and depression that brought them to therapy had lifted. They now felt a strong connection to one another as well as to their community resistance group and the corporate resistance circle. The question the couple had raised during their intake session about needing antidepressant medication was never mentioned again.

Reader: *Were they able to stop the toy manufacturer's distribution center?*

Authors: No. The community group wasn't successful in thwarting the warehouse construction project, but Daniel and Amy continued their organizing activities, broadening their focus to take on related environmental concerns. Resistance, even when unsuccessful, often energizes and activates people to keep struggling. We've repeatedly witnessed the truth in words from Alice Walker's novel, *Possessing the Secret of Joy*. Walker writes that "resistance is the secret of joy!" We know, too, that when people join together to challenge oppressive forces in their lives, they become healthier at multiple levels and less likely to require pharmaceutical interventions.

The therapist's role in putting social justice at the center of the therapeutic process is to foster critical consciousness, empowerment through concerted action, and accountability to primary relational responsibilities rather than identifying and treating just the presenting problem. Daniel's connection to George and the corporate resistance group helped him focus his priorities on his relationship with Amy, his extended family, healthy patterns of living, and bringing accountability to his work site.

Reader: *But when you expand the context and direct people to readings and community affiliations that have such obvious political leanings, aren't you imposing your own views on your clients? Doesn't that compromise therapeutic neutrality? Also, how did you manage to connect Daniel and Amy to the man who became Daniel's mentor without compromising the couple's confidentiality?*

Authors: We don't believe it's possible to deliver communication or therapeutic intervention that doesn't include a political message. Just how obvious the political slant of a communication is really depends on the degree to which it resonates with or deviates from a culture's dominant values.

Imagine that a 14-year-old boy tells his therapist he has a secret crush on a girl, and the therapist encourages him to ask her on a date with his parents as chaperones. Because the mainstream in the United States affirms heterosexual dating among teens, most people would not see any political agenda in the therapist's suggestion.

But what if the object of the boy's affection was another boy? Or what if the boy belonged to an ethnicity or religious group that frowned on dating? In those cases, the therapist's encouragement might be seen as advancing a political agenda. In fact, when therapists pretend that there is no political content to their interventions, when they subscribe to neutrality, they are likely to intervene in ways that consistently affirm mainstream values, including sexism, racism, and homophobia.

Reader: *Quite a few family therapists have written about therapeutic neutrality. When you say that there can be no genuine neutrality in a world that assigns different power dimensions to people according to gender, are you referring to the work of Rachel Hare-Mustin and James and McIntye's challenge of Bateson's concept of both/and?*

Authors: Yes. And in addition to gender issues, we expand the focus to include aspects of identity that carry added power implications, such as race, sexual orientation, and economic class. Let's say that a young black woman, distraught at finding out she did not get the workplace promotion she believed she merited, engages a black female therapist. The therapist empathizes with her client's anguish and encourages the young woman to emulate the communication and work styles exhibited by people who get ahead at her company.

The therapist knows that her client, as a black female with a working-class background, is vastly different from her senior colleagues, who are mostly upper-class white males. She also believes these differences have something to do with the challenges her client faces. But the client hasn't mentioned these differences, so neither does the therapist because she fears that raising such matters would compromise her neutrality.

Reader: *I think a narrative therapist might also struggle with a concern that she or he could be imposing his or her own position on the client.*

Author: As Dee Watts Jones (2002) stated in her article, "Healing Internalized Racism: The Within Group Experience," there are therapists who, not wanting to "impose" their own struggle with internalized racism, assume what they consider a posture of neutrality. These therapists would not challenge the client to consider the larger sociopolitical context of her dilemma. Instead, the therapist looks for "unique outcomes" within this young woman's narrative, moments when she was successful in fitting in. The therapist helps her client work to refine her behavior to increase the frequency of such moments.

Memmi (1967) might say that both therapist and client are falling for the colonialist myth of assimilation, which promises that if the young woman becomes similar enough to the colonizers—such as her employer— she will be accepted as one of them and could be as economically viable as they are. Memmi describes this as a cruel joke that colonizers use to exploit the colonized.

In her misguided effort to maintain therapeutic neutrality, through her silence, the therapist in effect decides not to help the young woman evaluate whether or not racism contributed to her lack of a promotion.

Reader: *What should the therapist have done differently?*

Authors: The therapist could ask how many women executives of color there are at the firm and what its promotional patterns are in terms of gender, race, and sexual orientation. She could coach her client on how to navigate the corporate system strategically in order to access this information. The therapist could help her client embrace with critical consciousness the concerns she may be silently harboring.

It would also be helpful to contrast the client's current dilemma with the corporate culture of sexism and racism that has allowed white men to profit from the labor of women and men of color for centuries. If the therapist referred the young woman to the work of Terry Kupers on *The Politics of Psychiatry: Gender and Sexual Preference in DSM IV* or Angela Davis (2000) on the prison industrial complex, she would help her client expand her viewpoint on the current state of oppression of people of color in the United States. These explorations would expand her view of the continuum of racism and sexism against which her personal dilemma is played out.

When the therapist keeps her client's personal narrative separate from the larger collective narrative of society (under misguided notions about subjective truths and the importance of neutrality), she is using her power to leave patterns of oppression invisible and unchallenged.

Reader: *So you would replace a commitment to neutrality with an effort to foster critical consciousness. Is it really fair to say that therapeutic neutrality is a euphemism for therapeutic practices that are politically conservative and seriously harmful to some?*

Authors: Exactly. In this example, accountability would include considering options after the client had fully examined the possibility that racism and sexism might have contributed to her stalled career development. Suppose the client learned that people of color were woefully underrepresented at the senior levels of the firm and that a similar pattern applied to promotional patterns. She would be encouraged to explore internal and external grievance procedures and the pros and cons of legal action. She would be referred to professional associations for people of color where she could get additional support and guidance. She might also be coached to seek employment with more progressive employers or launch her own business enterprise. Clients need to be informed about antiquated corporate policies that have not kept up with the needs of contemporary families.

Suppose, on the contrary, she learned that over the past 15 years, the CEO and 30% of senior partners at the firm had been women of color; that company policy mandated strong representation of people of color, women, and GLBT people at all organizational levels; and that promotional patterns indicated the absence of a glass ceiling. This knowledge would free her to seek a mentor within the firm without the lurking suspicion that racism and sexism would forever hold her back.

We therapists also need accountability. In this example, the therapist would not have made the mistakes she did had she been held accountable by consultants who have worked to gain critical consciousness and who represent the experiences of colonized people, including women of all colors, working-class people, and those who work at the poverty level. Such consultants would have challenged the therapist's silence regarding differences of power related to gender and race and the implications of these differences.

Just as social justice–based therapy expands the focus of the therapeutic endeavor, accountability of the therapist requires an expanded of system of delivery.

Reader: *In this case, the minority race and gender of the therapist did not mean she demonstrated a progressive approach to therapy. You're saying that even nonwhite, lesbian, disabled, and elder therapists can benefit from connection to consultants who hold them accountable.*

Authors: That's right. Every day, each of us faces a barrage of messages and rewards that push us to go along with the mainstream agenda. We all have blind spots. And when we occupy a position of power and responsibility in an institution, even a relatively marginalized institution like a domestic violence shelter or a mental health agency, we may slip into patterns of "power over" rather than "power with." That's why we all need a therapeutic process that fosters accountability through connecting us to consulting professionals who hold advanced critical consciousness.

Reader: *How can we respect confidentiality while expanding the definition of who interacts with the family in the therapeutic context and who knows the details of the case?*

Authors: When we think of our clients as being interdependent with others in their world instead of being in charge of or at odds with them, the function that confidentiality plays in collective and individual healing becomes more complex. The rule-driven, one-size-fits-all standard of confidentiality often makes things worse rather than better.

We mentioned extensively in previous chapters that when families remain isolated, they tend to believe that their life problems flow from their own flawed selves and the decisions they make. However, when they are connected to one another and empowered toward critical consciousness, the impact of gender, race, class, and sexual orientation become evident. The question *What's wrong with me/us?* is replaced by *Why am I buying into all these societal messages about how we're supposed to live, and what other options can I pursue?*

Most clients readily accept referrals and expansions of their therapeutic circle when their therapists clearly and convincingly explain the rationale and potential benefits in doing so. When an anguished family is told that meeting a sponsor or cultural consultant may offer them relief, they rarely decline the opportunity. Similarly, most clients have no problem allowing additional therapists into the process for consultation. In fact, it appeals to their sense that more is better. Most men end up embracing sponsors and peers within a culture circle and experience a sense of camaraderie and support that they have not felt since adolescence.

We believe that expanding the boundary of the therapeutic encounter presents more of a conflict for most therapists than for most clients. Therapists may resist including additional therapists as team members or consultants and may be adverse to including sponsors, cultural consultants, and the development of culture circles because doing so

- Involves changing the way one practices, and change is rarely welcome.
- May feel like it will end up being more work.
- Exposes their previously private interventions to a larger field of scrutiny.
- Involves sharing power and control within the therapeutic process.

But when therapists are able to make the adjustments needed to expand the therapeutic process, there are clear benefits for their practice and their clients. We strongly suggest that therapists in all settings challenge themselves to expand the treatment unit from one individual to a collective.

Personal and social liberation can occur only when collectives of individuals and families begin to decipher the mechanisms of power, privilege, oppression, and dehumanization. Then they can begin to understand how power relationships shape people's perceptions and experiences and identify how they can assume a role in social change.

For example, a coalition of women can empower the individual woman. When working-class people join together, the individual is empowered. Simultaneously, an individual man needs a coalition of men who will challenge male privilege and support him as he struggles to examine his socialization into masculinity.

Coalitions like these can alter the boundaries and power dynamics that preserve the status quo of family and community life. Grouping women or men together may seem like a simple intervention. However, the result is powerful when people begin to go beyond their personal stories and see themselves operating in the social and political world as a conscious community of listeners and responders.

Changing the way we practice will be challenging and frightening. Clients learn from their therapists what they should expect in therapy. They buy into the private clinical session because therapists do. If we redefine therapy, clients will see the benefits in what we offer and will follow suit.

Reader: *If therapists who practice in an agency, hospital, or other institutional setting start inviting cultural consultants and/or creating therapeutic teams and culture circles, they will be going against long-held traditions, and such innovations may simply not be allowed by their higher ups.*

Authors: Change certainly presents challenges, and change that leads toward more justice may upset "higher ups." Remember, the right for mental patients to be treated as human beings did not come without a fight. The transition from individual to family therapy did not come without enormous backlash. New developments in therapy will always be met with such resistance. Courage, persistence, and subversion are essential when seeking social justice. The phrase "better to ask forgiveness than permission" is the credo of risk-takers in the corporate world, and it also applies when practicing transformational family therapy.

One of the authors works with a corporate employee–assistance program. He enjoys great support from his immediate supervisor, even though he frequently delivers training, consultation, and clinical services that include social education components unlikely to please business leaders. He has never been challenged, however, because services that gain praise from employees—precisely because of their truthful and subversive content—draw little scrutiny from higher ups. His credibility among employees and managers buys him goodwill that has enabled him to foster the development of peer consciousness-raising networks and an array of supports for domestic violence survivors.

When therapists worry that the new model of treatment will make them have to take on more work, they should consider the case involving Daniel and Amy. Referring Daniel to George's downsizing survivor circle and the community action group actually reduced rather than added to the therapist's work. In the long run, helping clients build such networks invariably lessens rather than increases the therapist's workload.

Creating a team or consultation group requires self-disclosure and trust on the part of therapists. But our responsibility is to provide the highest possible level of service to our clients, and don't we owe it to our clients to practice what we preach?

We therapists are rooted in the same world they are. We learn many things that mislead us. Opening up our work to scrutiny and recognizing that the choices we make as professionals can be changed and do not define our value as human beings helps us approach our clients from a posture of collaboration and humility rather than authoritarian control. This kind of power sharing and accountability serves us all well.

Reader: *What you describe isn't just a set of new strategies that I can add to my repertoire of therapeutic tools. It's more like a reformulation of the basic premises of how one practices therapy.*

Authors: That's right. It's about changing the structure and the methods of therapeutic practice, bringing them more into line with the passion and commitment of the very people who practice in mental health. Therapists from all disciplines enter the field to ensure justice at some level for all individuals, families, and communities.

Some therapists worry that they may dilute their bond with their clients by including sponsors, cultural consultants, and other laypeople. We urge you to remember that establishing a circle of support leads to changes that would be impossible to foster in the confines of the private conversation that usually happens between one client family and one therapist. When clients experience healing that exceeds their expectations, they recognize the value of their therapist.

Reader: *Does this approach to practice apply to all presenting concerns? Should we work with all client families and for every presenting problem in a manner that fosters critical consciousness, accountability, empowerment, and social action?*

Authors: We believe you should because injustice shapes every aspect of our society and therefore has significant impact on all families and individuals. Typically, we do not think about the air we breathe. So, too, we often take for granted and accept patterns of injustice, which makes it a challenge to even notice them and look for possible alternatives. Critical consciousness and community, rather than individual, options redefine problems and broaden the range of possible solutions through empowerment and accountability.

Reader: *Can you give me an example?*

Authors: An 18-year-old black male client was denied a federal student loan because he earned $9,000 while a senior in high school, which was over the eligibility limit. He had no family members to cosign a Sallie Mae loan application, leaving him $4,000 short for tuition and expenses at the college of his choice.

In an agency mental health setting, his therapist might advise him to explore community colleges or to work for another year in order to save money. His psychiatrist might prescribe antidepressant medications to control the young man's sadness and frustration and to ensure that these emotions would not spill over into rage.

When the young man sought treatment in a social justice–based practice, his culture circle discussed the institutional unfairness that prevents youth of color, who are disproportionately from lower-income families, from gaining access to the quality schooling that white upper-middle-class youth claim as a birthright.

The fact that he had no family to cosign his loan application had the potential to block this young man's transition to college. Neither the school nor the financial institutions were willing or able to bridge the gap in his funding. Some of the privileged members of his circle spent hours on the phone with various institutions trying to break down the barriers confronting this young man. Ultimately, two middle-class white members of the young man's culture circle cosigned his Sallie Mae application. Other culture circle members, filling in for the family he did not have, celebrated his launching by giving him school supplies and gift cards from the university bookstore.

Reader: *In this case and the case involving Daniel and Amy, clients came to ther-*
apy feeling depleted and seemed to expect to be diagnosed with depression or some
related disorder. Yet, once they connected to communities that supported them,
they became involved in social justice. Is this where therapy that puts social jus-
tice at its center most frequently leads?

Authors: That is the hope. In many models of family therapy, clients are
simply consumers. The client buys the undivided attention and expertise
of the therapist and in return gets a better adjusted and more productive
fit with the world.

By contrast, social justice–based therapy says, "Let's look at what
bothers you and how it may be connected to an unjust world order."
Clients are empowered to reclaim their lives as their critical consciousness
grows. Isolation is replaced by a social network that demands and supports accountability.

In some cases, this mobilization is mainly directed toward making
choices within one's personal relationships and is guided by ethics-driven
deliberation instead of blind compliance with mainstream prescriptions.
In other cases, clients are motivated toward activism on a larger scale and
focus their efforts on organizing and working toward making a more just
world.

We cannot stress enough how important it is to bring the input of the
larger circles into the healing process. Remember Susie, the biracial 10-
year-old in Chapter 7 who was struggling to cope with her parents'
divorce and her mother's coming out as a lesbian?

As we finish this book, Susie is 13 and a prime example of what the
social justice approaches offer. She is an adolescent female navigating the
difficult terrain of an acrimonious divorce, her father's sexual immaturity
(he parades his numerous partners through his daughter's life, and he
pays more attention to those courtships than to connecting with or parenting her), the homophobia of her peers toward her mother, and her own
desperate desire to grow up in heterosexual normalcy. Susie's mother was
guided to change her parenting to include others in her daughter's life.
Together, mother and daughter have followed the evolving lives of the
other parents and children in their circles. Addressing the complexities that
Susie had to deal with was certainly daunting, but they were able to successfully utilize the resources of a community with critical consciousness.

Like most 13-year-olds, Susie creates hook-ups, falsifies events, lies
about where she's going, gets caught, and fights with her mother about
appropriate limits. Her father vacillates between colluding with her and
being punitive. Eight months into this whole process, Susie hinted to her
mother that she needed to set some "boundaries" with her boyfriend.
Supported by her culture circle, the mother was able to gently probe this
highly charged terrain and discovered that the boy had made many unflat-
tering comments about Susie's body and was inconsistent in the attention
he paid her.

A few months later, her mother overheard Susie's end of a phone conversation with her boyfriend. Susie sounded calm and strong, telling him, "I am disappointed with the way you have been treating me, so I think it is a good idea that we get some space."

After a pause for his response, Susie told him, "I know you have had a difficult life because of your parents' divorce. But so have I. And it is not okay for you to tell me you will call me back and then you don't. It is not okay that you say you will meet me at my locker, but you don't show up."

After another short pause, Susie said, "I am taking back my life space for now," and she hung up. Then she got off the phone singing, ran a bath, and asked her mother if they could watch a movie together!

This is a case in which a young woman has been able to deal with the complex and interconnected ways that race, gender, and sexuality affect the most vulnerable as well as the most resilient aspects of her identity. We were able to harness the combined force and wisdom of a community that shares a collective morality of inclusiveness. This positive context went a long way toward neutralizing the toxicity of patriarchy, racism, and homophobia for Susie.

Our view of social justice–based therapy is that all families, those who have access to good care as well as those who don't, suffer from the compartmentalization of their life's problems. Bringing down those walls creates a stronger and more enlightened path for the next generation.

REFERENCES

Bateson, G. (1972). *Steps to an ecology of mind*. New York: Balbdire.

Davis, A. (2000) *The prison industrial complex*. Audiobook (CD-ROM). Edinburgh, Scotland: AK Press.

Hare-Mustin (1986). Autonomy and gender: Some questions for therapists. *Psychotherapy, 23*, 205–212.

International Forum on Globalization. (2002). *Alternatives to economic globalization: A better world is possible*. San Francisco: Berrett-Koehler.

James, K., & McIntyre, D. (1983). The reproduction of families: The social role of family therapy. *Journal of Marital and Family Therapy, 9*, 119–129.

Klein, N. (2000). *No logo*. New York: Picador.

Kupers, T. (1995). The politics of psychiatry: Gender and sexual preference in DSM-IV. *Masculinities, 3*(2), 67–78.

LaDuke, W. (1999). *All our relations: Native struggles for land and life*. Cambridge, MA: South End Press.

Memmi, A. (1967). *The colonizer and the colonized*. Boston: Beacon Press.

Monblot, G. (2003, October 21). The flight to India: The jobs Britain stole from the Asian subcontinent 200 years ago are now being returned. *The Guardian*.

Roy, A. (2001). *Power politics*. Cambridge, MA: South End Press.

Walker, A. (1993). *Possessing the secret of joy*. New York: Pocket Books.

Watts-Jones, D. (2002). Healing internalized racism: The within group experience. *Family Process, 41*(4), 591–601.

Zinn, H. (1995). *You can't be neutral on a moving train: A personal history of our times*. Boston: Beacon Press.

INDEX